Goodbye History, Hello Hamburger
The Tall Building Artistically Reconsidered:
  The Search for a Skyscraper Style
Kicked a Building Lately?
Will They Ever Finish Bruckner Boulevard?
Pier Luigi Nervi
Classical New York

ARCHITECTURE, ANYONE?

ARCHITECTURE, ANYONE?

ADA LOUISE HUXTABLE

University of California Press

Berkeley   Los Angeles

University of California Press
Berkeley and Los Angeles, California
© 1986 by Ada Louise Huxtable

Library of Congress Cataloging-in-Publication Data

Huxtable, Ada Louise.
　　Architecture, anyone?

　　Reprint. Originally Published: 1st ed. New York:
Random House, © 1986
　　　　　1. Architecture, Modern--20th century.
I. Title.
NA680.H89　　　1988　　　724.9'1　　　87-10930
ISBN 0-520-06195-0

Manufactured in the United States of America

First Paperback Printing 1988

Designed by Jo Anne Metsch

3　4　5　6　7　8　9

CONTENTS

INTRODUCTION

In 1982, after eighteen years of crisis-oriented, deadline-controlled, daily and weekly reportage and commentary as *The New York Times* architecture critic and as a member of its Editorial Board, I left to embark on a broader and deeper involvement with architectural and urban issues—to return, in a sense, to the more scholarly pursuits with which I started my career.

The opportunity to do so came through an appointment as a MacArthur Fellow by the John D. and Catherine T. MacArthur Foundation, a grant that carries with it the extraordinary gifts of freedom and time. There comes a moment, in even the most rewarding of jobs at the most prestigious of institutions, when one craves freedom and time with a consuming passion. To be in a position to pick themes independent of their value as news or trends and to investigate them at leisure seems like the ultimate unattainable luxury. To be able to bring to them the kind of experience provided by New York City and *The New York Times* is both an advantage and a privilege. I welcome the chance to think about what I have learned at the center of the urban storm in a city where the winds of profit and power blow at steady gale force. The enormous amount of building and occasional work of architecture produced in New York through manipulations of money, law, politics, and morality make Machiavelli and the Medici seem like simple country folk. The critic on a respected and influential newspaper has had an awesome responsibility and incomparable experience. In bringing together this collection of essays from the last years I worked on *The Times,* I have taken the advantage of this new perspective to expand, clarify, and update some of them; the opinions and judgments have not changed.

It would be normal at this point to indulge in some kind of retrospective stocktaking, but I have never been one for keeping score. I can think of nothing more futile than to try to list the successes and failures of two decades of critical writing, to record the buildings or movements supported or embraced, the campaigns won or lost, the disasters averted (usually temporarily), the reputations aided (wisely or unwisely), and the visible or lasting monuments, if any, of my tenure. Battles are fought over and over again in wars that are rarely won. I can count at least three skirmishes on East Sixty-second Street, for example, and such choice and handsome pieces of Manhattan land will always call out the most ingenious developers' ploys. That this land is not exactly up for grabs since the designation of the Upper East Side Historic District is a victory of sorts, but the continued presence of the street's handsome houses owes more to the economics of luxury co-op conversion and preservation tax credits than to architectural appreciation.

How would you score the failure of New York's much-admired and emulated incentive zoning amendments, whose uncalculated side effects are a disaster in terms of bulk, density, light, and air—the amenities the original law was designed to protect? How can I explain my own failure and just about everyone else's to foresee the unprecedented changes in building and investment economics and the manipulative skills that would transform the patently impossible into the all-too-real, turning the 1961 zoning reform law into a Frankenstein instrument for creating monsters? It has become impossible to measure the cleverness and cupidity of New York's developers and lawyers. There is a sophisticated kind of corruption and erosion of the planning process that goes beyond the uncomplicated Tammany Hall tradition and the conventional campaign contribution. Zoning is being used in New York as a bargaining chip, as a monetary instead of a planning tool, to encourage development rather than to control it. The "accommodations" promote exactly the kind of overbuilding that the rules were meant to outlaw and that the city's antiquated infrastructure can no longer support. (No, New York will not die; it will simply rot away beneath its glittering veneer while the deals are cut.)

On what point system do you mark the moment when survival no longer seems like a fun game for the fittest? Just when and how a city becomes unviable is a subjective matter; it depends on one's standards and stamina. Because New York masochism is as celebrated as its skyline and pastrami, the "natives" continue to congratulate each other on their endurance and fortitude, while City Hall and Madison Avenue sing "I Love New York" hopelessly off-key. The view from the co-op and condo fortresses remains superb. But I do not see how one can count victories when religious and cultural institutions work steadily to undermine the city's hard-won landmarks law. Or take heart from civic groups that used to fight like tigers for "lost" causes and now cannot reach a consensus on safe-enough campaigns. There is simply no plausible way to sort out the successes or failures, satisfactions or frustrations of the critic's job.

All this, however, comes with the territory; it does not cancel out the challenge and fulfillment of dealing in the broadest terms with a vital art that literally shapes our lives. During the years that I have been observing the built world, epic changes have taken place in the construction of cities and in the art of architecture. Preservation of the past has become an urban and environmental force for the continuity and character of our cities and towns. Modernists are arrayed against postmodernists, with critical questions being asked about the style, use, meaning, and impact of building in a surge of provocative debate, design, and construction. This has made architectural criticism an incomparably stimulating, rewarding, and sometimes hectic activity, with little time to look back. I tend to have the long, and often unfashionable, view.

Obviously, I have enjoyed the work, and I have also enjoyed the rewards. I was alone when I started—the first and only full-time architecture critic in the American press—a fact that is generally forgotten along with *The Times*'s brave gamble on establishing the position, based on the belief that the quality of the built world mattered at a time when environment was still only a dictionary word. Now there are cover stories and full-color treatments of buildings and architects and state-of-the-art articles in the weekly news journals. Architecture has taken its hyped-up place on the world stage of celebrity journalism, and developers have discovered the market value of designer labels. There are legions, or battalions, of critics and would-be critics, with vision ranging from the flyspeck to the apocalyptic, in fashionable pursuit of architectural answers to questions that purport to address the hot topics of art and life. To them I say, with feeling, lots of luck.

Still, I cannot avoid a sense of some pluses and minuses, some beginnings and ends. In general, I do not believe that anything has really improved, measurably or permanently, nor would any rational, reasonably sophisticated person expect to see either utopian progress or the end of the world. The perfectibility of man is the shattered dream of the twentieth century. That a lastingly better existence or environment could be established as the result of anyone's crusading labors, in architecture or anything else, is an arrogant and foolish hope, not only unachievable but quite beside the point. History consists of holding actions. There are the familiar, immutable, unfailing, dependable constants: ambition, vanity, greed, insensitivity, enduring opportunities for the sellout, and the consistent inability to learn from the past—all those components of human nature that are as immortal as any kind of art. What has been added is a certain unique talent and highly developed specialty that turns evil inside out as a sort of good, publicly dignified and admired as the practical well-orchestrated compromise, or deal, in which gargantuan profits are seriously balanced against the public interest as if both were coins of equal legitimacy and value.

Not surprisingly, the art of building is no better or worse than it ever was; since the well-publicized renunciation of modernism and the value system that included socially responsible design, there is probably more opportunity for a vastly enlarged range of abuse and ineptitude. Politicians do not change: some are always more venal or virtuous than others, and all are forced at least occasionally to pay lip service to environmental issues and the quality of life. Policies improve to the degree that official agencies embrace elevated standards for a while, usually under pressure, and then backslide to payoffs, pork barrel, and rigid bureaucracies once again, leaving a small legacy of better buildings behind, to be kicked around when tastes change. It is a predictable roller coaster, and I have been up and down on it too many times not to recognize the cyclical nature of good intentions, history, and art.

What, if anything, then, has twenty years of architectural criticism achieved that is worth putting on the record? I see one enormously important difference with a significance and influence beyond challenge. In these last few decades, there has been a universal consciousness-raising, an awakening awareness of the components, and the effects, of what and how we build, a recognition of far-reaching aesthetic and environmental values. The climate in which the critic operates today is totally unlike the climate of twenty years ago. There has been a basic, radical change in the way people see and respond to their surroundings; they are tuned in to elements that were previously unnoticed and ignored. A kind of vision has been established that cannot be lost again; it is a phenomenon of a particular time and place, a historical absolute that is now an integral ingredient of the received, contemporary culture. This is an unprecedented and irreversible conceptual advance. To have helped this happen is surely reward enough.

With these new attitudes, we accept the city as a rich and contradictory place of the designed and the accidental that operates on many complex functional, sensory, and historical levels. We know how valuable and how fragile the urban fabric is, and how susceptible to the interventions of man. This understanding is the background for a sophisticated kind of preservation that is far removed in its responses to twentieth-century urbanism from the nostalgia and knee britches of the Williamsburg-type restoration. This perception is behind increasingly thoughtful strategies for controlling development and the quality of urban life through policy and law. The individual landmark saved or sacrificed, the construction projects defeated or brought to fruition, are only transient, peripheral events in this larger revolution. My hope, and prayer, is that this will not all be lost in the current proliferation of meaningless arguments about style.

The real hope lies in the fact that the consumers of our urban culture are a savvy group today, with an educated expectation of public "entitlements." The holdouts and the dinosaurs and the born-again believers in laissez faire, who look remarkably like the old real estate crowd, no longer have either the conventional wisdom or an unquestioning acceptance on their side. Too much has been learned by too many about the destruction and impoverishment of cities through painful empirical experience. The loss of community and place wrought by clean-slate urban renewal remains clear, as do the errors of the philosophy behind it. The traditional pieties—you can't stop progress, new is better than old, and that investment canard with the spurious sound of Mosaic law which claimed the highest and best use of land to be its most profitable use—now sound like con games or blasphemies. It takes courage to revive them with a straight face, but that does not stop those who know that if they can't play it straight there is always the end run. Only enormous political muscle can push through a project as reactionary as the proposed redevelopment of Times Square. The rape of the city can no longer be carried out in crude or overt fashion. The possibilities for more sensitive solutions exist in much greater variety. But building at the changing scale and for the inconstant needs of modern cities will continue to be an empirical and hazardous process, with no easy or obvious answers. The real issues have been joined, however, and officials and investors can never hide behind ignorance or innocence again.

In this climate the need is greater than ever for those who will raise their voices and use their abilities to identify the issues and keep some standards of art and decency operative in the design and construction process. The critic is the link between people and the buildings that make the public realm; the critic's view of the art of architecture must embrace the policy and the culture that are inseparable from it. It is the repeated messages and small improvements in these relationships that make the difference. There is a critical responsibility to keep an eye unwaveringly on the values and quality that cannot survive compromise and to turn the spotlight on those involved in compromising them. It never hurts to hold a few feet to the fire. That kind of vigilance is lonely and even eccentric work. It does not advance one's connections or popularity. But conviction and credibility, backed by the essential facts, can be more effective in defining and deciding issues of public policy—and it is impossible to divorce architecture from policy because of its public impact and the reality of its public regulation—than the most adroit legal or political maneuvering. As history has generously shown, principle and print are among the most powerful tools in the world.

Unfortunately, much of the present theoretical and critical discourse has renounced this public role for a cop-out definition of architecture as a formal object that bears no relationship or responsibility to forces beyond its own forms. There is talk of symbolism, metaphor and typology, and a great deal of genuflecting to history with a thin veneer of stagy style that mocks the history it pretends to recall. Still more serious, there is a general acceptance today, in architecture and elsewhere, of the obsolescence and abandonment of value judgments, and a concerted effort to fill the vacuum with a well-screened—one might even call it an élite—populism or pluralism. Bombarded as we are with every kind of message, evaluations of meaning or worth are more important than ever. It is only the judgments based on the wistful oversimplification and willful blindness to the realities of the human condition which so flawed the modernist ideal that stand condemned. It is pious simplicities and paternalistic prescriptions based on false premises that are obsolete. The desire to pit a limited and artificia¹ academic order, whether historicist or modernist, against the disorderly inequities and gritty vitality of the real world, is a shallow, fruitless act. Today we recognize infinite complexities and subtleties; a world that consists of, not many shades of gray, or carefully orchestrated colors, but intensely clashing hues, almost beyond our ability to name them. It is this incomplete, irreconcilable, fractured, and fragmented, but vastly enlarged view with its enormous potential that is characteristic of our time. This view has led to the investigation of many problematic areas and unfamiliar and even heretical themes, from the riddles of conscious and unconscious behavior to galloping revisionism in history, literature, and art. The physical landscape and the inner landscape have taken on meanings and established relationships unknown to any other age.

Still, not all is cosmic or catastrophic. And if I have no "final" reckoning, I must confess to continuing small pleasures and quiet satisfactions. There is, for one example, the Bronx Grit Chamber. This late, late work (1936) from the successors (or ghosts) of McKim, Mead and White always cheered me on my trips through the detritus of New York's outer-borough architectural fallout during the years I was struggling with my curious urban epiphany. The building seems like a miraculously misplaced Parisian work by the early-nineteenth-century French visionary, Claude-Nicholas Ledoux. A brick pediment and unadorned stone architrave top an odd number (seven) of attached flat columns or pilasters along the front. The pilasters alternate light and dark bands of brick and stone; between them are large bays topped by lunette windows framed in round arches of well-laid brick with proper keystones. This strong, serene structure, so conspicuously out of touch with its time and place, gave (and gives) a maverick dignity and extraordinary presence to a shabby Bronx street.

Dignity is not to be disdained in the South Bronx. But you had to be just a little bit strange to admire that building twenty years ago; both its romantic classicism and its unromantic function suggested a distinctly offbeat taste. A grit chamber is a sewage plant, and only disposal trucks go through those classical bays. It took a kooky kind of courage to believe that something so consummately ordinary could suggest qualities of architecture and man that rise above sludge, that endure beyond transient hopes, tawdry structures, and endemic debris and decay. Today, the Bronx Grit Chamber is an officially designated New York City landmark. Our perception, our values, and our vision of the city have come a long way. For me, that is the real bottom line.

Ada Louise Huxtable
New York City
November 1985

ARCHITECTURE, ANYONE?

ARCHITECTURE,
ANYONE?

I f you are ever driving on I-91 through Connecticut, don't
miss the Colt Firearms Building on your way to New
England diversions. You can't miss it anyway; how many
expressways offer a view of a deep cerulean-blue onion dome,
gilt-trimmed and studded with stars, set on a crown of white
columns, atop a large nineteenth-century brick factory with a
mirage-like twentieth-century Hartford behind it?

I have been watching that building, en route, for a good part
of my life, and I find that these places seen in transit through
a car window, with the changing vision of motion, have a
special kind of image. The eye is really a camera, and the image
is kinetic and transient, but timeless in the way it makes cinema
a haunting art of transfixed, passing shadows. Perhaps because
these buildings are a repeated and anticipated experience, such
places and structures that may touch our lives only tangentially
stay permanently fixed in the mind's eye.

But they change, from one year to the next. Over the
decades I have watched the Colt Firearms Building (which
instantly tells me that I have gotten to Hartford) transformed
from a shabby relic to renewed splendor, with growing general

recognition that it is a superb example of what art historians now call industrial archeology. An anonymous admirer, whose name is supposedly unknown even to Colt, donated $5,000 to put back the stars on the dome that have been missing for the last fifty years. The stars were part of the original building of 1857, which burned in 1864 and was reconstructed in 1874; they disappeared around 1920.

Obviously, Colonel Colt was quite aware of the symbolic and status value of architecture. The Hartford Architectural Conservancy, in its notes on the building, tells us that he meant the exotic dome on its circle of decorous columns to be seen by travelers passing through Hartford by barge on the Connecticut River. Today they see it from the thruway, at high speed. They may miss the details—the gleaming gold ball at the top is surmounted by a casting of a rearing colt, and there are eighty stars. But the fine vernacular brick building, a prime example of typically pragmatic and handsome nineteenth-century design, has even gained in visual impact.

I find, when I think of it, that I have a set of such landmarks —personal, transient, and indelible—that mark the stages of my journeys and the stages of my life. I wait for these particular places on trips year after year; they are all old friends. It is more important than I have ever consciously admitted that they should be where I expect to find them. If they are gone I have a real and shocking sense of loss; if they have been refurbished I am suffused with joy.

Sometimes I admire these buildings for years without knowing what they are or anything about them. They can be encountered on country roads or on those curious routes by which one is forced to leave large cities. They can loom up along New York's potholed avenues that turn abruptly on to bridges of surpassing beauty or lead to boulevards of oppressive banality. The city's exits and entrances are a surreal landscape of scales and references from graffiti praising Bessie Smith on the crumbling wall of a corner bar (recently painted over and replaced by a co-ops-for-sale sign) to pocket-handkerchief gardens bordering a superhighway and anonymous public-housing wastelands where even grass and trees despair. The omnipresent urban glue is dust, litter, and weeds.

Just past the cemeteries on the approach to La Guardia Airport, with their legions of carved angels like stone hiccups from the same mortuary sculptor's pattern, is the Bulova watch factory, a long, streamlined Art Deco structure that never ceases to delight. (It has recently been rediscovered by those who deal in stylish styles.) Time stands still there in more ways than one; the building is a frozen custard of architectural optimism—these were the soft rounded forms of the world of the future in the 1930's—and the entrance clock no longer has its hands.

Another building that I look forward to seeing on New England excursions is a factory in Beverly, Massachusetts. This, too, is one of those structures that always elicited a pleased "there it is" long before I knew what it was. An early reinforced concrete–framed industrial building, with great expanses of many-paned sash, it stretches far along a meadow with singular assurance and surprising grace. Impressive and pleasing proportions combine with the direct expression of structure to create a naturally superior aesthetic.

Many years ago, when I was doing research in innovative concrete construction in the United States, I found an illustration of the United Shoe Machinery Plant in Beverly, Massachusetts, designed by the pioneering American engineer of reinforced concrete, Ernest Ransome. It was a picture of my building. And the dates were an astonishingly early 1903–5—putting it slightly in advance of the Detroit automobile factories by Albert Kahn always celebrated as the first examples of the type. To find that the structure which so pleased my eye also rewrote an important chapter of architectural history has increased my contentment on every subsequent viewing.

These are some of my personal landmarks, and there are many more. I am catholic in my tastes, possessive and passionate in my responses. And response is the key word—the point of these buildings that become one's geographic and cultural signposts is that it is impossible to be neutral toward them. From high art to high camp, they are a source of satisfaction and delight. I am as fond of Violet's Lounge, a humdrum little house raised to spurious glamour with mauve plastic panels and a glittering silver sign at a busy intersection on Massachusetts Route 114 (I always wondered what Violet was like), as I am of Colonel Colt's extravaganza. Violet's Lounge disappeared a few years ago. Not even stars are forever.

June 26, 1977

THE PAST AS
FUTURE

Whatever happened to the future? I mean, the world of the future, as it was envisioned in those future-happy days just after World War II. The promises and visions began, actually, during the war, for those who remember, when the architecture magazines were filled with dreams that were supposed to become reality as soon as the fighting stopped and construction could begin. The illustrations featured boldly cantilevered and streamlined saucers and spirals connected to other futuristic wonders by skyways and bridges. There were always bubble-domed automobiles in the streets. The style was pure, ingenuous space age. The message was clear: by the 1980's a Martian would feel at home.

What really happened was enough to give futurism a bad name, but that is never a very hard thing to do. A few flying saucer–type structures appeared in cities as disparate as Stamford, Connecticut, and Bordeaux, France, tarted-up with wall-to-wall carpeting for corporations, banks, and bureaucracies. Somewhere along the way the space age was dumped. The direction today is full speed backward. Architecture is rushing pell-mell into the mists of history; galactic symbolism has given way to the trappings of tradition. Younger architects, and some more mature ones, too, are retreating bravely into academic convention and nostalgic revivals. The wave of the future has turned out to be the wave of the past.

The newest thing is anything that's old, and the hottest trend of all is classicism. I have seen the future—in buildings, books, and exhibitions—and this time it is not courtesy of Captain Marvel; it is straight out of Quatremère de Quincy and Banister Fletcher. (The first was a godhead of the École des Beaux Arts and the Academy, and the second was for years the standard academic reference for the history of architectural styles and orders.) Banister Fletcher was bumped by Sigfried Giedion's revolutionary text on modern architecture. Giedion now languishes on the shelves or is being attacked by revisionists, and Banister Fletcher has been reprinted. The trick today is to know a string course from a spandrel, a plinth from a *piloti*. The dream house is no longer a Dymaxion by Buckminister Fuller. By some neat trick of fate and futurism, the avant-garde is busy reinstating the centuries-old Western classical tradition that the modernists so vehemently rejected.

At this moment, everywhere, the future is being repealed. From Casselton, North Dakota, for example, come before and after pictures of the Casselton State Bank. One view shows a typical late-nineteenth-century, small-town main-street building of arcaded red brick; the other shows the same building refaced with a "modern" front. For years, one could have reliably concluded that the old building was "before" and the modernized building was "after." Not so now. Shuffle the pictures. "Before" is the refaced 1959 version, when the bank embraced, in its own words, "the Space Age and the modernistic style." "After" is the restoration of the original facade, twenty years later, when the bank was remodeled again. This time the "modernistic" front was stripped off, and the handsome old brickwork that had been covered over was revealed and restored. The bank had come full circle—from its modestly stylish, nicely detailed Sullivanesque vernacular of the nineteenth century, through the faceless anonymity of the Great Manufacturers' Cover-up of the 1950's and 60's, to the blinding rediscovery of its institutional roots and architectural history today.

8

If the Casselton Bank's rehabilitation is a tribute to the past, those postwar remodelings were a tribute to the hard sell. The advertising pages of the architectural journals were full of "artists' renderings" of before-and-after buildings Kawneered and Johns-Manvilled to extinction in the destruction of the Main Streets of America. This was the kind of modernization that gave modern a bad name. You, too, went the four-color message, can update your old, outmoded, stubbornly unmodern Victorian storefront or other honest and interesting bit of Americana by covering it with truly nondescript panels sold and applied by the shoddy, characterless, and highly profitable mile. "But before is better," I used to object silently and angrily to the glossy pages. "But after is progress," said the text. Progress—constantly invoked in those days for architectural sabotage and bulldozer demolition—should have sued.

No one pretends to know what progress is anymore, or whether the conventionally accepted premise of change for the better means looking forward or backward. Another before-and-after sequence of a building in Manchester, Connecticut, remodeled by Allan Greenberg, is a provocative performance of born-again classicism. The before picture is of a supermarket —one of those typical horizontal suburban warehouses or roadside shopping boxes with an asymmetrical glass facade and cantilevered roof canopy. Without its familiar graphic adornment of weekly special signs, it bears an uncanny resemblance to some examples of austere Italian modernism of the 1930's —the *rationalismo* in current revival. (There are more ambiguities and ironies here than meet the eye.) In the after view, the supermarket has become—presto change!—the State of Connecticut Superior Court Building. Same box, different facade: a pedimented entrance and arched windows in a brick front, with stone quoins and courses—somewhat oddly proportioned, but that is another of the cultivated ambiguities of postmodern classicism. Inside, there is a marble-paneled corridor with cove lighting above classical columns and architrave.

This is no A&P Colonial; it is a knowledgeable use of a traditional vocabulary with established conventions that undeniably impart scale and interest and symbolic suggestion to the box. It is a lot more sophisticated than the Kawneer cover-up; but is it really very different? Instead of modernizing, we have classicizing. At best, the result, and the response, is superficial and ambivalent. Is this design artful and dignified, pompous or pop? More to the point, which way does it want to be read? Because that is never quite certain the result is never fully convincing.

Today, the classical vocabulary is often treated as a means to an end. Its practitioners like allusive references as much as literal quotations; the aim can be a pure or hybrid, solemn or witty product. In the work of such architects as James Stirling, Hans Hollein, Charles Moore, and Michael Graves, classicism becomes something very unexpected, and very unsettling at times, used in totally individual and personal ways.

Certainly the Golden House of Nero or Hadrian's Villa is not where anyone expected to be at this particular moment in architectural time. The retreat is interesting; the direction is neither forward nor backward, but distinctly oblique. If there is any lesson in all of this, it is the familiar one that life and art confound analysis and defy prediction. The world of the future is where you find it.

June 14, 1981

MODERNISM
REVISTED

REAPPRAISAL AT PESSAC

I n 1981, I went to Pessac to see the future as it was envisioned fifty years before. Pessac is the town near Bordeaux, in France, where Le Corbusier designed and built a community of fifty-one houses in the 1920's under the sponsorship of the French industrialist Henry Frugès, who meant them to be a laboratory of new domestic, structural, and aesthetic ideas.

I went to Pessac prepared for the worst. Everything I had ever heard about it led to expectations of a failed experiment and an aesthetic slum, a testament to the miscarriage of modernism and the arrogance of its architects. This did not turn out to be the case. The Pessac housing, a landmark of early modernism, looks, and doesn't look, like Le Corbusier's original design.

These are not "landmark" houses in the usual sense. They were not commissioned by those who were to live in them, and they are not, like Frank Lloyd Wright houses, objects of curatorial pride, a responsibility that has led some owners to divorce or flight. Pessac was built as experimental "workers' housing"; there was no personal contract between occupant-patron and famous architect in which the owner's tastes, and

Le Corbusier

Quartiers Modernes Frugès, Pessac, France, 1926

Strong enough to adapt and survive

Jean Didier

even lives, were subordinate to the maintenance of a work of art, in which any change would be a violation. With half a century of additions and remodelings, Le Corbusier's houses have been "violated" over and over. They have come a long way from his *prisme pur,* or "machine to live in," and even from their concept as a social experiment. But Pessac is alive and well today and making an entirely different kind of history than intended.

The Quartiers Modernes Frugès, as the project was called, has been put down in the literature of modernism almost since the day it was built. In his avant-garde 1929 book, *Modern Architecture: Romanticism and Reintegration,* the historian Henry-Russell Hitchcock referred to Pessac as a "serious disappointment." He had some praise for the variety of the planning, which embraced detached, semidetached, and row houses and three-story multiple dwellings that the Bordelaise called skyscrapers, all with individual gardens. But he scorned the interiors of the houses as "uncomfortable for the small-salaried employees for whom they were designed," and called features like roof terraces more suitable for the artists and millionaires who were usually Le Corbusier's clients.

"Effective Pessac admittedly was," he wrote, "but practical not at all, even in elementary matters. . . . As the first executed housing scheme of the New Pioneers in France it has actually done more harm than good to the development of modern housing there." Over the years, by way of the pilgrimage grapevine, have come vivid descriptions of how disgruntled and uncomprehending occupants have sabotaged the architecture.

With this background, Pessac has become a convenient whipping boy for those who are currently busy singling out every defect of the modern movement while declaring its demise. Pessac is the model failure. Say Pessac, and you have said everything there is to say about all that ever went wrong with modern architecture. It is grouped ritually with that other example of modernist housing failure, Pruitt-Igoe, the public housing project in St. Louis that was dynamited after severe socioeconomic problems, for which it was never designed, made it uninhabitable. Pessac was supposedly finished off by the occupant's rebellious rejection of Le Corbusier's doctrinaire modernist aesthetic and elitist ideas about how they should live.

This neat doomsday script is favored over more complex realities by those rewriting history. It was the scenario presented in Robert Hughes's visually stunning television series on architecture, *The Shock of the New*. There is, of course, nothing more effective in the shock department than blowing it all up, à la Pruitt-Igoe, even if that means compromising art and history for a tidy knockout punch.

And so I walked down the Avenue Frugès and Rue Le Corbusier in Pessac on a late January day expecting the shock of the old, or the future that died, but the script didn't fit. I tried blaming the springlike sunshine and the wines of Bordeaux as I found myself thinking, If this is so bad, how can it be this good?

The scale and relationship of the houses to one another and to the gardens are excellent; the shapes and proportions of the buildings are still strong and good. There is a feeling of a cohesive whole. Even with the loss of key elements of the "pure" Corbusian style—the precise repetition of open and closed geometries, the visual sense of a thin membrane, the painterly abstraction of the original colored facades—Pessac retains an impressive and recognizable integrity. This is a very pleasant place to be. And the houses are clearly survivors.

It is also clear that Pessac is a survivor precisely because of its architecture. Its strong identity absorbs almost anything time and residents can inflict. Structurally, the houses are incredibly solid. One can read the original features and then read the way they have been used or assimilated. Pessac continues to give something to the eye and the spirit that only buildings shaped and informed by a superior and caring eye and spirit can. This still holds true, with all of the changes made by the occupants over the years.

Le Corbusier once said, in a statement usually turned against him, "You know, it is always life that is right and the architect who is wrong." This was not a confession of error as much as the recognition of the validity of process over the sanctity of ideology. Few architects are capable of making that observation, because it speaks not to some fixed ideal, but to the acknowledged complexity and incompleteness of architecture, to how life and art accommodate to each other. And that is what Pessac is really about.

The process of accommodation has been thoroughly documented in a study published in 1972 called *Lived-in Architecture, Le Corbusier's Pessac Revisited,* by a French architect, Philippe Boudon. Boudon carried out a systematic analysis of exterior and interior changes and attitudes toward the architecture through extensive occupant interviews. I acquired the book only after my visit, although I remember scare pictures of the "failures" in an architectural journal at the time. The study was almost universally misunderstood—or just not read—by those who considered it proof that Pessac had been destroyed. Photographs of garage doors where there once were open entrances, small shuttered windows replacing large expanses of glass, tile roofs, and endearing touches of kitsch were cited as evidence of failure. But "the Quartiers Modernes Frugès were not an 'architectural failure,' " Boudon wrote. "The modifications carried out by the occupants constitute a positive and not a negative consequence of Le Corbusier's original conception. Pessac not only allowed the occupants sufficient latitude to satisfy their needs, by doing so it also helped them to realize what those needs were."

Breathes there the householder who has not revised, revamped, expanded, or added a little class or space to his home in dream or actuality? Pessac's radical open plan of the 1920's could be (and was) reorganized and subdivided in many ways; a terrace could be roofed over for that extra room that all families eventually need; windows of one's choice could be fitted into the large openings without knocking out a wall; a garage fitted neatly between *pilotis*. There is no sense of "the architect's will imposed," or of an unyielding authoritarian design. The houses rolled with the punches. The transition from a cool, uniform, and surprisingly colorful International Style to personalized, somewhat Mediterranean-looking villas has led to an air of solidity rather than openness; of individuality rather than uniformity; of enclosed volumes rather than screen walls. Because the planning is good, each owner has a sense of privacy, with no loss of a collective ensemble, or community.

One row house resident, who generously invited our small sightseeing group inside, discoursed knowledgeably on the strength, solidity, and longevity of Le Corbusier's reinforced concrete construction, while we stood on a roof terrace that had been resurfaced in fancy colored tiles. Downstairs, a closed corridor had been created from the front door to the living room, and a formal dining space had been added by extending the living space into the garden. There were flowered wallpaper, overstuffed furniture, and the accessories of a comfortable bourgeois lifestyle.

Another owner, according to Boudon, had never heard of Le Corbusier, but he was busy "restoring back" the interior of his house to the original open plan by removing earlier partitions; he cited, as his own, Le Corbusier's rationale of space, light, and view. But many speak with reasonable understanding of Le Corbusier, and most of the residents are aware and rather proud that the houses have been "listed" for their aesthetic and historical importance. None feel that they have attacked the architecture. They have found it accommodating and are proud of the results.

Like all of Le Corbusier's houses, these were based on five design principles that he enunciated repeatedly: the raised ground floor, wide windows, roof terraces, open facades, and open plans made possible by the uniquely strong and ductile new material, reinforced concrete, which freed the architecture from the traditional restrictions of thick masonry walls. Corners could be breached, openings placed almost anywhere and made much larger, spans increased and walls treated as screens, rooms opened to each other and to the light and view; the building could even be levitated to become a six-sided prism.

The unprecedented structural and design freedom was intoxicating. But if it created the challenge of a new kind of architecture that was to make the twentieth century unique, it also led to wildly overreaching ideas that went beyond making better buildings to making better cities and better people. This assumption was more innocent than arrogant and, like all utopian dreams, it was doomed.

Le Corbusier's vision of the city of the future proved exhilarating and seductive in such an atmosphere of optimism. But it never ceased to amaze me that his superblocks of slabs and towers raised above flat landscapes laced to the horizon with superhighways were ever taken seriously. Those of us who refused to take them seriously were branded as hopeless unconverted heathens. The converts who lived to see the sterile fallout in our cities are now bumping into each other recanting.

But Pessac, even if it had been built to double its size, as intended, was no helicopter view of the world of the future; it was housing on a small, intimate scale. Its module was human and it was both strong and flexible enough to endure. Many of its features have long since become standard. It was truly designed in the measure of man.

What everyone remembers with varying degrees of distress was Le Corbusier's announced wish to build "a machine to live in," based on the early twentieth century's enchantment with the belief that technology, in itself, was good, that the "machine to live in" would free its inhabitants for higher things, and that the savior of the cities would be mass produced housing. What has since been forgotten is what he said in the next sentence. "But since men also have hearts," reads his dedication speech at Pessac in 1926, which contained that notorious phrase, "we have also tried to ensure that men with hearts would be able to live happily in our houses." They have.

March 15, 1981

LOOKING BACK IN BOSTON

For a city identified with Bulfinch, Boston espoused modernism early, and with characteristic intellectual conviction. In 1980 twenty-two landmark buildings chosen by William Curtis and shown in photographs at Boston's Institute of Contemporary Art, with a catalogue by Professor Curtis, re-created a unique chapter in art and architectural history. Boston played a leading role in the practice and dissemination of a movement that changed the face of the twentieth century.

The list of the examples in "Boston: Forty Years of Modern Architecture," is a litany of familiar icons: the tradition-shattering houses of the 1930's by Walter Gropius and Marcel Breuer, Alvar Aalto's 1947 Baker House dormitory at the Massachusetts Institute of Technology, Eero Saarinen's 1955 MIT chapel, Le Corbusier's 1960–63 Carpenter Center for the Visual Arts at Harvard, and the second generation of 1960's work that included Kallmann, McKinnell and Knowles's competition-winning Boston City Hall, Philip Johnson and John Burgee's Public Library extension, and the design of I. M. Pei and Henry N. Cobb's John Hancock Building. Most of the examples, including those by the "native" firms of Hugh Stubbins and Benjamin Thompson, are in the doctrinaire modern tradition, something currently being attacked as full of flaws and failures.

Le Corbusier

*Carpenter Center
Harvard University
Cambridge,
Massachusetts,
1960–63*

*A high level of
innovative art*

The buildings may be flawed, but they still measure up—most as creative milestones and some as works of art. Aalto's dormitory, for example, which puzzled and disappointed many by its lack of bombast and approved modernist mannerisms, looks extraordinarily good—and undated—today. The subtleties of a design that outstripped current clichés and the architect's easy mastery of a style that is both personal and universal are far clearer now than they were then.

It is fascinating to be able to see these buildings as a group; they reward hindsight. By affirming the excellence of what is now unfashionable, the exhibition becomes something of a counterrevolutionary gesture; it takes courage to be out of step. But once we are free of the polemical restraints that produced these structures, we can understand them better. They have their place in history at a high level of innovative art. It is quite possible now to judge them independently of their unrealized utopian aims. People have successfully resisted salvation by architectural or other means for centuries, and civilization feeds on the process of rejecting and remolding the past, creating rich layers of cultural mulch. The last example in the show, a suave reinterpretation of the International Style by the Gwathmey, Siegel firm, for Knoll headquarters on Newbury Street, brings modernism full circle from established orthodoxy to thoughtful renaissance. The process continues.

Most of these early modern buildings were brought to Boston by something else that the city's intellectual leadership has specialized in—enlightened patronage. Strictly speaking, Boston's great educational institutions, Harvard and MIT, were the real crucible in which American modern architecture was formed. When Walter Gropius left the Bauhaus in the late 1930's in response to Dean Joseph Hudnut's invitation to chair the Architecture Department of the Harvard Graduate School of Design, he brought the International Style with him. Marcel Breuer followed, and the houses that the two men built for themselves in Lincoln, Massachusetts, in 1937 and 1938, had an extraordinary impact. Although the style already existed on the West Coast in the work of such émigrés as Neutra and Schindler, it was the conversion of the eastern establishment to the new architecture that determined the course of serious building in this country from then on.

It was in the Harvard-MIT crucible that several generations of architects who became the leaders of the profession and the setters of the style were trained. Nor was that style exclusively orthodox. The same sources produced the monumental corporate manner of Gordon Bunshaft, the rational formalism of I. M. Pei, the precisely defined refinements of Edward L. Barnes. It was a step away from these "correct" interpretations, but still under the influence of the same masters, to the romantic, concrete brutalism of Paul Rudolph and the literate, gadfly practice and catalytic patronage of Philip Johnson. The list is long and impressive.

Today we see these buildings with different eyes. In the early houses, the conscious effort of the European pioneers to blend the radical import with native architectural traditions produced an intriguing hybrid that is not nearly as "pure" as previously assumed. But functionalist doctrine and the gestures to local custom were soon overcome by increasing rigidity and a desire for monumentality—an instinct that is hard to kill.

What happened in Boston was the architectural shot heard round the world. It is a fitting gesture for the cradle of American culture, and a testament to the passage of time, that the once-shocking Gropius house has been acquired by the Society for the Preservation of New England Antiquities. The latest in the line that began in Lincoln, Gwathmey, Siegel's Knoll headquarters continues the local tradition of civilized controversy, handsomely at home in the Back Bay.

September 28, 1980

ENDURING ART:
ALVAR AALTO

A lvar Aalto died in 1976 at the age of seventy-eight. The retrospective of his work at the Cooper-Hewitt Museum three years later was an import, like the pale birch furniture that has become his trademark; it was organized by the Museum of Finnish Architecture in Helsinki, where Aalto lived and worked for almost all of his career.

The avant-garde buildings of the 1920's and 30's—the Turun-Sanomat newspaper office in Turku of 1928–30, the Tuberculosis Sanatorium at Paimio of 1930–33, and the Viipuri Library of 1933–35—share the familiar Aalto themes: the open, skylit, layered space that counts social interaction as high among its functions, the wood details that bring nature to high art, the architecture that is at once coolly aesthetic and warmly human. The highly personal manner that Aalto perfected in the 1950's and 60's, as he moved away from the International Style to something more individual and quite overtly romantic, is traced through such outstanding structures as the Town Hall at Seinäjoki and the Technical University at Otieniemi, as well as the libraries, churches, concert halls, and community centers that he built in and outside Finland during those years.

Aalto's American work, which has never become familiar to the general public, consists of a handful of buildings and interiors. While he had many commissions from large companies in Europe, his atelier-type operation attracted institutional rather than corporate clients here, and the jobs were on a less ambitious scale. An early much-admired work, which brought Aalto to American notice, was the Finnish Pavilion at the 1939 New York World's Fair; an expressionistic use of wood served as a romantic evocation of Finnish forests at the same time that it displayed Aalto's personal design philosophy. The Baker House dormitories of the Massachusetts Institute of Technology were carried out under the pressure of the war years 1947–48, when the Woodberry Poetry Room was designed for the Lamont Library at Harvard. The Edgar Kaufmann, Jr., conference rooms were done for the Institute of International Education in New York in 1963–65, and the Library for Mount Angel Abbey, a Benedictine monastery in Portland, Oregon, was executed from 1965 to 1970.

These buildings frequently made even their admirers uneasy because they were so far out of the modernist mainstream. Critics struggled with their disappointment when so few of the expected International Style hallmarks appeared. It has taken the much-bruited "demise" of modern architecture to make it clear what rich and vital design this is when seen without preconceptions, even in the more limited American translations, and when it is understood on its own—and Aalto's—terms.

Aalto's style, in fact, was a very complex and sophisticated mix. His work moved from neoclassical beginnings through a sleek mastery of modernism, which he used quickly and astutely to become Finland's acknowledged avant-garde leader and to build an international reputation, to a reevaluation of native and romantic sources. His final integration of all these influences was done with an exceptional sensibility and an impeccable twentieth-century eye. The resulting aesthetic owed a great deal to a variety of factors, but was wholly his own. In later years, with the design of Helsinki's Finlandia Hall from 1962 to 1975, he seemed almost to revert to the near-classical quality of the Finnish "national style" of his early

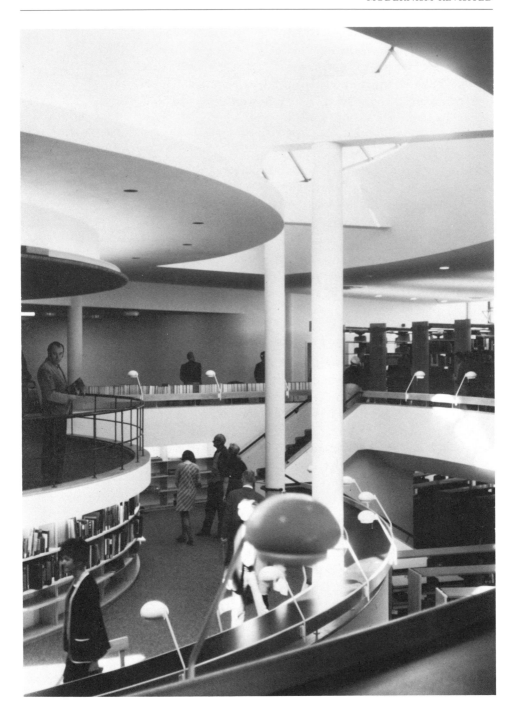

years and training. No throwback, however, this is a suavely assured masterwork. Someone has said that only Aalto could use marble without being pompous.

He was not an austere architect, despite his reduction of elements to calculated essentials. His plans and spaces curved and fanned out freely from the basic box—he was almost alone in his ability to translate the influence of Arp and Miró, using those free forms destined to become the most banal of clichés —into fresh and convincing design elements. Nor was his sensuosity any less strong for being so elegantly understated; he attended equally to the selection of clear, silky, almost-white birch and its lamination and bending into his stylized "tree forms," and to the exact color and profile of the dark blue wall tiles that change subtly as the viewer walks around them. His characteristic palette of white, natural, honey beige, dark blue, and black has a subtle richness that makes bright colors seem cheap and gaudy and quite unnecessary. A stair rail or a door handle becomes an event.

A lover of nature, he never allowed it to upstage him; there were surprisingly few views where one expected them in his buildings. The balance between art and nature was carefully controlled. The way he used natural light to shape and suffuse the multiple levels of a building is his luminous spatial hand-writing. His free forms became everyone else's camp. His way with wood, of course, is legendary: the undulating, slatted ceilings, the columns of bound saplings, the gracefully bent forms, the details that greet the eye no less than the hand, the soft, light finishes and pale natural color that make American wood products look like plastic.

The exhibition and a number of books attest to Aalto's increasing importance and influence on the architectural scene. The kind of total examination of his work that is in order now, long enough after his death to see it whole, is under way. For at least two generations, talented practitioners have paid a kind of quiet homage to his vision, incorporating elements of it that go beyond style or mannerism, as appreciation has risen for his combined aesthetic and environmental skills. There are echoes everywhere, but the understanding and admiration of younger architects for aspects of his sensibility foreclosed to their elders

Opposite page:
Alvar Aalto

Mount Angel Abbey
Portland, Oregon,
1965–70

A door handle or a
stair rail becomes
an aesthetic event

Garth Huxtable

continues to grow. The way in which Aalto adopted and capitalized on the theoretical strengths and technological innovations of the International Style and then, for all polemical purposes, became a dropout looking for alternate architectural expression, is more understandable now.

In retrospect, Aalto was clearly an artist who always knew exactly what he was doing. A small, wise, dapper man, he was a charming maverick in everything he did. Elegant, witty, and convivial, in later years he held increasingly bibulous bull sessions in his studio with staff and visitors in which wine and ideas flowed freely, often into the next morning. He could be courtly; I was always addressed as *"chère madame."* He liked to take people to the Savoy Restaurant in Helsinki, which he had designed in 1937 and which remained satisfyingly unchanged; there he would invariably order delicately cured fish and a very fine red wine. The combination broke all the rules, and so did his architecture. That is exactly the point, of course. Some people need rules; some do not.

Aalto buildings are a rare paradox: they combine intimacy and monumentality with deceptive ease. His structures are full of their own "complexity and contradiction." At the same time, they are most strictly and subtly ordered, and they rely on an almost tyrannical refinement—exactly the right detail to evoke the right sensation and relationship for the right job. Because they deal in a kinetic, sensuous experience rather than in bold exterior images, few of his buildings are particularly photogenic; in an age when reputations are made through images, this has been a disadvantage. It is absolutely essential to experience Aalto firsthand.

His buildings wear their excellence with grace. Above all, they are humane environments in which man is the measure of art. Few architects who walk through them remain unchallenged and unchanged.

July 17, 1979

MISREAD ROMANTIC:
WALLACE HARRISON

I n 1980, a year before his death, the Institute for Architecture and Urban Studies held the first retrospective exhibition devoted to Wallace K. Harrison, the architect who did so much to shape New York's twentieth-century landmarks. It provided unexpected insights into Harrison's work and the period in which he practiced.

The material, most of which had not previously been seen publicly, or had not been seen for a long time, was organized by Rem Koolhaas, a Dutch architect who lives in London and is fascinated by New York. His rather amazing sense of Manhattan produced an earlier, offbeat book and show, *Delirious New York*. Koolhaas deals in mythology—his own and the city's. He has a wonderful sense of the rich, dense disorder that makes New York a uniquely vital urban phenomenon. He understands its criteria of power and disposability. But I do not think he understands Wallace Harrison—at least not in the intimate terms in which Harrison related to New York's peculiarly political architecture. Still, Koolhaas sees Harrison and his work freshly and unconventionally, and that is good when a reputation has hardened into clichés. But he has an oddly distorting lens.

The presentation was supposed to "rehabilitate" Harrison's reputation, which had not been high among hard-line modernists and critics, in spite of his involvement with the city's most important architectural and planning projects since the late 1920's. These include Rockefeller Center; the 1939 New York World's Fair, for which he created the Trylon and Perisphere theme; the United Nations; and Lincoln Center. This list could not be more prestigious or more indivisible from what is perceived as central to New York life. As friend and builder for Nelson Rockefeller, he was the closest New York ever had to an *architecte du roi,* with commissions including a number of Rockefeller residences and the gargantuan and horrendous Albany Mall.

The revealing group of drawings and photographs at the exhibition covered Harrison's vision and working methods over six decades. What was revealed by this overview was surprising, but it was only in part what Koolhaas believed it to be. He saw this work as postmodernist, forty years ahead of its time. No one would have been more surprised than Harrison, the true believer in the gospel according to Le Corbusier. Few have believed that Harrison's aesthetic interpretations, however, were as significant as his aesthetic power-brokering: his ability to bring the right people together under the right auspices at the right time and to turn compromise into architecture, or at least into a reasonable facsimile, is beyond dispute. These were not inconsiderable talents, and they have had a lasting impact on our times.

Koolhaas's curious conclusion was that those features considered dubious or vacillating in Harrison's work then are to be seen as virtues now; what was scored as weak or uncertain in his designs was translated in this interpretation into a kind of courageous foresight, an ability to move boldly beyond modernism. If Harrison really had a design philosophy or method it was, if at first you aren't sure, try, try again. Courageous foresight and unswerving conviction were not his thing; charm, intelligence, a suave hand and an understanding heart for all, but in particular for the rich and powerful, the ability to make a smooth porridge out of a mixed stew, and an unquestioned dedication to the highest objectives of building for art

and the public good were his unique talents, admired then and now. He practiced an unparalleled architectural diplomacy.

In a characteristic display of preliminary sketches, he touched base with a variety of ideological persuasions, a working method that seemed indecisive to some but earned praise as undogmatic by Koolhaas. The soft curving shapes that clearly owe so much to the modernist artists Harrison knew and admired, called hedonistic and voluptuous by Koolhaas, have been labeled superficial and derivative by others. The

Wallace Harrison

New York World's Fair: Trylon and Perisphere, 1939

An architecture of ideals and images

houses described by Koolhaas as "virtuoso exercises in curvilinear predilections" have been characterized as low to medium camp, lacking any central design conviction. Times change. Camp is very much à la mode among postmodernists. For those who believe that they have invented, or reinvented, sensuosity, curves and color, Harrison, supposedly, beat them to it. So there.

What emerged strongly from the exhibition was the fact that Harrison was a supreme romantic—a light in which he has not previously been examined. This is the key that makes his work all fall in place. Romanticism, of course, was the architectural love that dared not speak its name for most of this century, and one's attitude toward the Harrison taste and style is clearly a matter of timing and natural inclination. His education and training in this country actually predated the acceptance of modernism. The year he spent in Paris at the École des Beaux Arts, 1920, reinforced his traditional concepts of beauty and grandeur, just at the time that the European avant-garde was agitating against them.

Harrison sought beauty, consciously and primarily, all his life. He was quite single-minded about it, while others were involved in the pursuit of a revolutionary modernist, sociostructural morality. When he embraced modernism, he was never fully radicalized by it; he always saw Le Corbusier's towers in a park in a luminous radiance, behind softening scrim. He was influenced not a little, like others of his generation, by the American architect and delineator Hugh Ferriss, whose atmospheric charcoal renderings of an ideal, scaleless, romantic city of the future virtually created the American skyscraper style of the late 1920's and early 30's as opposed to the more austere style developing in Europe. Those soaring and shadowed towers and slabs, their romantic masses gleaming in morning mists or crepuscular half-light, stand halfway between the Beaux Arts tradition and modernism, in their own half-world. Even when the trappings changed, the mood remained. Harrison's late lunar landscape for the Albany Mall is an updated Buck Rogers version of the world-of-the-future utopian dream of the visionary twenties. Sheldon Cheney named it, at the time, "the poetry of daring." Call Harrison the Joyce Kilmer of modern architecture.

Aspects of Harrison's work that merit attention may have been ignored or misunderstood; it tends to defy categorization. But it is stretching things to call him an early breaker of modernist taboos; if he broke them, it was an act of unconscious backsliding, or sideslipping, not a great leap forward. It takes a suspension of credulity to see him as the originator of the "forbidden" effects being loudly touted today.

It is not fair to use his architecture to fit a current popular thesis. What is needed is a more objective kind of research and analysis made in the context of the ideals, objectives, practices, illusions, and influences of the architect's own times. For these large and important projects, we need to know the interaction of the practitioners involved and the background against which they worked; we should try to find out whether the systems of design and the plans they devised satisfied, or failed to satisfy, those urban, social, and symbolic purposes that architecture ultimately serves. Distance sharpens vision and understanding, and reality beats second-guessing every time. What is particularly distressing about today's revisionism is that it is so often propagandistic or self-serving rather than information-seeking, with valuable new data forced to fit dubious polemical arguments. All this is troubling, but most disturbing of all is that art and history are being warped out of shape by those who were not there, and who prefer to invent what happened. In Wallace Harrison's case, this simply isn't the way it was at all.

January 6, 1980

FORGOTTEN PROPHET: CLARENCE STEIN

The American town planner Clarence S. Stein is in the position of a prophet not so much without honor as one totally forgotten or taken for granted. He is caught between a younger generation that has never heard of him and an older generation that is suffering the stigma of being ideologically out of fashion. That gave the Clarence Stein commemorative exhibition at the Washington, D.C., headquarters of the American Institute of Architects in 1977 a certain poignance—at least to those who knew him as the early champion of the neighborhood, the greenbelt town, and of regeneration within cities.

The irony, of course, is that as a planner and a humanist, Stein prefigured everything the younger generation throws at the older generation about community, amenity, and the quality of life—concepts so overworked and underpracticed today that they are almost dangerous clichés. He was a man of his time, and ahead of his time, a social reformer who carried out his ideas of bettering the human condition through community design. He understood the kind of relationships between the built world and people's physical and spiritual needs that transcend statistical and demographic data, and his plans were sensitive to those needs in the most primary and heartwarming sense.

Working with his partner Henry Wright, he was responsible for the now-classic (and still extraordinarily pleasant) schemes of the 1920's for Radburn, in Fair Lawn, New Jersey, and Sunnyside, Long Island, for the noble federal town experiments of the 1930's in Greenbelt, Maryland; Greenhills, Ohio; and Greendale, Wisconsin; and for Chatham Village in Pittsburgh and Baldwin Hills Village in Los Angeles. Stein and Wright set goals and patterns that still serve as models. These are the planning prototypes for the best of the postwar British and Scandinavian New Towns and for America's two (ultimately) successful new communities, Reston, Virginia, and Columbia, Maryland.

The hallmarks of all these pioneering projects have become basic to good planning everywhere. They include separation of pedestrian and vehicular traffic, superblock streets with interior green space and houses on traffic-free culs-de-sac. They have connecting footpaths and overpasses. There is always a progression of related outdoor areas from private gardens to landscaped public circulation and shared common land, and a town center combining shopping and leisure activities.

Many of these principles permeate new towns from Stevenage and Harrow in England to Vällingby and Färsta in Sweden. They are found as far afield as Chandigarh in India and Wadi Faliq in Israel. Stein's innovations are simply accepted, like sliced bread.

The fact that the recent rise in environmental consciousness barely recognizes this pioneer is a sad commentary on history and memory. But it is sadder still that when the planning debt is beginning to be acknowledged and the planning need is clearer than ever, the economic, political, and ideological obstacles to rational development in the United States are so great that Stein's aims and principles may be close to unattainable. Certainly the difficulties are far more serious than they were even in the frightening depths of the 1930's, when the government was inclined toward great social experiments and dollar costs and the national debt were far less.

But it is not enough for an exhibition to serve up the planning pieties that passed for public education at an earlier and more innocent time in a truncated text and platitudinous photographs of happy children and contented old folks in traffic-free green surroundings. One can, of course, read Stein's book, written in 1953, *Toward New Towns in America,* which draws together his rich experience. Reissued in 1956 and 1966, it is still pertinent today. Stein owed much to the ideas and practice of the English garden city planners; he was a student of Ebenezer Howard, Raymond Unwin, Patrick Geddes, and, in this country, Frederick Law Olmsted. He had numerous and devoted associates and allies; in addition to his partner, Henry Wright, there were Burton MacKaye, Stuart Chase, Catherine Bauer, and Lewis Mumford. They all endorsed a kind of sensitive and humane planning that was part of the climate of the 1920's and 30's, when the answer to many of the ills of society seemed to be a better place to live. It was a rational, compassionate, idealistic, and somewhat simplistic and naive philosophy. It worked for the middle class. And it is not without relevance now.

But it is an ideal that has been exploded by racial tensions and by the discovery that social malaise lies in a bedrock of complex human problems and deep-rooted inequities to which better physical planning offers few, if any, answers. And some of its most basic and widely used principles—the public ownership of land, for example, to avoid speculative exploitation and to provide the service infrastructure and community facilities that require long-term, up-front investment—are still generally unacceptable in the United States. Because of the inadequacy of this kind of commitment, this country's new town experiments of the 1960's failed.

Stein was not unaware of these complexities, or of the need to press for constant change. He offered no formulas, no certainties, no universal cures. "The planner's shield should be a simple device—a question mark," he wrote. "When an idea becomes conventional, it is time to think it through again."

January 16, 1977

BEYOND
MODERNISM

ALDO ROSSI:
MEMORY AND METAPHOR

I n 1976 the Italian architect Aldo Rossi created one of the
most compelling images in architecture today with his
competition-winning design for the Modena Cemetery. A
rectangular space surrounded by a timeless wall-like structure
reduced the architectural components to an elemental simplicity; repeated voids of blank, empty windows suggested a place
from which all life had fled forever. The image is unforgettable. Its spare, surreal geometry invokes a haunting symbolism
of death and the eternal with an extraordinary intensity. In
avant-garde circles the Modena Cemetery achieved instant status as an almost legendary work of art.

  This is so strong a design, in fact, that its impact has been felt
internationally; in architectural schools here and abroad,
Rossi's work is much imitated by the young. Not only is his
austerely reductive style immediately identifiable, it also seems
to call forth a universal set of emotional responses. There is a
distinct and recognizable "Rossi world." Entering that world
through his projects and drawings—there are only a few executed works—is like going through the looking glass, leaving
reality behind for something that transcends it. One finds his
vision incorporated into one's own, imposed as a kind of uni-

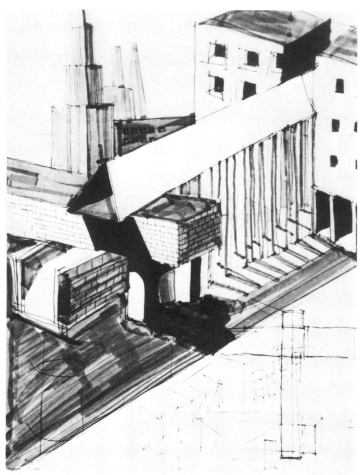

versal experience on a landscape that will never be innocent
of it again.

Whether Rossi's world is art or architecture or a purely
visionary excursion into private terrain, whether it is a structural, political, philosophical or poetic act, is the subject of
much debate. But he has a way of attracting the kind of critical
comment that makes his work seem simple and open by contrast—which it obviously is not.

A concentrated sampling of his work was brought to New
York in 1979, in two concurrent Rossi exhibitions: "Aldo
Rossi—Architectural Projects," covering built work and proj-

ects, and "Aldo Rossi in America: 1976–79," devoted to a series of drawings made on trips to the United States. The double showing reinforced the uniqueness of his product, but it did not make it any easier to categorize it within conventional definitions.

I am not sure that comprehension was aided by the two handsome catalogues that accompanied the shows. One, with an essay by Peter Eisenman and a statement by Rossi, is part of the excellent "Oppositions" series published by Rizzoli and the Institute for Architecture and Urban Design. The other, a Centro Di catalogue edited by Francesco Moschini, with an English translation from the Italian, is also distributed by Rizzoli. Both are daunting flights of aesthetic and philosophical interpretation. Rossi himself expresses surprise about the views of his work offered by the critics. His eyes widen at the theories propounded. But his projects invite this kind of exercise. He is not uninvolved in the arcane debates on typologies and metaphors that his work inspires—based on the idea of universal and timeless buildings that are enduring containers of meaning and memory in architecture.

That wise-child gaze suggests as much of an inward vision as an eye attuned to the world around him. How else to explain a style that contains a chillingly beautiful imagery of cell blocks and towers of concentration camp intensity, raised to forms of elegant abstraction, combined with lyrical touches of striped cabanas and flying pennants that keep recurring in his drawings like elements in a dream? You know that Rossi does not see these stripped barracks of buildings in anything resembling either human or inhuman terms; he is quite surprised at the suggestion that this might not be an architecture of joy, or that its forms might relate tenuously or arbitrarily to its programs. For him, this insistence on what turns out to be a subtly sinister or highly suggestive vocabulary is the elimination of "easy art" (for which, I suppose, read "bourgeois art") for a "true art" reduced to the basic essentials of form (as in "rationalist" architecture). What is important is that these forms then take on an overwhelming visual life of their own.

Much has been made of Rossi's apparent preoccupation with death, and of his Marxist politics, or at least with the kind of

Marxist philosophy fashionable in artistic and intellectual circles. For devout Marxists, however, who see the art of building in service to what they consider obsolete and oppressive institutions, architecture has lost all public validity and meaning; its only possible role at present is a destructive or nihilist one. To those practicing architects who still believe that building is a positive, creative, and problem-solving necessity, requiring specific answers rather than cosmic gloom, the Marxist architect is not an architect at all. The bottom line, however, is that Rossi is a building architect, whenever he gets the chance. By the conventional yardsticks of successful design, Rossi's is an uncompromising art of singular theoretical consistency—but it is neither pure nor simple. When he builds, the results are remarkably unsettling. In his elementary school of Fagnano Olona in Lombardy, the forms and images are searingly memorable, from the crematorium-like chimney to the round, baptistry-like "common classroom and library" pierced by a few strategic openings, placed precisely in a small walled courtyard. Meticulously minimal, these are unbelievably eloquent forms, and they are not without echoes in some of the bleaker and more compelling Italian landscapes.

To Rossi, this kind of design is a pleasant evocation (or typology, or metaphor, if you will) of the town square in the city; to others it looks more like a jail or a gas chamber. I have a hard time imagining children in this school. In photographs, the *poverini* who are committed to it look cheerful enough; in reality, it may not be too far from the more austere local vernacular. Rossi expresses a considerable affection for the ambience he creates. But it is obvious that it is totally that "life of their own" of these forms that he values. In his writings he has made it clear that such buildings are the vessels of the culture of cities. His insistent minimalism, repeated without variation, however, makes his housing in Milan look like a penitentiary block. But it also suggests the spectral magic of a De Chirico painting. Rossi's understanding and manipulation of basic geometry for its visual and emotional content is immensely skilled. Whatever else, it is a natural for monuments and cemeteries.

What interests Rossi increasingly is the series of drawings he calls "Analogues of the City." I think that it is safe to say that these are essentially drawn and painted collages of elements stored in his mind, all of which relate to various cities and landscapes, and the way such memories are kept and conditioned by personal experience and a sense of history. The repeated motifs become so familiar as to seem like trademarks or a kind of design signature. These are not easy ideas to express, and Rossi does not make it any easier by saying that "the idea of analogy can never be fully possessed by the conscious and rational mind." If he means that the juxtapositions and relationships of our visions of the built world are made as much by instinct and unconscious memory as by calculated intent, that seems obvious. And so is the outpouring of subjective interpretations that this makes possible.

Without apologies, then, I offer some superficial responses that may at least have the merit of comprehensibility to those who read and run. Certain objects appear in Rossi's work repeatedly—towers, chimneys, arcades, trusses, small discrete structures like baptistries or farm buildings, the upraised arm of a saint from a baroque statue, a giant coffeepot, palm trees, long arcaded structures often on stilts, those boxlike bathhouses and banners, all seen as a set of special images that have burned their shapes into Rossi's mind at some point in his life. The palm trees, for example, are from Spain; the bathhouses are from Elba. Many complex explanations are offered for these choices and their meanings. Rossi's own explanation is much more direct. "These are the things that I remember, that I have seen in my travels, that have stayed with me. These are things that I like and use over and over again." They are indelible images; I can never, for example, pass a certain sand and gravel plant, with its sharp sheet-metal shapes raised on thin trussed stilts, without seeing Rossi.

It is the way in which he uses these things—obsessively, lyrically, evocatively—that ultimately makes it possible to define his work. Rossi is a poet as much as he is an architect. He is making poetry out of visual devices, as a writer uses literary or aural devices. As words become symbols, so do objects; the architectural world is an endless source of symbols with unique ramifications in time and space. Architecture has given Rossi his poetic and artistic vocabulary.

It is the power of Rossi's poetic images that explains why students copy his work without understanding his sources, or, necessarily, his meanings. There is a kind of universal memory in those images that transcends everything else. That is why flights of interpretive rhetoric invariably accompany all of his drawings and projects. And it is how the boundaries of art continue to expand.

October 7, 1979

LEON KRIER:
THE RADICAL PAST

The deceptively benign and very beautiful architectural drawings by Leon Krier do not at first glance look like a revolutionary statement. But they are, in fact, a manifesto—a renunciation of the modern city and a call for a return to the urban traditions that the modernists disrupted.

The traditions the modernists chose to ignore were embodied in such places as Paris's Place des Vosges and Place Vendôme, Rome's Piazza Navona, and the formal symmetrical squares and crescents of Bath; those ceremonial public spaces, surrounded by churches, palaces, and low-arcaded buildings of brick and stone, were declared monuments to a past way of life. The Renaissance vocabulary of columns, pediments, and pilasters, put together by hand and in the measure of man, was considered inappropriate in structure and style to the needs of an industrial age. Classical architecture was dismissed as obsolete. According to the modernist credo, the new needs, which included offices, factories, and housing on an unprecedented scale, were to be met by the new technology of concrete, steel and glass, which was to create a better and different world of skyscrapers and superblocks. Le Corbusier envisioned tearing out the heart of old Paris, to replace it with a dozen huge towers in a park.

Leon Krier

A world seductively rendered with a radical view of the romantic past

Max Protech Gallery

Today, architects like Krier want to go back to the old ways and the old forms, to construct again in the classical manner and at the human scale of the block and the neighborhood that endured from the sixteenth to the nineteenth century. With an enviable combination of art and nostalgia, and an all-too-wise innocence, they would roll back the twentieth century.

Leon Krier and his brother Robert, born in Luxembourg, are part of the European branch of an international architectural avant-garde that reaches across borders and oceans. They stand for the most radical form of the current rejection of modernism. With other like-minded architects, such as Rossi and the North Italian group called La Tendenza, they are dedicated to a return to a more "rational" way of building.

But their position, which sounds reasonable enough, is ex-

treme rather than moderate. Leon Krier is convinced that technology and industrialization and the innovations of modernism have destroyed everything good about the city—its cultural continuity, its appropriate social patterns, its proper architectural scale and symbolism—for the creation of ugly and alienating wastelands. To restore these qualities, he concludes, one must go back to the kind of construction and the older building types that produced them. In other words, the modernist dictum of "form follows function" becomes "function follows form." "Typologies" in intellectual discourse, they are historical revivals in practice.

Many of Krier's drawings are for the "reconstruction" of parts of Luxembourg, London, Paris, and West Berlin on models that would have been accepted routinely a century ago.

Some of the plans are well-known competition entries, others are the result of his own intensely personal pursuit, in infinite detail, of this "countercity" style, which he promotes assiduously as the proven way that cities have been built over time. The superhighway, the skyscraper, the shopping mall are unacknowledged and expendable.

Most of these assured exercises in classical and vernacular forms are idyllic and serene depictions of a familiar kind of environment common to older European centers. Cleared miraculously of chaos, they offer a comforting small scale, arranged in established patterns of blocks, streets, and squares. They are absolutely without the bombast or shock value of the schemes with which the modernist revolutionaries of the early part of this century announced their rejection of the past and their manifestos for the future.

Only at first glance, however, are they comfortingly familiar. After a while one notices that the idyll is steadily infiltrated by something that can be as sinister as it is seductive. The classical order of these streets and structures is based on strong images of stringent formalism that are eerily manipulative of space and the spectator. There is obviously a lot more going on than immediately meets the eye. The work has a distinctive and haunting quality of its own that is neither of the present nor of the past. There are echoes of Boullée and De Chirico; this is the imagery of an obsessive visionary. And the plans make as clean and ruthless a sweep of the buildings of the twentieth century as the modernists would have—and often did—make of the monuments of the nineteenth-century classical world.

Deceptively conservative, this radical work is meant to be an equally radical political statement. It belongs to the long and complex history of the relationship of politics and art. What is being renounced by Krier, along with modernism and industrialization, is capitalism and the economic, political, and power structure that it embraces; in short, everything that has brought the modern city, with its disruptions, dislocations, and architectural aberrations, into being.

As an architect, Krier's natural extension of this belief is to reject the built world that these conditions have created, and to refuse to function as part of it. This is an act of simple, clean, nihilist logic. "Venality, innovation, and quick profit now destroy Europe's most beautiful cities and countrysides," he tells us. "We can choose not to participate." Thus we have the ultimate revolutionary stance: it is better not to build at all than to contribute to the malaise and monstrosities of modern urban life. The only real architecture, as he defines it, survives from earlier periods. "I do not build because I am an architect," he says, in a marvelously loaded pronouncement. Nor will he compromise. And he has the lost or rejected commissions to prove it.

Unlike the Futurists, who wanted to destroy the culture of the past, Krier wants to save and reconstruct "civilized society." And unlike the modernists, he offers no total and instant utopia. His solution is to go back to the preindustrial city; he believes that all the problems of architecture were solved before the Industrial Revolution. His plans are incremental bits and pieces on a neighborhood scale; he picks up and continues the arcaded streets and public squares and their masonry and timber buildings as if the art and technology of the twentieth century had never happened and no time had intervened. Only traditional crafts and the classical style and its vernacular versions are used.

This is what Paul Goodman used to call, for its convincing logic in total conflict with reality, "crackpot realism." These simple, rational and appealing schemes make perfect sense if you bypass existing methods of construction, financing, and control and discount the whole complex mechanism by which politics, investment, and special interests respond to an assortment of needs, tastes, and priorities.

Surely one would have to be naive not to realize that the processes by which we build and govern are faulty, and blind not to know that these processes have both disrupted and debased the established tradition and amenities of scale, style, and ambience that distinguished the city until the industrial age. It is not necessary to invoke Marx or Marcuse; capitalism is not the only culprit. All political systems have used industrialization badly. There is no beneficent, progressive technology; we are aware of the incestuous relationships of power, profit, and politics that have shaped the twentieth-century world so badly.

But to say that architects, by abandoning the classical tradition, left themselves no way to oppose the abuse of the environment by the interests of money and power is to ignore the fact that these interests have been equally well served by classicism and the Academy; the glory of ancient Greece and Rome and the derivatives thereof have been no proof against corruption and no guarantee of democratic ideals. That point, ironically, was basic to the modernists' rejection of classicism. And to think only in terms of craft methods today is to ignore the irreversible conditions of contemporary building technology. This is truly awesome irrationality.

But if Krier's world is unworldly, it can be surpassingly lovely, and it is still susceptible to rational interpretation. As the critic and historian Kenneth Frampton points out, Krier's emphasis on "the cultural importance of place" has already proved significant. His plans have been influential far beyond their unexecuted state for the way in which they have reestablished a lost vision. There is an increasing preoccupation with critical problems of preservation and new construction in terms of the existing historical fabric of cities—a growing understanding and valuation that owes a great deal to his urban essays. Not the least reason for this influence is that Krier is a talented architect and magical delineator. In the years that Krier worked in England in the office of James Stirling, it is hard to tell who influenced whom, but there are distinct echoes of Krier's personal vision in Stirling's work today; they share an erudite, quirky set of references to the past, and Krier's unique renderings have become absorbed into the Stirling style. But while Krier moved steadily and relentlessly back to post and lintel, column and beam, Stirling's industrial aesthetic took on a classical cast and components for a startling and remarkable stylistic marriage.

Krier makes the point that no commission has ever tempted him to alter his position or beliefs. When his plans for a school at St. Quentin-en-Yvelines in France came in 200 percent over the budget, he gave up the job rather than change or cheapen the character of his design. But if he does not compromise, he does temporize somewhat; one notes that he says he does not build "for the time being."

And so he draws—superbly and with consummate art. His exquisitely controlled, delicate ink, pencil, and wash renderings create a world of evocative magic. An airy pavilion overlooks the misty hills of Tuscany, and one knows that it is morning; faded red flags flutter in a wooden frame, and one feels the breezes through them; minimalist perspectives trap one in eternal abstractions of measured urban space. The cool clarity and sheer beauty of these drawings is breathtaking. The poetry, without the politics, is pure.

February 1, 1981

JAMES STIRLING: HIGH-TECH HISTORY

The creative processes in architecture have less to do with the muses of inspiration than with the painstaking resolution of site, program, structure, and plan. That procedure can be understood fairly easily; what is less clear are the aesthetic and cultural impulses that account for those very personal decisions that give the solution its specific shape and style.

For anyone interested in both aspects of the process, James Stirling's design for the expansion of Harvard's Fogg Museum provides considerable insight. This is the Harvard architectural event of the 1980's, which parallels Le Corbusier's Carpenter Center as the architectural event of the 1960's. A great, gray concrete presence that bursts from its constricted site near the Fogg with massive exuberance, the Carpenter Center represented the arrival on American, or Harvard, soil of the work of one of the great architectural talents of the twentieth century.

There are those who see the British architect James Stirling as a member of that same exalted company. His firm, James Stirling, Michael Wilford and Associates, has a number of commissions in this country—an addition to the School of

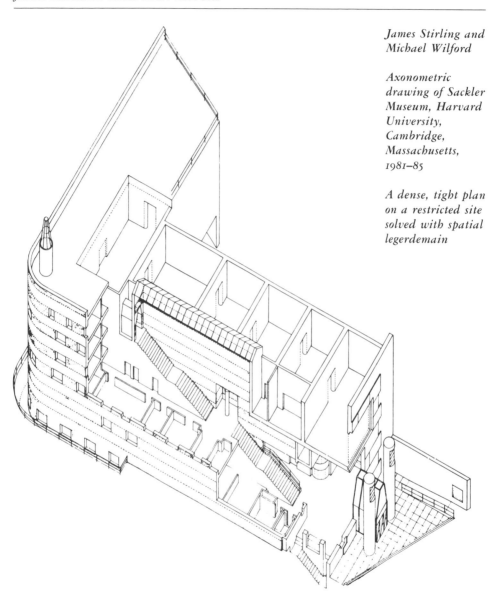

James Stirling and Michael Wilford

Axonometric drawing of Sackler Museum, Harvard University, Cambridge, Massachusetts, 1981–85

A dense, tight plan on a restricted site solved with spatial legerdemain

Architecture at Rice University in Houston, a performing arts center at Cornell University, and the Fogg, which is being carried out with Perry, Dean, Stahl and Rogers of Boston. Stirling has not been a prolific builder, but such structures as the Engineering School at Leicester College and the History

Faculty Building at Cambridge, England, have been viewed as architectural landmarks, with as many visitors, as the saying goes, as buildings have mice, and as many problems as daring design, experimental technology, questionable fabrication, and deferred or delinquent maintenance can create. The functional flaws of these buildings have been as notable as their much copied stylistic trademarks.

A high priest of high tech in the 1950's and 60's, Stirling has moved on to explore historical and classical sources in a radically personal way that would set academicians spinning in their Beaux Arts tombs. With his switch from less-than-tried-and-true technology to more traditional methods and materials in recent years, the buildings seem to be holding together better. And his unconventional combinations and juxtapositions have resulted in a provocative, idiosyncratic style that recalls the strengths and eccentricities of another unconventional architect, Nicholas Hawksmoor. Stirling's creative energy, powerful images, and masterful treatment of space, light, and procession, as well as his handling of the formal relationships of art and use, put him at the top of today's list of architects, in company with the best of the century. Not least in today's context is his ability to use these devices in innovative, ahistorical ways while still invoking the lessons of the past.

Today's innovators are a more numerous and diversified group than they were in the High Modern period; introspective rather than heroic or universal in their ambitions, they are moving closer to a human scale and context. The new work is not only literary and eclectic, it is often obscure and puzzling in its use of symbols and historical references. It favors image, style, and language over social and structural concerns. Nothing could be more instructive about these changes in architectural theory and practice than the two Harvard buildings.

With hindsight, it becomes obvious that this has been a steady, ongoing, evolutionary transformation. It is also evident that the changes are crystallizing into a new architectural style. What is on the line now is the kind of modernism in which an abstract concept of geometric beauty was reduced to its simplest visual and structural terms, carefully and rigorously detached from the traditions and restrictions of the past. It was an architecture that made a bold, revolutionary statement about art, technology, and the perfectibility of the world. We have become a sadder and wiser society. But even the miscalculations of modernism can be impressive.

Both life and art tend to be messy and lacking in moral consistency. This is a truism that turns out to have certain architectural virtues, as Robert Venturi has reminded us, since the mess is a rich accumulation of cultural acts and accidents. The espousal of messiness, under the names of inclusiveness and complexity, has followed. But what has also followed is that the architect still creates order, by the very process that organizes and resolves the problem and its parts. Show me ad hoc architecture by an architect and I will show you relationships that may be subliminal or subversive, but they are there. Or it is not architecture—but that is a serious matter for another time.

James Stirling has dealt in a very high kind of order and organization in the design of the Fogg; this is a dense, tight plan on a small restricted site that brilliantly solves administrative and gallery needs. The building is remarkable for the creative virtuosity with which its functions are accommodated while suggesting a monumentality that belies its actual dimensions. Stirling was lucky to have as a client the director of the Fogg, Seymour Slive, who understood this achievement immediately. Professors John Coolidge and Neil Levine complete a formidable triumvirate of sympathetic experts.

But if there is functional clarity here, there is also a great deal of aesthetic ambiguity. Stirling's current preoccupation is with oddly scaled and strangely evocative elements of archaic and classical periods, with fragmentary historical references wrought large and mysterious; he displays an attachment to the tomb and the crypt and the monuments of the far-distant past —not as scholarly archeology, but with the more romantic flavor of cinema. At the same time, he has not lost his infatuation with the trappings of technology. In fact, he has put the two together for an extraordinary classical-technological eclecticism that creates a startling imagery. The classical elements are deliberately distorted and stripped of their original structural rationale for strange and unsettling effects. He adds to this a Pop palette of strong colors, from pea green to purple. The results are not easy to forget.

The entrance facade of the Fogg extension, called the Sackler Museum, is just such an image. It is also currently the most disliked exterior in the Harvard architectural hierarchy, a dubious honor previously held by its immediate neighbor, Ware and Van Brunt's rich Ruskinian Gothic plum pudding, Memorial Hall. The entry to the Sackler is a slant-sided, flat-topped enclosure of glass and metal, flanked by two monumental cooling towers, like a space age pair of classical columns. This high-tech element is framed by overscaled classical quoins that surround the doors and an opening just above, which may or may not be used for a connecting bridge to the older building. The quoins flaunt their nonstructural character; it is their visual and evocative impact that counts.

The small entrance space is expanded vertically with a high ceiling emphasized by lighted false columns, which are used purely as a scaling device; this bit of heresy works spectacularly well. The verticality is further stressed by a central stair on a direct line with the entrance, which sweeps narrowly up to the building's full height. It is flooded with daylight from the top. These dramatic organizational skills turn small space into a marvel of suggestive grandeur; it has something of the same luminous legerdemain as the Soane Museum.

The stair is the spine between offices and galleries that provides both visual and processional space; it is tightly flanked by five floors of offices on one side and three double-height galleries on the other, separated by a polychrome wall. The offices are random sizes, reflecting staff preferences and needs, which, in turn, are reflected in the fenestration. Stirling ignored the standard modernist practice of establishing a modular system for a uniform office measure and formal street elevation—one imagines that he accepted the dictates of individual academic intransigence with considerable glee. Instead, he has matched random windows to the random offices, and then used some fast brickwork to contain the irregular window patterns within polychrome bands. His sketches show that he would prefer purple or green to the more discreet coloration that the authorities have selected; but the device unifies the openings into a horizontal composition that totally transforms the facade's emphasis and balance. Because the steel exterior is an office wall, however, it offers no ceremonial facade; the formal entrance, on the short side, almost explodes its small dimensions, and until, and if, a planned connecting bridge is built to the Fogg, it will remain ambiguous and unresolved.

Look carefully at the design of the exterior, and it becomes evident that those colored brick bands are meant to suggest the Victorian polychromy of the architectural fruitcake just down the block, Ware and van Brunt's Memorial Hall. Look again, and those horizontal bands will pick up the projecting levels of John Andrews's High Modern and equally distracting and disjunctive Gund Hall, the Graduate School of Design, just beyond. But this is no modest act of deference to a neighborhood that is commonly considered an architectural zoo; it is simply a way of living with the animals—now known as contextualism.

Nor do these references make Stirling's design any less positive a statement of his own intentions, which clearly include the need and desire to disturb the established way of seeing. High on his list is the wish to push the senses to the rediscovery of some of the grandest and subtlest tricks in the architect's bag, traditional and otherwise. He does this in the most provocative way possible, with a very private and internal sensibility and some willfully skewed history. He does not play it safe and he can blow it here and there. But he rarely blows it all, and the strength of this work makes the better publicized postmodern buildings look like prissy exercises in designer dandyism.

The critic Charles Jencks has characterized Stirling's recent direction as an enigmatic and perplexing conjecture on the past. Stirling prefers to see his juxtapositions of the unexpected as "delightful ambiguity." He favors an architecture that is "neither ancient nor modern, primitive nor technological." What he admires most is "a free-wheeling constructive manipulation of elements" in the manner of Hawksmoor or Schinkel. As a philosophy and method, it is anything but risk-free.

In sum, this is not easy architecture. And it is not innocent architecture. It is knowledgeable, worldly, elitist, difficult, and even quirky architecture. The emphasis is on myth and monumentality rather than on the old partnership of form and function. But whatever the conspicuous departures from modernist practice, it is in the expressive use of basic spatial and structural combinations that Stirling and Le Corbusier share common ground at Harvard in other than their physical contiguity. Nothing substitutes for this synthesis of idea, means, and image. Call the new architecture postmodernism, revisionism, or revolution, the fact remains that you've got to be as good as Stirling to pull it off. It takes an extraordinary talent to combine reference and invention with the creative force that moves architecture into a new age.

May 31, 1981

JOHN HEJDUK: FABLES FOR THE FUTURE

I n 1980, John Hejduk was the subject of two simultaneous exhibitions. "John Hejduk: Seven Houses" revealed a painstaking investigation of the elements underlying architectural form, carried out as a series of house studies made over a period of nine years, from 1954 to 1963. Another show, "The Works of John Hejduk," consisted of later projects, of the 1960's and 70's, in a totally different vein—intensely personal, visionary, and poetic schemes where architectural forms are primarily vehicles of mystery and metaphor. Call them frightening fairy tales for the malaise of our times.

The two shows and the two themes illustrate two sides of a very complex and talented man. Nor are these two sides of vision mutually exclusive—like night and day they are part of the same quotidian cycle, a theme of contrasts that Hejduk likes and has explored, incidentally, in a scheme for a "day and night" house. There is a good deal of crossing over between these poles of expression.

John Hejduk is equally concerned with vast mysteries and the most impeccably calculated structural details. In the seven-house project (done with the help of a Graham Foundation grant while he was teaching at the University of Texas in Austin), he was working on the reduction of a basic architec-

John Hejduk

*House study
drawing*

*Defining structure
as abstract poetry*

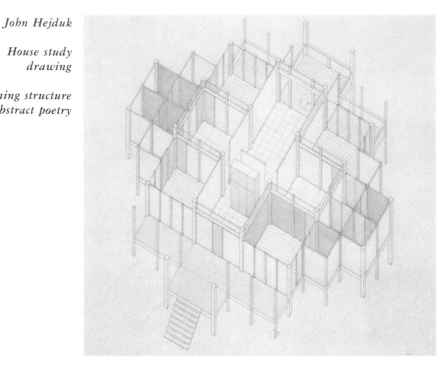

tural object to its most absolute elements. The houses are all composed of nine squares, with a seemingly infinite analysis of how columns, piers, walls, and panels create related enclosures within an ideal symmetry, carried to the point where it succeeds in demonstrating how complex the search for basics can become. It was a nine-year, one-man investigation of the architectural generators of form. This required a mind of Euclidian curiosity and the transcendental attitudes of a saint; John Hejduk has both.

It is clear from the meticulous drawings that he is in love with the art of architecture and filled with awe and admiration for those who have raised it to its highest level. There are echoes, in these houses studies, of the villas of Palladio and Le Corbusier; there is homage to Mies. It is also clear that he is a mystic and a poet; there are suggestions of everything from the solemn fears instilled by a Catholic childhood to the discovery of the suave beauties of the Italian landscape encountered during a Fulbright year abroad. And he has indeed become

62

best known for his narrative fantasies—architectural metaphors and morality tales with titles like "Silent Witnesses" and
"Cemetery for the Ashes of Thought," and for the lyrical
drawings and paintings that express these ideas.

But what is not too well understood is that he is a fine
architect, very much overpublicized as a dreamer and under-
publicized—and undercommissioned—as a builder. As head of
the Cooper Union School of Architecture in New York, he
remodeled, with Peter Bruder and Ed Aviles, the historic
Cooper Union building, displaying great skill in the creation
of new spaces within a landmark structure. It is a restoration
and conversion of unusual elegance and style.

To point up the dichotomy of his work further, the house
exercises at the institute are precise line drawings in black and
white, or more correctly, in shades of gray, executed in extremely fine hard pencil. These detailed explorations of the
language of architecture are technically exquisite—it would be
hard to find more beautiful renderings.

The other work is free, fanciful, executed in a variety of
media and full of color. The colors are so lovely and light-
hearted that they are like candy coatings on timeless themes of
infinity and dread. Picture thirteen tall, close-ranked towers on
a bare Venetian plaza containing thirteen men condemned to
dwell in them for a lifetime, with one house for another
dweller who will take the place of the first man who dies. And
then imagine, on another solitary square, "the house of the
inhabitant who refused to participate," where the functions of
living are reduced to a punitive simplicity, exposed to the gaze
of strangers, in an obscure symbolic world somewhere between the eye and the mind. This is a series called "The Thirteen Watchtowers of Canareggio." A script provides the
explanation, but the images have a life of their own.

Peter Eisenman, writing in one of the Institute for Architecture and Urban Studies' publications, has summed up this work
superbly; he characterizes Hejduk's house studies as "a synthesis of abstraction and reality [using] a reduced vernacular of
the 20th century in the 16th-century manner." He points out
that this rational simplicity "contains a conceptual overload, a
density and compaction of themes." It is evident that when

Eisenman says that these designs "articulate an intrinsic architectural language," dealing as they do in a basic geometry of space and form, he means it as an object lesson to those who are busy today articulating such things as decorative detail or historical recall.

There are also some interesting statements by Hejduk himself. One refers directly to the period of the Texas house project, and its observations and sentiments are a delightful indicator of his particular sensibilities.

> In 1954 . . . I returned from the landscape of Italy to that of the hill country of central Texas. . . . The landscape of Texas is sparse; objects take on a clarity and remoteness. There is a magic moment in the fall after weeks of intense dry heat when the Blue Northern comes down across the northeast plains. Temperatures drop 50 degrees within minutes and the air becomes cool and crystal clear; the shadows deepen. It is also a time when you can run after armadillos. Now armadillos appear to be hard, but in fact they are soft and they shed tears when you catch them by the tail; so you let them go.
>
> There are a lot of things you let go of in Texas. You let go of old visions and old romances, you let go of city-states and northern broodings. But, in letting go, other things and other moods are captured, such as the meaning of isolated objects, of void spaces. You capture the horizontal and you capture a flatness, a flatness which impregnates your thoughts and fills you with an anticipation—an anticipation of the solemnity of detail and construction.

The Texas house studies are solemn, isolated objects created in precise structural detail. They have severe limitations, the result of formal restrictions that are scrupulously self-imposed. But in their response to a special time and place and their total preoccupation with the genesis of form, they represent that part of architecture that transcends practical reality. His is the kind of vision that transforms structure into poetry and art.

February 3, 1980

MICHAEL GRAVES:
A PERSONAL LANGUAGE

A 1979 exhibition of work by Michael Graves at the Max Protech Gallery documented some of the most significant changes going on in the art of architecture today. A charter member of a loosely allied group of younger practitioners of quite wide diversity who have become known as postmodernists, Graves has moved from an intricately mannered modernism to a romantic historicism of equally complex artfulness.

Graves's ideas were effectively exposed in this exhibition, which consisted of fully developed schemes from intimate early sketches to detailed renderings and models, plus a selection of photographs of completed work, a sampling of sketchbooks, and the mural-size abstract paintings that he executed both for his buildings and for his own continuing exploration of color and form. Graves's painting and architecture stand on their own merits. In fact, one of the distinctive characteristics of his work is that the two arts partake of each other's nature in a way that adds a dimension to each that neither would have had without such interaction. This is, in effect, a hybrid art, exploring new architectural horizons.

Graves has built some houses and parts of houses in New

Jersey and Indiana (he came from Indianapolis by way of Harvard and is currently based in Princeton), and is engaged in the design of some larger and more important buildings. One of his most interesting projects was for the Fargo-Moorhead Cultural Center, a remarkable concept that would have joined North Dakota and Minnesota in a single structure spanning the Red River. This powerful, poetic Ledoux-like design shattered a lot of ideas about what such a building, or any building, should be like. Even without that distinction, it is probably one of the most beautiful architectural drawings of recent times. The Fargo-Moorhead Center appears to have aborted before construction, but an equally controversial structure, the Portland Public Service Building of Portland, Oregon, a competition-winning project, has been completed, to the noticeable disappointment of some of its more ardent champions, who hailed the design as the postmodern beacon of the eighties. There have apparently been enough crippling economies to make the building less than a perfect exemplar of Graves's intentions.

This is the sort of work that sends the viewer away with the sense that some kind of breakthrough is being made, and that the art of architecture has been moved a step further along its creative and historical path. A departure of this sort, arrived at gradually over the years in Graves's case, can lead to a dramatic expansion of design possibilities or to an overemphasis on surface effects. It will shock and puzzle anyone grown comfortable with the "tradition" of modernism. Radical change that readjusts vision and meaning this deeply ruptures easy understanding and carries enormous risks.

A Michael Graves facade may look like a pastiche of building parts, or a kind of jigsaw of trompe l'oeil materials and historical references. But traditional elements are never copied directly; they are filtered through the interpretations and reinterpretations of centuries of changing vision and culture, to be recombined in an intensely personal and abstract way. They can be wrenched out of context, like the removal of the keystone of an arch from the entrance of a house, to have the form reappear as another part of the structure. These buildings are like films that use flashbacks and events seen through many eyes to tell a story of ambiguous and multifaceted meanings. Graves speaks of his "diaries and sketchbooks of remembered things," of sources that range from antiquity to the International Style. But the details that he records are treated more as inspirational archetypes; he seeks the essence of walls, doors and rooms, the way in which style and association shape our sense of being and place.

On the most universal level, this is an architecture that is meant to create perceptions of special relationships between the worlds of man and nature. In Graves's eyes, the windowed interiors of a painting by Mantegna and the ceremonial doors and windows of a house by Palladio both reveal the "event" of the opening to the outside world in a very special way—an event that only architecture can properly celebrate.

Graves's early designs were tortuously preoccupied with the mannerisms of 1920's international modernism. Their thin screen walls lapped and overlapped and were embellished with a geometric fanfare of railings, stairs, and balconies. The work was so packed with ideas and effects that its intricacy verged on hysteria. Even so, Graves was always in control. Unfortunately, it was just this complexity for its own sake that younger architects chose to emulate.

But above all, Graves is a colorist. His sense of color is elegant and subtle and an integral part of his art. Those early "white" houses that were so well publicized were not meant to be left unpainted. Graves uses what he calls "representational" color, keyed to nature and the environment, with base tones in dark green or terra-cotta to suggest ground or brick, and blue tones above for sky. The polychromed wall always has a specific set of references.

It is important that all of these references, from color to metaphor and historical recall, serve a larger, unifying idea. Otherwise Graves's work would be no more than disruptive surface embellishment—something it skirts dangerously. What keeps it from being just "bits and pieces" eclecticism is the aesthetic intelligence that digests and transforms the sources into a consistent and unified language of design. Every age has its architectural vocabulary, based on its particular articles of faith. All architects build with such a set of principles, whether they invent them—as Graves does—or inherit them as received wisdom, such as the functional and structural determinism of modernist doctrine. That is how style evolves. Graves's architecture goes considerably beyond the borrowings from the past that are being thrown around like so much loose change today for a "historicism" that is no more than shorthand caricature. He is slowly, painstakingly, and lovingly resolving a different language of form and meaning, taking us into a realm of architecture where we have not been before.

If he has left some of the highly publicized decorative gropings of postmodernism behind, however, he must still demonstrate more than pictorial skills. The transformation of Graves's subtle and painterly collages of ideas, references, textures, and colors to important three-dimensional buildings is something one awaits with a mixture of hope and fear. The drawings are such elegant artifacts in themselves. But something happens in the translation from the picture plane to the real world, and the executed works simply do not read the same way that they do on paper; the intriguing aesthetic intelligence can turn into an architecture that is fussy, flat, obvious, or obscure. Graves's fully developed ideas have great subtlety and power, originality and elegance. Above all, they are expressed in a language of forms, colors, and details that are distinctly his own—a point of no small importance in a day when an identifiable style is the first step to recognition and reputation. How successful this stylistic language is as architecture is still an open debate; judgment can be made only on the basis of the completion of at least one major uncompromised work.

May 27, 1979

THE VENTURI
ANTI-STYLE

The Allen Memorial Art Museum at Oberlin College, a Renaissance palazzo out of Brunelleschi by way of Cass Gilbert and the Beaux Arts (1915–17), is a gem of a building for a gem of a collection. It has turned a small Ohio town into an extraordinary place.

When the museum needed to expand, the architectural assignment posed a special challenge. A perfectly cut and polished Cass Gilbert building is a hard act to follow. Robert Venturi, of the firm of Venturi, Rauch and Scott Brown, which was given the job, compares it to "drawing a moustache on a madonna. A wing on a symmetrical Renaissance villa, like a bowler hat on a Venus, will never look correct." Having thus succinctly stated the problem, he proceeded to solve it.

The solution is anything but standard. The work he has done with his wife, Denise Scott Brown, on the iconography of the Las Vegas strip and Levittown has made him the apostle of complexity and contradiction and the dumb and ordinary, in one or another combination, and the conscious practitioner of plain and fancy symbolism. But the image of the architect as a Pop guru is actually a cliché that serves him badly, and perhaps this building can help set the record straight. The

70

result, in fact, is urbane, cultured, deeply responsive to history and art, and unusually understanding of existing values—a solution of sophisticated, subtle, sympathetic, and sometimes wry sensibility.

The new museum wing is only a shocker to those with predetermined ideas of how such a wing should be designed or look. To anyone who examines it carefully, a thoughtful logic unfolds. It is not a statement of dogma or doctrine, although enough of that can be dragged in by the feet to make an interesting argument. The new building has been designed, above all, with a concerned and gentle hand. The solution is unconventional enough, however, to have raised a few hackles on campus where the Allen Museum is something of an icon, and to fuel the legend of Venturian perversity.

The new wing is a stepped-back block that joins the Cass Gilbert building at the side and rear. It connects directly to it without the kind of separating link that is considered a properly respectful signal of transition from old to new. It makes no obeisances to the original structure by repeating patterns of arcades or windows in "updated" versions. It jogs back on the site unevenly. It does nothing expected or obvious.

The facade closest to the old building is a "checkerboard" of rose and cream sandstone with strip windows; the design becomes a "pure" 1930's loft building as it sets back once again and changes functions from a gallery to school and laboratory. And although there are "reasons" for all of this— the kind of aesthetic and symbolic rationale for a Venturian philosophical exercise that can be both edifying and fun— everything works in purely architectural terms. The solution is successful in the justness and appropriateness of its visual, functional, and programmatic relationships, which is the test of good architecture at any time. Taste and judgment are the eternal elite verities that do the job.

Quite properly, use and a restricted site have determined the plan. This led to butting the new construction against the old and placing it toward the back of the land to gain the most space and still keep the Cass Gilbert design dominant. The transitional element is a large new exhibition space, the Ellen Johnson Gallery of Modern Art. Set slightly behind this gal-

*Venturi, Rauch
and Scott Brown*

*Allen Memorial
Art Museum,
Oberlin, Ohio, 1977*

*A cultured response
to art and history*

Tom Bernard

lery, the rest of the new wing houses the art school and library
and the labs of the Intermuseum Conservation Association.
The addition is crisply contemporary; its "recalls" of the older
building are, at best, artfully intellectual. A deep roof overhang only suggests the Italianate original; it is equally reminiscent of indigenous midwestern modernism. The checkerboard
wall is almost like a patterned fabric background for the beautiful Renaissance decoration of the Cass Gilbert design in the
same rose and cream stone. Asymmetrical windows stop carefully short of the classical structure.

The new building makes a point of its respect for the old one
and its conscious lack of pretentiousness. The meticulously
detailed strip windows and plain buff brick of the school and
lab section deliberately suggest a very classy loft building. It

is exactly the kind of building that suits working artists best. Inside, the new modern art gallery is a large, almost square room, sixty-one by fifty-five feet and twenty-three feet high. But this is not the average museum director's neutral, flexible container with all-purpose modular lighting and panels. It is an extremely dramatic space flooded with daylight, which holds contemporary art beautifully. The gallery insists on being architecture at the same time that it serves as a setting, and in doing so, it enhances the total aesthetic experience.

The daylight comes from high windows that run around the top of the room, controlled by the roof overhang and translucent Plexiglas panels that also screen out harmful rays. Outside, at a point between the new gallery and the enchanting Renaissance courtyard of the old, there is a typical Venturi touch—a symbol-sculpture of a giant Ionic column at trompe l'oeil scale. It has been made by applying stylized wood forms to a structural column.

The new gallery restates the main space of the Cass Gilbert building, a superb, classical sculpture court thirty-six feet high. The firm's work in the old building includes the installations of new lighting, air-conditioning and security systems, new graphics and paint colors, and the "rehabilitation" of spaces for print and drawing collections.

In this undertaking, as in all their work, the Venturis stress the need to follow simple and familiar models. What is not spelled out in their eclectic rule book, however, is how purpose becomes style, and that, rather than iconographic gamesmanship, is the prime lesson of the past. If this kind of architecture is "anti-style," then the Venturis have made the most of it.

January 30, 1977

THE MEIER
SUPERSTYLE

I

There are some buildings that the world watches, and some buildings that the profession watches. From the moment its construction began, an international assortment of journalists and critics, Japanese visitors by the busload, and local architects on day trips were beating a path to the Bronx Developmental Center by Richard Meier and Associates. The structure's sleek silvery skin and carefully machined look turned on most professionals and turned off most laymen. An object of controversy from the start, it was a landmark before its doors opened.

Meier's addition to the Bronx State Hospital complex, adjacent to the Hutchinson River Parkway, has been built for the New York State Department of Mental Hygiene by the State's Facilities Development Corporation. Until then, the architect had been known for a series of pristine white houses of complex and sophisticated artistry. This was his first large-scale public work. Representative of some of today's most progressive trends in architectural design, Meier's building stands on its own, and on its merits, as a distinguished work. That it was able to achieve such quality and status while dealing with a program in a state of total flux—the treatment of the retarded or mentally ill is one of the most embattled subjects of

Richard Meier

Bronx
Developmental
Center, New York,
1977

A disciplined use of
architecture in
conflict with
programmatic
change

Ezra Stoller

the decade—is remarkable in itself. After planning and during construction, a series of radical changes in attitude toward the care and treatment of those severely disabled both mentally and physically took place, and the debate still rages about whether they should be institutionalized or their treatment "normalized" within the community. According to Dr. David Kliegler, deputy director of the Bronx Developmental Center, nothing has been resolved; no one really knows what is best. But practices are being drastically revised. That the building's design survived this kind of programmatic and ideological chaos, and that it has done so with clarity and distinction, says much for the flexibility and durability of the building art.

The facility was originally intended as a center for training those mentally retarded who, it was hoped, could eventually learn to adapt to normal living; there is even a small "house" where they would live while this training took place. Now that the idea of the "holding" institution, or self-sufficient "community," has been cast into doubt and the resident population reduced, the almost monastic atmosphere has become an anachronism. The new conventional wisdom is to bus the pa-

tient out into the community as much as possible for education and services, and to mix residents, staff, and outpatients within the center. Almost every space in this building has been converted to some use other than the one originally intended. Clearly, the ultimate test of success or failure for this kind of structure will be in the adaptability of the physical plant to modifications of theory and practice and the degree to which the staff exploits its potential.

The architect has brought a rigorous intellect and a sensitive aesthetic to these nearly insoluble problems. The site is a triangular twelve acres of limbo bounded by railroad tracks, parkways, and scattered, scaleless construction. The plan consists of two parallel and connected four-story units about 565 feet long —a service and a residential section—joined across a landscaped court. By turning inward to this court, the complex creates its own environment. The main entrance is through the section for services, in which the treatment, therapy, and public spaces for both residents and outpatients are concentrated. The residential wing consists of slightly offset "houses" broken down into "family" units of twenty-four, further divided into groups of eight. All of the buildings are encased in a taut thin skin of flat, soft-finished silver-toned aluminum.

Immediately upon entry, the glass-walled reception area gives a view of the entire complex that makes its organization clear. The progress from public to private spaces is skillfully controlled, from reception, classrooms, clinics and cafeteria, across the court with its outdoor classroom extensions, sculptured steps, walls, slides and amphitheater, by way of a glass-roofed corridor or open walk, to the residential quarters. All of these uses are "coded" visually by the window types, the nature of the exterior skin panels, and the articulation of the parts. In this way, the whole building can be "read." The aluminum panels shift from horizontal to vertical, for example, from the classrooms with their elongated windows to a closed vertical stairwell. The windows themselves are round-cornered, like bus windows (curious intimations of a mobile technology) and are held rigidly flat with the wall surface in residential or classroom areas. In the more public dining, social, or therapy areas (pool, gymnasium, etc.) they become larger, slightly inset, mullioned glass expanses. There is a rhythmic fugue of fenestration, allied to a subtly expressive skin. No one really knows about the effect of design quality, but the intent is to create a "comfortable" physical and psychic environment.

In this building, Meier has gone beyond the lyrical abstraction of his white houses. There is a fusion of form and purpose in which style and function become a single thing. The elements of structure and skin, circulation and use, are put together like a fine expensive watch. (The building has been called a Patek Philippe on the outside and a Timex on the inside by one architect-observer; the interiors use limited stock parts livened by a diffusion of fragmented colors that cannot disguise their standardized construction.)

The whole project is marked by an extremely disciplined interlocking of logic and art. In spite of its fashionably "minimalist" components, this building has a richness of composition and a finesse and originality of form that mark an important new phase of Meier's design.

May 8, 1977

II

On the banks of the Wabash River, not far from the cornfields of Indiana, stands a gleaming white structure that is as radical an addition to the rural American heartland as Le Corbusier's Villa Savoie was to the French countryside at Poissy half a century ago.

Called the Atheneum, the building is the visitors' center for the historic town of New Harmony—the Indiana village that played a uniquely important role in nineteenth-century social idealism, religion, and science. This Atheneum is not, as one would expect, a classical place of learning; the name draws more from New Harmony's intellectual heritage than from the building's present functions. It is a reception and orientation center built around a series of exhibits and presentations through which the visitor is channeled. By the time the journey has been made from the ground floor to the rooftop terrace for views of the river and town, one has also become familiar with the story and spirit of New Harmony. At the same time, one has been exposed to an extraordinary series of architectural

Richard Meier

New Harmony, Indiana, Atheneum, 1979

Processional public space of intricate and subtle style

Ezra Stoller

impressions in which the sense of the past is heightened, both physically and poetically, by the experience of the present.

This latest building by Richard Meier and Partners—public, open, dealing in movement and process made visible—is the perfect vehicle for the architect's evolving personal, intricate, and highly sophisticated style. It carries his rigorous explorations of geometry and space about as far as they can go.

Middle America has mixed feelings about the Atheneum—a controversy that extends into professional ranks. There are those who call it inappropriate for the setting and the purpose, who find its striking forms just as strikingly out of place. But there are also those who consider the building a significant step beyond the accepted ways of composing architectural space for a whole new range of perceptions and experiences. The matter of suitability is bound to be an extremely subjective judgment. But I think the nature of the building should be weighed against the history and character of New Harmony, which is a very special kind of American town, and the unconventional approach to preservation that has guided its restoration.

New Harmony was founded, planned, and built by a religious sect, the Harmony Society, led by George Rapp from 1814 to 1824. As organized and orderly as its small straight grid of streets, the community prospered in its industries to become the affluent "wonder of the West." In 1825, Rapp decided to move closer to eastern markets. The town was sold, lock, stock and barrel, to the Welsh-born social reformer and industrialist Robert Owen. Owen had visions of New Harmony as a Utopian community—one of those admirable nineteenth-century experiments in social idealism. He brought together a group of eminent naturalists and educators, who were to create a model of egalitarian excellence. The Utopian ideal soon failed, but New Harmony became an important center of scientific research from 1825 to 1860. Owen's descendants were distinguished scientists, active in the geological mapping of the West and the founding of such national institutions as the Smithsonian.

Of the two phases of the town, the spiritual and scientific—

both so typical of the nineteenth-century New World—there are only spotty remains. But the size and configuration have stayed essentially the same. There is no single, cohesive character or style, however, and no richly uniform period architecture. What the town offers is a remarkable continuous history, with fascinating fragments of each of its phases from its founding to the present, and a sense of the character of a special place. Its preservation philosophy emphasizes the interpretive presentation of what was once there as well as what has survived, using everything from early nineteenth-century split-log houses to Victorian gingerbread. There is no arbitrary "cut-off date"; there is no attempt to create a homogeneous "place museum." Under the direction of Ralph G. Schwarz, president of Historic New Harmony, Inc., a combination of physical rehabilitation and skilled interpretive presentation has brought the community back to life in more ways than one; the past is being preserved as part of the present on a revitalized economic base of commerce and tourism.

The Atheneum can be seen as New Harmony's twentieth-century capstone—designed in the same spirit of creative inquiry and experiment as the town itself. Located at the northwest outer limit of the town, near the curving river's edge, the building stands on a low grassy podium above a flat green field that is flooded yearly by the Wabash. A traditional split-rail fence separates the site from the older historic section. To me, the building is suitable, quite aside from its unusual architectural interest. I see the choice as one between a legitimate artifact of our own time and a spurious or debatable, and ultimately, quite arbitrary, "suitability," since there is no real "New Harmony style" or even any overriding vernacular. I do not see the point of inventing one. Given the choice of such a fabrication, and a design of contemporary beauty and brilliance, I would opt for the latter.

The building is actually conceived as a circulation system. A reception and orientation area with computerized tour ticketing facilities leads to exhibition galleries, a theater, and observation terraces. Visitors follow a central ramp up to the theater and exhibition levels within a high open space that extends from the ground to the skylit roof. Because the ramp winds up on a five-degree diagonal grid, the interior is simultaneously perceived in different ways as the visitor ascends; the twist almost seems to set the building in motion. Everything that does not need to be enclosed, such as the theater, is not only visible, but visible from many levels and points of view. And as one moves, each view yields still more intricate patterns of a staggered and overlapping geometry of floor levels and indoor and outdoor spaces and outdoor vistas. There is a constant counterpoint of stairs, with an inner core containing a spiral stair as a sculptural object; that it is primarily for viewing is emphasized by the fact that this is the one area off-limits to the public.

Surprisingly, there is no sense of disorientation. It soon becomes evident that this striking interior is totally integrated with the purpose of the building—to tell the story of New Harmony. As that story and its artifacts are revealed along the visitor's route, so are corresponding views of the town, through glass walls or between white metal panel screens, or from the outdoor terraces. Standing in front of the model of the first New Harmony, for example, it is possible to see out to the fence-enclosed field of early split-log structures—also visible on the model—which have been moved back to their original site after numerous relocations. Thus they are seen both in the context of the present and of the nineteenth-century town.

There is a remarkable fusion of architectural means with the programmatic result. But it is not possible, of course, to be aware only of this process. At the same time, one is also intensely aware of the building. Never background, it fulfills its purpose while it plays skillfully with a new aesthetic, advancing conventional modernist practice provocatively. beyond established limits. Meier does not deny or reject modern architecture in any way, as is the fashion now; he uses its vocabulary and achievements to move into a new phase of exploration of those things that architecture has always been about: the controlled and purposeful manipulation of light and space, and the rewarding relationship of pragmatic and sensuous purpose. This is the kind of development that has always marked the change from one period of art to another. The point can be made that the creative spirit of this building is not far from the pioneering heritage of New Harmony. Frontiers are where you find them.

September 30, 1979

III

Any visitor to the new headquarters of the Hartford Seminary in Hartford, Connecticut, will have no trouble recognizing the building. Confronted by this glistening snowy structure, there is no question about which building one has come to see, or who has designed it. Richard Meier has developed this clean, but complex style through a series of recent buildings that have achieved a special significance on the international architectural scene.

Meier is surely one of the most accomplished practitioners of a difficult art in a period of controversial transition. His work is assured and accomplished on both the technological and design levels. It is moving modern architecture beyond its established achievements into a new realm of formal and functional expression. His recent projects—an addition to the Decorative Arts Museum in Frankfurt, West Germany, and a new building for the High Museum of Art in Atlanta, Georgia—are giving the architect far more scope than the houses that established his reputation. As exquisite as those dwellings were, and are, their demanding aesthetic can make severe claims on clients whose living habits are less than totally in tune. Many of Meier's ideas and images have seemed compressed in his earlier structures; the tension between angled and orthogonal planning, for example, can add confusion to complexity. The New Harmony Atheneum was almost too small to contain its wealth of visual and spatial effects. The Hartford Seminary, which is actually no larger than the Atheneum, refines and simplifies some of those themes and organizes them into a resolved and mature work that confirms the architect's attachment to a meticulously evolving style.

As spectacular as these gleaming white structures are, Meier does not create stage-set architecture. His designs grow out of a strong commitment to the essential relationships of plan and structure. This steel-framed, three-story, 27,000-square foot building is made up of intricately linked spaces and volumes derived equally from the plan and program and an acute awareness of its aesthetic and symbolic values.

The plan itself is surprisingly simple. The ground floor consists of a central entrance flanked by a library and bookstore on one side, and meeting room and chapel on the other. The second and third floors contain classrooms, conference rooms, and offices. How the plan is handled, however, is not simple. It is conceived three-dimensionally, with the volumes of the larger public spaces threaded vertically through the structure, and a circulation system that emphasizes the experience of those spaces at many levels. The white porcelain-enameled steel panels of the exterior set the building's three-foot module.

As in Meier's other buildings, much of this organization can be understood on the exterior, where precise and elegant architectural clues graphically indicate interior uses. The "box" on the wall to the right of the entrance, for example, turns out to enclose a chapel worthy of its exterior abstract sculpture. It also creates the building's **L**-shaped plan. Glass block indicates a stair tower. A shallow screen wall suggests an entrance arcade and subtly modulates the approach.

But these functions and features are revealed gradually, through a studied relationship of solids and voids. The screen wall through which one passes into a partially enclosed court on the way to the entrance provides a cloistered serenity. Other screen walls establish a pattern of receding and advancing planes; sometimes they extend beyond the building's corners to create modifications of space in much the same manner as the devices of Mannerism modulated the formal spaces of the Renaissance. Once inside, views of the outside are never lost; indoors and outdoors are played off against each other with courts, roofs, balconies, and terraces connected by bridges and walkways. Even interior spaces are suggested or revealed through glass walls and partitions. Balconies become viewing platforms of space for art's sake.

Meier is loyal to the vocabulary of modernism. He uses it in a way, however, that transcends and elaborates on precedent. He is much indebted to Le Corbusier and Aalto, whom he obviously admires, but he carries these references to new stages of interpretation only possible at this particular moment of hindsight and technological development. His effects are achieved through the careful interplay of solidity and transparency, of screens and openings, of interlocking volumes. They are enriched by the interaction of spaces perceived both simultaneously and sequentially, at different levels, and by the way they are brought to subtle and luminous life through the sources of daylight. This gives new and extended meaning to Le Corbusier's definition of architecture as the calculated play of forms in light.

In the last decade, the Hartford Seminary has moved from being a training college for the ministry to broader, interdenominational educational and community activities meant to serve both the clergy and the lay public. There have been no resident seminarians since 1972. Because the new program breaks with tradition, the president of the seminary, John Dillenberger, wanted a building that would break with tradition as well. It was hoped that the design could express the seminary's changing spirit and functions. The seminary's old buildings, a Gothic Revival group that the seminary had occupied since 1937—its fourth home since it was founded in 1834—were sold to the neighboring University of Connecticut Law School. The new building does not upstage them; white, after all, is not an unfamiliar New England color, and it pays the older structures the compliment of design quality and suitable scale.

Interestingly, a chapel was not originally included in the plans. It was added as a result of the architect's persuasive arguments that it would provide a symbolic focus for the building, and while it bears out this belief, it has also provided an irresistible architectural opportunity. In a sense, it is the key to the design. This high, white-walled, glowing skylit space is constantly transformed in color and mood by clouds and the course of the sun. If it is more coolly intellectual and hardedged, less gently or deeply sensuous than comparable chapels by Le Corbusier or Aalto, it is still a very special place.

The new Hartford Seminary is a disciplined, rigorous,

highly cerebral work that achieves a large measure of lyrical beauty. A pristine presence in a level green field, this dazzling structure is on the leading edge of the building art.

September 27, 1981

THE NEAR AND DISTANT PAST

VIOLLET-LE-DUC

I n any survey of out-of-favor architects least likely to be revived, an easy winner, until very recently, would have been Eugène Emmanuel Viollet-le-Duc. Probably no architect has been more consistently put down in this century; it is hard to look at a medieval monument in France, from the Cathedral of Notre Dame in Paris to the walled town of Carcassonne, without hearing imprecations against Viollet-le-Spoiler. He is the nineteenth-century French architect (1814–79) who spent his life elaborately reconstructing the buildings of the Middle Ages and who represents everything the twentieth century has disdained: the over-restoration of monuments, the popularization of quasi-historical styles, and, perhaps most unforgivable of all, the preeminence of the traditionalist in official art and culture. From the 1830's to the 1870's, Viollet-le-Duc was one of the most active, influential, and respected architects in the Western world.

On second thought, that would probably make him a prime candidate for revival. In today's spirit of revisionism, scholars seem bent on standing history on its head, with the rediscovery prize going to the most unexpected choices. Nineteen seventy-nine was the centenary of Viollet-le-Duc's death, a moment

Viollet-le-Duc

*Medieval
monuments or
metal technology
display an equally
ravishing hand*

when deflated reputations have a way of beginning to rise. Reassessment is in progress. The rumors, the research, the serious reappraisals all came together in a major exhibition at the Grand Palais in Paris, called simply "Viollet-le-Duc."

This exhibition was the first one-man show ever given to an architect in this prestigious setting, under the auspices of the French National Museums. The display took up three floors and included drawings, paintings, models, photographs, furniture, and objects of decorative art, material gathered from archives and collections all over France. The comprehensive documentation covers every facet of Viollet-le-Duc's extraordinary career—as restorer of monuments, builder and theoretician, artist and painter, champion of innovative technologies, master of decorative arts, guardian of the past and prophet of the future.

The viewpoint was neither the customary condemnation of Viollet-le-Duc as the dead and destructive hand of convention and violator of the past, nor the one-sided reading of such things as his vision of metal construction, which the modernists hailed as the key to a new architecture.

The extensive and evenhanded presentation gave a picture of a whole, quintessentially nineteenth-century man. If a little special pleading made him come off more heroically than necessary—he is still a far better theoretician than designer—we were finally able not only to see the true dimensions of his work but also to understand it in the appropriate context and framework of his own time. It was a complex time, with established traditions being shattered by political, social, and industrial revolutions, and it was not an easy time for architecture, which was caught between the poles of technological advance and cultivated practice. In France, under the Beaux Arts, that schism between architecture and engineering was particularly troublesome.

But aside from the contributions that the selection made to an understanding of the man and his period, there was a great deal of pleasure in the viewing; the drawings and paintings had a skilled and ravishing delicacy. In everything from the controlled curve of a carved acanthus leaf and the details of a stone grotesque peering from the foliage of a crumbling capital, to serene views of nature, these were refined and beautiful renderings by a man whose acute visual perceptions were accompanied by a freshly sharpened pencil wherever he went. He drew like a dream. In his travels through France, all during his life, he recorded mountains and monuments, landscapes and ruins, in meltingly lovely watercolors. And whether it was a design for sculpture or stained glass (an art he largely revived), a minutely detailed church steeple, a piece of furniture for his major antiquarian invention, the Château at Pierrefonds, the decorative woodwork and ironwork for the imperial train, or a sketch of a bat in flight, there was the ease and enchantment of a fine eye and great technical expertise.

The controversial restorations form a long and impressive list; among them are the monuments of Vézelay, Sens, Amiens, Beaune, Avignon, and Toulouse; there are churches, cathedrals, châteaux, and *hôtels de ville.* This work was based on the best archeological knowledge at that time, but the art and science of archeology have advanced immeasurably since then.

Viollet-le-Duc overreached, undeniably, and his confidence in his ability to re-create the past, to recapture the irretrievable, was boundless and naive. But his concerns, as recorded in his writings, were often surprisingly sound and sensitive.

One must remember that the preservation philosophies of the nineteenth and twentieth centuries could not be more unlike. Viollet-le-Duc's world wanted things put together the way they were, Humpty-Dumpty fashion; he played the delicate and dangerous game of "restoring back." The twentieth century stresses the value of whatever is left of the original fabric, from the original creative hands over everything else.

The important point is not how much of what we see today was put there by Viollet-le-Duc and his sculptors and artisans, but that without them, there would be little or nothing to see at all. France's superb medieval heritage was literally crumbling away, and sheer structural survival often made considerable rebuilding necessary. The recent rediscovery of the statues of the kings from the portal of Notre Dame in Paris reveals both how amazingly close to the originals Viollet-le-Duc and his sculptors were, and at the same time how critical the difference is in the tilt of an eye or the turn of a lip. The softer modeling and insidious nineteenth-century sweetness of the replacements lack the greater strength and sharpness and subtly exotic character of the earlier vision and style. It is that kind of thing that has given him his bad name.

But he has a surprisingly good name among modernist historians. Sigfried Giedion, in his account of skyscraper development in Chicago in the 1880's, quotes Leroy Buffington's claim to the "invention" of the steel-framed tall building based on the inspiration of Viollet-le-Duc's widely published and translated *Lectures on Architecture.* The French architect's earlier endorsement of the radical possibilities of the structural ironwork that was being actively pursued, and his emphasis on the visible materials and rational structure of medieval architecture and design, had a strong appeal for the aesthetic reformers of the nineteenth century. Viollet-le-Duc himself considered medievalism the most "modern" of all styles.

It is not surprising that the historian and critic Henry-Russell Hitchcock characterized Viollet-le-Duc's work as "curiously ambiguous." He praised the iron projects but called them paper boldness. He condemned the restorations as "no contribution to 19th-century architecture; rather they represent a furious diminution of authenticity in the monuments of the past." Even in the sympathetic display at the Grand Palais, Viollet-le-Duc's new buildings did not come off well. They remained correct and spiritless exercises in revivalist styles. It is not surprising that he lost out to Charles Garnier's flamboyant planning and theatrical sense of circulation and social display in the competition for the new Paris Opéra in 1860–61. Good show won over good form, to Viollet-le-Duc's considerable and lasting distress.

Still, the man who emerged from the Grand Palais exhibition is tremendously impressive. He was the architect-born, who never wanted to be anything else from the time he was a child. At sixteen, when revolutionary barricades were being erected in the streets of Paris, he gave advice on their construction. He bypassed formal education at the École des Beaux Arts to work in architects' offices as soon as possible, and his early travels in France and Italy established his taste for the past. A daguerreotype at the age of thirty shows him as vibrantly attractive and assured, with a dark beard and remarkably clear and observant eyes. His cross-legged position is debonair; there is a bit of stylish Scotch plaid on his vest and a gold chain and fob hung below a well-cut coat. Only his carefully combed hair displays any signs of youthful unruliness. This is already a confident and elegant man.

Photographed at sixty-five, the year before he died, the elegant air and clear gaze are undimmed, the beard and hair are white, and everything is still impeccably under control. Perhaps control is the key word for Viollet-le-Duc. His art was one of precedent, rules, and measure. It did not aspire to break out of tradition or to transcend expectations. He practiced architecture as the controlling art to which other arts were subordinate, and he practiced all of them exceptionally well. But he could neither control nor resolve the ambiguities of the nineteenth century, the split between the world of art and the world of technology that the twentieth century has devoted so much of its aesthetic energy to trying to heal, only to create more doubts and schisms. What he left us is a superb record of his delights and dilemmas, and the work of that rare kind of artist—the universal man.

April 6, 1980

IVAN LEONIDOV

The first exhibition in the United States of the work of the Soviet architect Ivan Leonidov (1902–59), held at New York's Institute for Architecture and Urban Studies in 1978, revealed one of the most radical talents of the early years of the Russian Revolution. The new material adds a previously unwritten chapter to modern architectural history, with all of the elements of genius and angst of a classic Russian novel. Leonidov is a remarkable artist whose eclipse today is equaled only by his fame within the Soviet Union in the 1920's. His story is a personal and aesthetic tragedy of epic proportions.

It is largely a story of unbuilt buildings; of all of the architect's spectacular projects, ranging from cultural palaces to new towns, only an ornamental stair built into a mountainside was constructed in 1937 in the Crimea. Oddly enough, this fact diminishes neither his significance nor his position in the official assessments of modern architecture. Because Leonidov's work has not been widely known and has been virtually inaccessible, that assessment is overdue. Except for a very brief initial period, Leonidov was systematically downgraded and deprived of his livelihood by the Soviet bureaucracy that controlled all architectural production. A series of portrait photos shows a young man of intense spiritual beauty reduced to a broken and eroded sadness by the end of his life.

Two Dutch architects, Rem Koolhaas and Gerrit Oorthuys, have painstakingly searched out the Leonidov documentation in the Soviet Union. On the basis of photographs of drawings, models, and paintings (none of the original documents could be taken out of the country), Leonidov emerges as one of the towering talents of the twentieth century, an idealistic and Olympian figure of vast romantic dimensions—a visionary in the classic definition. The clichés of the Russian temperament are all present—intellectual passion and imaginative ardor— but the reality that comes through is of an intensely creative mind devoted to the new ideals of revolution and abstraction.

Leonidov was a leading architectural light of the related Russian movements of Suprematism and Constructivism, in the company of, and indebted to, such artists as Kazimir Malevich and El Lissitzky. Among the influential architects of the time were Ladovsky, Ginzburg, the Vesnin brothers, and Konstantin Melnikov. For one exhilarating decade right after the revolution, it looked as if these men might indeed remake the world, or at least a part of the Soviet Union, in their image.

Actually, the aesthetic revolution came to Russia before the political revolution. The years from 1914 to 1917 saw the innovations of Kandinsky, Malevich, Tatlin, and the other originators of the geometric abstraction that was to have such a profound influence on Western art. In the early 1920's there was a sense of artists and society moving in the same direction in the Soviet Union, sharing the same radical means and goals. Architects were exhilarated by the irresistible idea of building a new state.

Building types called "social condensors"—workers' clubs, palaces of health and culture—were invented to serve new social and state needs. Workers' housing and new towns were planned. The radical designs were often beyond the economic and technological reach of the new government. But most major Soviet cities have at least one or two Constructivist monuments of the 1920's, such as Golossov's remarkable Zuyev Club in Moscow of 1926–27, and a wealth of documents remain from the constant competitions that became the established Soviet way of choosing public designs.

The new Soviet architecture came to outside attention

Ivan Leonidov

*Competition
drawing, Ministry
of Heavy Industry,
Moscow, 1933*

*Visionary futurism
of a short-lived
Soviet avant-garde*

through Konstantin Melnikov's much-admired Paris Exposition Building of 1925, which was greeted by European professionals as an aesthetic revelation. "They carried me on their shoulders," Melnikov recalled in 1967, a few years before his death. By 1930, the conservatives regained power and set out to destroy the radical art styles. The progressive architectural organizations, Asnova and OSA, were dissolved by Stalin in 1932 and replaced by the State Academy of Architecture. In 1937 the Congress of Soviet Architects established the familiar wedding-cake classicism as the official academic style.

The most vicious attacks of all were leveled at Leonidov. The whole range of subversive strains to be purged were lumped under the epithet "Leonidovism." He had been graduated as a star student from the Vkhutemas, the experimental school that predated the Bauhaus, in 1927; he was acclaimed and lionized for his talent from 1926 to 1929. Totally discredited by 1930, he lost both his teaching position and his apartment and became ineligible to build anything at all. A life of temporary shelter in friends' apartments and offices began for him and his family; in later years he worked as a taxi driver and a painter of lampshades. He continued to enter the endless competitions that he had no hope of winning.

Two projects, one near the beginning and the other at the end of Leonidov's career and life, are compelling examples of his mastery of art and symbolism. Once seen, the powerful images of a 1933 competition entry for the headquarters of the Ministry of Heavy Industry, the center of all Soviet planning, cannot be forgotten. The plan would have cleared Red Square of such structures as the GUM department store to create a vast space almost twice its present width, to be crowned, in part, with what Leonidov called "a sheaf of towers" on a podium base. These towers are three symbolic skyscrapers overshadowing the Kremlin and St. Basil's Cathedral. But Leonidov saw this as the proper aesthetic culmination of the "subtle and majestic music" of the architecture of the Kremlin and Red Square—in fact, he viewed it as a historical necessity in terms of the supremacy of the Soviet state.

The three tall clustered towers are rectangular, triangular, and circular in plan. The rectangular tower, a grid of masonry and glass, is topped by a dynamic linear abstraction of stainless steel masts meant to hold platforms for "sky performances." An external elevator soars up one side. The triangular tower has stone piers and curved glass walls. The round tower tapers like a smokestack and is of black glass blocks, luminous at night, with projecting gold-colored "viewing platforms." All are connected by aerial bridges. Next to this overwhelming Constructivist fantasy, Futurism looks tame. The freehand sketches that preceded the formal drawings are very beautiful; they have an almost Renaissance calligraphy.

Leonidov's last project was "The City of the Sun," which he worked on from 1947 to his death in 1959. This consisted of a huge tent, for which many fanciful studies were made, with a satellite suspended over it in an intricate and delicate geometry. Whenever world peace was achieved, the satellite was meant to be released to rise and float indefinitely in the sky. It would be appropriately and darkly Russian to equate the satellite with Leonidov's spirit and to dwell on metaphors of peace and freedom. But it would be unnecessary. Leonidov's art has obviously been its own symbol and tragic necessity.

February 12, 1978

VIENNA MODERNE

Some of the most interesting architecture is the most ambiguous; the transitional period from about 1890 to World War I, never quite free of nineteenth-century tradition while straining spectacularly after a new twentieth-century vision, is full of genius and contradiction.

That remarkable quarter of a century accommodated everything from the suavely sinuous Art Nouveau to the spectral solemnities of Charles Rennie Mackintosh and the passionate renunciations of Adolf Loos. It is a time when art and morality form a strange alliance. One by one, we are picking up these overlapping movements that came so rapidly on each other's heels and reexamining them in terms of the struggle between aesthetic roots and radical theory. Today we find these real and false starts as fresh and challenging as they seemed in their own time and just as rewarding as the full-scale modernist revolution that they fostered.

The peculiar duality of this period is one of the fascinations of an exhibition held at the Cooper-Hewitt Museum in New York in 1978 called "Vienna Moderne; 1898–1918," subtitled "An Early Encounter Between Taste and Utility." According to the show's guest director, Jan Ernst Adlmann, this was a time when the creative mind was torn between the wish and the commitment to simplify radically and the irrepressible urge to decorate. The Viennese managed to have it both ways. For two vital decades, they were the force behind an evolving style that was consciously "functional" in its programs, materials and forms, at the same time that it was embellished by a rich, but restrained ornament that stressed an intrinsic, rather than applied, character. This style was largely the work of the Wiener Werkstätte, the Vienna Workshops established by the architect Josef Hoffmann and others in 1903, following the lead of the Vienna Secession, the group that broke away from the academic mainstream in 1897 under Gustav Klimt and Otto Wagner. The avowed purpose was to elevate the arts of design to the level of the fine arts; the ultimate objective was a "totally designed" environment.

However, this was not a movement that preached populism or espoused mass production or a machine aesthetic; it was a limited handcraft production for an elite clientele. Its high point was reached in the coordinated details of Hoffmann's Palais Stoclet in Brussels of 1904–11, one of the most elegantly opulent houses of the century. Only Adolf Loos attempted to break completely with the taste and standards of the past, in his famous denunciatory coupling of ornament with crime, a position that seems ironic seen against the details and materials of some of his designs.

The pioneering Werkstätte style straddled the ornamental orgies of Art Nouveau and the strict asceticism of the Bauhaus. It had an oddly eclectic background, combining an admiration for the English Arts and Crafts movement and the work of Charles Rennie Mackintosh in the years just before and after the turn of the century, with memories of Biedermeier and the Austrian baroque. Signals bounced from Vienna, to Glasgow, to Amsterdam, and back again. The result was a rich design stew. Those influences, fired in the unlikely crucible of moralist-aesthetic theory, laid much of the groundwork for later Dutch and German design, as well as for the modern movement.

For two important decades after 1900, the Viennese artists, architects, and artisans produced some breathtakingly beautiful ambiguities. The metalwork, ceramics, glass, furnishings,

and fabrics are a wonderfully mixed lot. The objects made of rectilinear metal grillwork, called *Gitterwerk,* or screenwork, are crisply abstract. Some furniture, such as a series of Hoffmann chairs done just after 1900, is almost primitively conceived and clumsily made. A Loos table embellished with onyx and brass-tipped feet seems to be walking off in several directions. Kolo Moser's superb amber-studded silver vase of 1905 and the glass and ceramics done under his tutelage, or Hoffmann's later magnificent silver fruit bowl of 1918, owned by Cooper-Hewitt, are marvelously lush in their sensuous shapes and surfaces. From the merely curious to the seductively beautiful, it is hard to find an uninteresting piece or a design cliché. In its second decade, the Werkstätte's restrained functionalism softened, its production dominated by Dagobert Peche's more conventionally ornamental but extremely handsome designs that foreshadowed the Art Moderne taste of the 1930's.

Revolution, with hindsight, becomes nostalgia. Just as the Mackintosh rooms installed in London's Victoria and Albert Museum some years ago seemed less radical than redolent with "the scent of heliotrope," these furnishings and objects evoke Vienna's worldly and very fashionable pre–World War I avant-garde. In the confrontation between Style and Functionalism that marked the Vienna Moderne's two brief brilliant decades, Style clearly won. Style always does.

November 26, 1978

THE FIRST
HUNDRED YEARS

McKIM, MEAD AND WHITE

The name McKim, Mead and White is to architecture
what J. P. Morgan is to banking and Dom Perignon is
to champagne. To the public, it means monuments,
mansions and millionaires, and the glamour of high society and
high life. It also means Evelyn Nesbit and Harry K. Thaw and
a crime of passion on the roof of the former Madison Square
Garden—a McKim, Mead and White building, of course.

The victim, the architect Stanford White, is remembered as
a celebrity, *bon vivant,* man about town, creative genius, and
fashionable arbiter of taste—a *Fountainhead*-like image (establishment rather than maverick division) of the sort that occasionally propels architecture into the popular imagination. So
great is the power of the legend that local mythology credits
any opulent and elegant turn-of-the-century house to Stanford
White, who could not possibly have designed them all, while
every sufficiently grand public building is assigned to Charles
McKim.

Scholars are busy sorting it all out. The early monographs
have been reissued, and in 1979 a major show at the Brooklyn
Museum, called "The American Renaissance," dealt with all of
the arts and many of the artists of the period from 1876 to

McKim, Mead and White

Municipal Building, New York, 1914

Changing fortunes of a famous American firm

David W. Dunlap

1917; the Brooklyn Museum, appropriately, is a grandly colonnaded McKim, Mead and White building. Previously unexhibited documents from the collection of Columbia University's Avery Architectural Library offered fascinating sidelights on the principals' work and personalities. They were displayed in Low Library, a Pantheon-like space with massive columns and marbles, and also a McKim, Mead and White building.

The firm of McKim, Mead and White was founded in 1879, when the young Stanford White joined Charles Follen McKim and William Rutherford Mead in a practice that would soon become the most important and influential of its time. Domestically, it ranged from the large shingle "cottages" of the New

England aristocracy to the marble châteaux of the Newport overachievers; institutionally, it included the civic centers, state capitols, universities, libraries, and museums that represented the political power, cultural ambitions, and philanthropic ideals of the day. The period of the firm's ascendancy was called by most of its art world participants—few of whom could be faulted for modesty—the American Renaissance. It involved a collaborative effort in all of the arts, based on what was fondly believed to be the Italian Renaissance model. Instead of noble and papal palaces, McKim, Mead and White built mansions for the new millionaires. Ambitious projects were initiated over lavish meals, fine wines, and Havana cigars in exclusive clubs, naturally, by McKim, Mead and White.

The architecture built in this spirit still looms large on the landscape. But the taste for it has had its ups and downs. From a high point around the turn of the century, it reached its low point during the modernist revolution, when its eclectic classical design stood for all the things that modern architecture was rebelling against. Everything this work represented—the borrowings from the past, the trappings of the conservative power structure—had to be destroyed if the revolution was to succeed. Although much that was rejected was tiresome and pretentious, the good, unfortunately, was jettisoned with the bad.

Today's young "radicals," in revolt against orthodox modernism, are looking for some of the lost symbols and skills that were grounded in so many centuries of a highly developed tradition. What they have found are the Academy, the Beaux Arts, and the American Renaissance. Only something that has been so completely out, could now be so far in. In fact, celebrations of the work of McKim, Mead and White would have been virtually impossible not too long ago. Or it would have been a very small party. Admirers of the American Renaissance, like Henry Hope Reed, Jr., and John Bayley, the founders of Classical America, a group devoted to the appreciation, study, and revival of the classical style, have been trying for many years to roll the firm's reputation back uphill with Sisyphean determination. Their major vindication came with the Museum of Modern Art's large Beaux Arts exhibition in 1975, which gave academic architecture the stamp of the establishment again. And now the unthinkable has happened; some young architects are actually designing in the "new classicism."

No one would have been more surprised at the changes in their fortunes than McKim, Mead and White. Certainly humility was not part of the imperial manner. There is the story about the planning session of artists and architects for the Columbian Exposition of 1893, for which McKim, Mead and White set the image that was to turn the Chicago fairgrounds into a great white City Beautiful. In a fit of aesthetic euphoria, Augustus St. Gaudens turned to Daniel Burnham to sum up the feelings in the room. "Look here, old fellow," he said, "do you realize that this is the greatest meeting of artists since the fifteenth century?" It is not recorded that anyone demurred.

A far less sanguine observer at the time was Louis Sullivan, who, almost alone, did not espouse the classical revival that was to sweep all else before it after the phenomenal success of the fair. The golden arches of his Transportation Building were neither snow-white nor indebted to Greece or Rome; their bold forms and interlaced ornament were meant to be a creative contribution to a native American development. The fair helped break Sullivan's cantankerous heart. His often-repeated observation was that its reactionary design would set back the course of American architecture fifty years or more.

He was right, of course, and he was also wrong. We eventually got the best of the Academy and the best of the brave new world, and the worst of both. We are standing at the point where we no longer have to choose sides. This is the moment when the two faces of art—the academic and the innovative—are finally being put back together, and we are once again looking at history whole. Now, if we can just look at it straight. The range, in nineteenth- and twentieth-century academic work, is from the magnificent to the perfectly dreadful. That which lacked content or meaning filled the void with lifeless pomposity. The craftsmanship and materials were often superb, which can do a lot for mediocrity, but some of the embellishing art definitely makes one queasy.

The work of McKim, Mead and White maintained a superior standard and has provided buildings that are among the chief ornaments and richest adornments of our cities. The norm was a cultivated competence, however, rather than greatness, and many of the later buildings were as cold and spiritless as they were maddeningly nonfunctional. It is now up to the scholars to call the hits, the misses, and the errors.

December 2, 1979

HOLABIRD AND ROOT

It probably shouldn't, but it still comes as something of a surprise to find American architectural firms celebrating their hundredth anniversaries. The centennial of the founding of the office of McKim, Mead and White coincided nicely with what might be called the "rediscovery" of its work or, at least, its reappraisal. One hopes that the same reexamination will be accorded the Chicago firm of Holabird and Root, which has also celebrated its centennial. As Holabird and Roche, this firm was central to the development of the skyscraper in the thirty years from 1880 to 1910, and to what is known, internationally, as the Chicago School.

Probably no single firm reflects more accurately the complete span of American architectural practice over the last hundred years, which includes a varied and quite valid sequence of styles. It has had its aesthetic vicissitudes. The office began with the practical and innovative emphasis on engineering and design pragmatism that characterized the early Chicago skyscrapers. This changed to the fashionable and sometimes strained eclectic conceits with which tall buildings were clothed just before and after World War I. That was followed by the original and elegant "modernistic," or Art Deco, designs of the 1930's. A return to something akin to the early structural pragmatism brought the firm full circle with the "modernism" that followed World War II.

As appreciative as I am of the grand achievements of McKim, Mead and White, give or take a fair number of impressive potboilers, I find myself more interested in the history

*Holabird and
Roche*

*Old Colony
Building, Chicago,
Illinois, 1894*

*The useful and
beautiful alliance
of structure and
expressive style*

Hedrich Blessing

of Holabird and Root. This story lacks the catalogue of lordly masterworks of the eastern establishment firm, but its tells us a good deal more about invention, adaptability, changing taste, and the struggle to survive as part of the American architectural mainstream.

I like the kind of tradition in which two and three generations of distinguished architectural names like Holabird (father, son, and grandson in the one Chicago firm) and Root (father and son, anchoring two Chicago firms) continued to practice in the same city—particularly a city that has claimed, proudly, to deal primarily in progress and change. I confess that I like it better than the instant academic tradition in which a firm like McKim, Mead and White wrapped itself so splendidly and successfully, and sometimes spiritlessly, in later years.

Holabird and Root produced sound rather than spectacular buildings. Even at its time of greatest strength, from 1880 to 1910, there were other firms and individuals in Chicago, from William Le Baron Jenney to Louis Sullivan, who made the great leaps forward in structure and style. But if other architects built greater buildings, few built consistently better ones. The office's claim to fame is based on that most interesting and important chapter in American architectural history, the development of the skyscraper, a field of design and construction in which it held a leadership position for a surprisingly long time. There were changes in partners and philosophy over the years, but it continued to produce top-rank tall buildings right through the 1920's and 30's.

Chicago's great contributions in the 1880's and 90's were the technological achievements of steel-frame construction and related engineering advances, and the handsome visual expression of that new technology. The Chicago Style became one of the strongest aesthetics of modern times. Holabird and Roche specialized in the careful, logical adaptation of structural means to functional ends—which resulted in the creation of a distinct design formula for the new large business buildings whose rise skyward was made possible by the metal frame, the elevator, and other service and construction technologies. The historian Carl W. Condit has characterized that formula as "a basic norm or type exactly developed to fit a particular set of conditions." Historian and critic William H. Jordy calls it an architectural type virtually beyond "design," something so well suited to its use that it led inevitably and properly to mass duplication. He makes it clear that it was "a superb type." The formula became the skyscraper style. To a stroller of Chicago's streets today, these early buildings still have an extraordinary impact. The visible scale and pattern of their structural frames, filled with the generous glass bays known as "Chicago windows," have an architectonic clarity and force that is only achieved through a sensuous and rational reference to structure. Architecturally, this is a hard act to follow.

It was a style exactly suited to the needs of business and builders. Boldly stated in Holabird and Roche's Tacoma building of 1886–89, the formula was carried further in the Marquette building of 1894, which definitively established the supremacy of the supporting structural frame. The solution was at its most refined in the Republic building of 1904–09. (The Tacoma and the Republic were both demolished in the 1960's.) With a Boston builder named Peter Brooks, Holabird and Roche laid out the fundamental principles of the new commercial construction. They stressed the provision of light and air, and the importance of the quality of public facilities, like lobbies, elevators, and corridors. Above all, there was to be no second-class space, because it cost as much to build and operate as first-class space. Proper materials and details were to simplify operation and maintenance.

Like so many others, Holabird and Roche succumbed to the avalanche of eclecticism after 1910, but the firm never had a sure hand for academic revivalism. In 1928, after a change of partners, the office emerged as Holabird and Root, and in the 1930's it produced a brilliant succession of "modernistic" skyscrapers of a radical streamlined or highly original eclectic elegance that included the Chicago Board of Trade, the Palmolive, now Playboy Building, and a "modernistic" masterpiece, the Chrysler Building at the Chicago World's Fair.

The 1940's brought the war, and the postwar 1950's saw a lot of uneven and pedestrian work. In the 1970's some of the senior partners retired, signaling a period of self-examination.

The firm is now embarked on a search for quality and style that is yet without a name; it reflects the newer, younger partners and the aesthetic pluralism of current architectural trends, in Chicago, as everywhere else.

The British magazine *The Economist,* in a feature on Chicago's historic architecture—which is more appreciated abroad than at home—deplored "the loss of many of the buildings that have inspired reverence for the city." Centennial celebrations are brief. The second hundred years are the hardest.

March 2, 1980

LATE ENTRIES TO
THE TRIBUNE TOWER
COMPETITION

I do not know quite how or when I acquired the original publication containing all of the designs for the Chicago Tribune Tower competition of 1922, but the book is one of my treasured possessions. It is a substantial volume that tells a great deal about the relationship of art and ambition at a time when the skyscraper was still young, and ideas about it were ambiguous and uncertain.

The competition held by the Chicago *Tribune* for its headquarters building was one of those benchmark events that have subsequently taken their place in architectural history because they embody the full range and spectrum of a particularly significant moment in the development of an art—in this case, the transition from centuries of the familiar Western classical tradition to the unknown abyss of modernism. The confusion and promise of the moment are summed up in the designs in that book, from examples of Beaux Arts formalism to International Style daring and a great deal in between. I am endlessly intrigued by the mix of certainty and uncertainty, of the adventurous and the *retardataire,* the sophisticated and the naive, the doctrinaire and the fanciful.

Whatever the idiom, however, most of the architects knew

exactly what they were doing; they had set out to fulfill the Chicago *Tribune*'s specific mandate to create "the most beautiful and distinctive office building in the world." They went about the assignment perfectly seriously and with no visible self-doubt, spurred on, undeniably, by the prospect of a munificent $100,000 in prizes and the understanding that the winning design would be built.

One of the most interesting things about the results is that so many of the designs were so very good. The entries were marked by an extremely high level of competence. Most of the contestants understood the relationships of mass and detail; they handled scale with ease. But even the bummers and the curiosities are fascinating and informative. And there is a surprising amount of what is called "commentary" today, a role not unknown to architecture historically, that is receiving far more emphasis than ever before. Most of this comes under the recognizable head of symbolism, although there were a few essays into irony, such as the tower in the shape of an Indian with uplifted tomahawk submitted by Mossdorf, Hahn and Busch of Leipzig, and Adolf Loos's notorious skyscraper as an overblown classical column.

The Chicago Tribune Tower competition had absolutely everything, and its continued fascination is that it can be read on a different level of meaning and significance almost any time you approach it. As modernism became the accepted way of building, it was fashionable to deplore the blindness of the judges who passed over Walter Gropius's radical Bauhaus-type tower from Germany for the "reactionary" Gothic Revival solution. I find the group of about a dozen Dutch entries, stylistically somewhere between Berlage and De Stijl, particularly interesting, largely uncelebrated exercises in stylistic innovation. Interpretation is the most ephemeral and intriguing of intellectual activities; its only truth is to the needs of its own time.

The winner, of course, stands in Chicago today, a skilled Gothic Revival skyscraper by John Mead Howells and Raymond M. Hood, who went on to do another remarkable landmark tower, the modernist Daily News building in New York. The unbuilt second-prize design is of even greater interest because of its design excellence and transitional character; in fact, it stunned the jury when it finally cleared customs just as the decision was about to be made. This was the proposal sent by Eliel Saarinen from Helsinki, where he was already the acknowledged master of a romantic quasi-historical modernism that was seen at the time as a brilliant step from the nineteenth to the twentieth century.

Obviously, I am not the only one to be entranced by the Chicago Tribune Tower competition or to find multitudes of meaning in it. Because we are in a comparable transitional period in the state of the art once more, when all the rules are being suspended again, there are very timely parallels. Among those who have found those parallels irresistible are two Chicago architects, Stuart Cohen and Stanley Tigerman, and a Chicago art dealer, Rhona Hoffman. Almost sixty years after the event, in 1980, they organized an invitational event called "Late Entries to the Chicago Tribune Competition," which elicited seventy American and foreign responses. (The original competition pulled over two hundred entries from twenty-three countries.) The idea of the new competition was to "redo" the Tribune Tower from today's point of view.

I took Stuart Cohen's word, from his catalogue essay, that a certain seriousness was inevitably lost because there was no prize money and everyone knew that nothing would be built. For better or worse, that led to a heavy emphasis on commentary, fantasy, and irony, which was, in a sense, both invited and expected, by the choice of participants, the approach to the project, and today's fashionable attitudes toward design. Many of the entries were really observations on the art of the skyscraper or the current state of architecture, highly personal responses to the original competition designs, or expressions of social and cultural attitudes through designs that stray far from conventional definitions of building.

There was, for example, Helmut Jahn's tour de force in which the flattened case, or skin, of the actual Gothic building was shown shot up into the airspace above it, like a projectile in a burst of light. Robert A. M. Stern's sophisticated vulgarization of the classical column idea could be read as an exposition

of postmodernist design and as a play on the famous Adolf
Loos scheme. (There were actually two versions of the build-
ing-as-column entered in 1922.) Walter Netsch gave us his
ultimate piece of compulsive geometry and Thomas Beeby
offered a shaft hidden in a Stars and Stripes wrapper topped by
a burning funerary urn. Jorge Silvetti's intersecting volumes
patterned with an elementary window grid was a surprising
recall of the similarly reduced fenestration of an Italian entry
of 1922 by Arturo Tricomi. And, as they say, much, much
more.

What none of the entries apparently attempted, or was
remotely concerned with, was the original challenge seriously
accepted by all of the contestants to produce a building of
distinction. Stuart Cohen tells us that the new architecture
deals more in "communication." It is full of metaphors and
messages. It is quite clear that the later competition departed
from the traditional making of a building for the making of
"images." This concern with images is supposed to be something new, or the revival of something old, because, theoreti-
cally, the modernists were forbidden to worship images of any
kind. It is also supposed to be the link between the first Tribune designs and the "late entries."

But there are images and images, and these are pretty thin
stuff. Literary allusion or naughty adolescent wit, architectural
division, is no substitute for knowing how to unite volume,
space, and setting in a significant architectonic whole, for the
creation of a work of art. Even the modernists, hiding behind
functionalism and often hobbled by abstract formalism, never
stopped trying for the big prize. Breathes there the architect,
who, in his secret heart, doesn't really want a crack at producing a great building rather than a commentary?

Everything has changed, and nothing has changed, in the
intervening years. The skyscraper has come of age. We have
pushed both structural technology and its aesthetic interpretation to extraordinary limits. It is even possible that we have
reached a dead end. Some thoughtful architects, dismayed by
the impact of gigantism on people and cities, have renounced
the tall building completely. Others are attempting to civilize

it by restoring it to history. But the skyscraper is still the leading image of the twentieth century and an irresistible bid for immortality. We won't see the last late entry to the Tribune Tower competition for a long time.

June 22, 1980

CITIES

NEW YORK:
BUILDING THE CITY

ZONING: THE END OF THE LINE

I

In an attempt to legislate an impossible balance between a profitable city and a livable city, New York has created a monster—call it Frankenstein zoning. The process by which good intentions and innovative practice are turned into an urban nightmare has been gradual and technically arcane. But what has been happening, insidiously and overtly, is that the whole idea of zoning has been turned upside down. It has been subverted from a way to control building bulk and size to a method for getting bigger buildings than ever.

If that seems like an anachronism, it is; exactly the kind of overbuilding is being encouraged that the law was designed to prohibit. The result, which is just beginning to be visible, is the rapid appearance of ranks of oppressively massive, sun- and light-blocking structures of a size that we have never seen in such concentration before. Their outline and impact appeared first on Madison avenue from Fifty-third to Fifty-seventh Street, with the forty-two-story, block-long Tishman building from Fifty-third to Fifty-fourth Street, another tower across Madison at Fifty-fifth Street, and the gargantuan AT&T and IBM buildings, from Fifty-fifth to Fifty-sixth, and Fifty-sixth to Fifty-seventh Street. This enclave of blockbusters was joined by the huge Trump Tower looming on the Bonwit Teller site at Fifty-sixth and Fifth.

When the first of these immense projects designed under the city's revised 1961 zoning regulations appeared, such as Olympic Tower on Fifth Avenue or Citicorp on Lexington, they seemed unique; as singular structures they were more interesting than overwhelming. As a standard to be replicated, however, they have become cautionary examples. The four-block stretch on Madison Avenue is the showcase of the new superscale. What must be understood is that this wave of bigger-than-ever New York buildings is not some overreaching passing fancy. It is the new and future norm. Nor is it just the product of the current state of ambition and economics; even the aspirations of builders and the high costs of development are ultimately controlled by the city's zoning. The bottom line is that the developers build what they are permitted to by law.

These new buildings, therefore, are equally revealing of the manipulative, negotiable, and mutable art that New York's zoning has become. And because what New York does in zoning is emulated by the rest of the country, whether it is innovative and constructive or dangerous and foolish, other cities will probably follow an example that has evolved from a reasonable system of controls, including creative attempts to balance restraints with public amenities, to an ad hoc exercise in horse-trading that is a clear environmental disaster.

Zoning, after all, is meant to be a set of rational regulations that puts restrictions on the size and nature of construction in a city, in the interest of such essential things as light, air, views, density, and the urban quality of the whole. These considerations are understood to be in the larger community interest to a degree that justifies the control of private enterprise, in this case, the operation of real estate. During the more than six decades in which zoning laws have been made and tested in this country, the courts have upheld both the need and the constitutionality of such controls.

What New York has done is to turn restrictive zoning, in the traditional sense of prohibitions or limitations, into a kind of permissive, or give-it-away, zoning, negotiated on a case-to-case basis. The controls have been undermined by discretionary changes in the law aimed at everything from increasing the tax base to promoting better architectural design. The solid shafts that now rise straight up from the street without set-backs, thanks to the Planning Commission's routine special permits, sacrifice the sky plane requirements of zoning (the building setbacks meant to permit light and air to reach the street and other buildings) to arguments of abstract architec-tural aesthetics and the corporate taste for enormous, comput-er-friendly floors. Seeing the sky in New York is a high-priced privilege, but the height and bulk of the new construction will affect not just the views of the affluent; these blockbusters are rapidly reducing the remaining sense of openness that makes the overbuilt city bearable.

These profitable glittering prizes are going to the developers and their lawyers, who specialize in end runs around the city's rules. Part of the game is to see how close the developer can stay to the letter of the law while flouting its intent. For exam-ple, glass doors with inconspicuous signs indicating the hours of access can completely camouflage the fact that the thru-building passageways, for which the builder earned the bonus of extra floors, are designated public space. Strategically placed planters, gates, and curb cuts implicitly deny access or use of apartment house plazas, although these public spaces have also been provided at the cost of increased building size. The ir-reconcilable objectives of the city and the developer, of permissiveness and restraint, have created a classic Catch-22 dilemma, which the builder, as usual, has succeeded in exploit-ing wherever possible.

The situation has become disturbing enough so that the City Planning Commission undertook a zoning and development study in 1980 aimed at correcting some of the most glaring defects and abuses; it was a sophisticated document with some useful recommendations that did not go nearly far enough and avoided the basic issue. Generally, it just pushed the overzon-ing around. An attempt to reestablish the limits of the zoning established in 1961 by cutting back on the snowballing bonuses is a "reform" that has a certain irony, since those limits were far too generous at the time, and have led to most of the damage. Those who soon realized that the formulas were grossly large were told that market economics would never support full use of the theoretical possibilities. That assumption has been a casualty of time and inflation, which have made every inch of prime Manhattan land worth developing to the maximum—from needles and slivers to blockbusters.

Technically, the guide to the permitted size of a building in New York is known as the Floor Area Ratio (FAR)—the size of the structure figured in terms of its total floor area as a multiple of the size of the site. Over the years this mysterious and magical number, which gives the permitted total square footage, has risen from a proposed standard of FAR 15 to a universal FAR 18 and a not uncommon FAR 21.6. These increases have supposedly been balanced by requiring the provision of public open space by the builder, or the inclusion of such things as theaters and shops to maintain the character of special districts. A number of these features, such as arcades and midblock passages, have turned out to be far less desirable than anyone thought, particularly as trade-offs for increased bulk and density. In addition, builders find it more to their liking, and either inconsequential or more advantageous to their bookkeeping in these huge investments, to leave the mandated, "enlivening" ground floor stores empty and to keep the "public" spaces unused, thus avoiding problems of security and maintenance.

But this is all small change. A sophisticated builder can pile up bonuses and utilize special legal tricks in ways never envisioned by the writers and revisers of the zoning law, to parlay them into monstrous zoning packages. Some truly outrageous practices are commonplace. A building that piggybacks bonuses for special district features and/or automatic bonuses for plazas and arcades or their amenities may also add floors acquired through air rights transfer from a neighboring smaller structure. Trump Tower is a prime example. When these extras are figured in terms of a very large plot put together through something called zoning lot merger, where all calculations and their multiples are based on the oversized piece of land, the resulting structure is staggering. When the city tells you that no more than 20 percent can be added to the building size through such devices it is like asking how high is up? And when the developer and his architect tell you virtuously that at the city-approved limit of 21.6 they are still below the amount that can be stacked up by this zoning con game, a new definition of chutzpah has been born.

The concerned observer of this game has a growing sense that the 1961 zoning act, with its subsequent amendments, is creating a dangerous cumulative overload on the city's services and antiquated infrastructure, an impression not allayed by the constant bursting of water mains and public transit in terminal stages of decay. There is, in addition, a cutoff point for a city's human and environmental pleasures.

However, forget the technicalities and the abuses for a moment. Instead, consider these facts. The history of New York zoning began in 1916 with the completion of the Equitable building at 120 Broadway, a forty-story structure built solidly and straight up, covering 100 percent of its site except for a few light wells. The immediate reaction was shock and a successful rush for tax reductions by Equitable's neighbors, on the grounds of reduced property value and lower rental income owing to the obstruction of light and air. The Equitable shadow covered four streets to the north and led to New York's, and the country's, first zoning law.

The legislation that was enacted established the building's height by a formula based on the width of the street, and required setbacks above a certain height, following the imaginary line called the sky exposure plane as a guarantee of light and air, and to eliminate shadows and obstruction. This produced the familiar New York ziggurat, or if the builder preferred a tower to setbacks, he could have one that covered no more than 25 percent of the site, usually with a kind of shaft on a blocky base. When the building pace accelerated after World War II, even these restrictions seemed too permissive. After several attempts at change, the 1961 revised zoning law was passed.

This zoning reform was sold—falsely, as it turned out—on the basis of reduced size and density for commercial buildings. But its Catch-22 character began with a provision for an automatic bonus of extra floors for a tower that provided a plaza or arcade. This immediately established a larger building type as the norm.

To encourage the tower and plaza, the Planning Commission gave special permits that waived height and setback restrictions. To offset the detrimental effects of the greater bulk and density that inevitably resulted, something called incentive zoning was devised. This procedure was meant to sweeten the bigger buildings by requiring public amenities at street level. To get the amenities, more bonuses were given. That, in turn, made more big buildings, and the creation of special districts with additional bonusable features made the structures even larger—like Olympic Tower on Fifth Avenue. Virtually all had to be individually bargained for with the Planning Commission.

The result has been gradual erosion of the city's real overall amenity on a large scale, even as small amenities have been provided. Anyone except a real estate investor knows, and is troubled by how much more crowded and less pleasant New York has become in recent years. One is constantly forced to balance the city's unparalleled attractions and increasing discomforts. When congested streets become obstacle races and the new towers turn them into cold sunless canyons on winter afternoons, when one fights vicious downdrafts across those plazas and getting anywhere ceases to be any fun at all, size and density are clearly part of the problem. There are also good arguments that overbuilding in midtown contributes to the city's economic woes, rather than correcting them. As Stephen Zoll pointed out in his essay on "Superville" in *The Massachusetts Review,* "As the center builds up, the perimeter crumbles." That often irreversible disinvestment does not appear in official development calculations.

The high cost of building is driven up by the high cost of land, and the price of Manhattan land is driven still higher by permissive zoning and even more permissive granting of special permits. The developer pays prices for land that gamble on those increases in size and bulk that he thinks he can "negotiate" from the city with deals that include the sop of a star architect or the lure of a desirable corporate client. The irony, and the dilemma for the critic, is that some of these buildings are far better architecture than before. We are getting designer-label, brand-name abuses. The process has ceased to be one of limits and controls; it is a giant poker game with constantly changing rules in which the developer always ups the ante and holds the aces.

This brings us to the ultimate Catch-22. Today's buildings, born out of the most complex regulatory processes, either repeat or exceed all of the original sins that made the need for the first restrictive legislation clear in 1916. Sky plane exposure is now routinely flouted by special permits. Land coverage constantly exceeds legal limits. Jonathan Barnett, the original head of the city's Urban Design Group, states in an article in *New York Affairs* that the new Philip Morris headquarters has higher tower coverage, and both the IBM and AT&T buildings have taller walls going straight up from the building line, than the Equitable building had in 1916. Some construction has gone back to 80 to 100 percent land coverage. Traditional zoning restrictions have simply been set aside and mocked. Barnett asks, not at all rhetorically, "Are these minor infractions of the zoning? And does it matter?"

It matters. When the Equitable building covered close to 100 percent of its site with walls rising from the street without setbacks, corrective controls were enacted. Now we have managed to "reform," amend, and manipulate these controls to make it legal to do exactly what was outlawed in the first place. The only difference between then and now is the even more monstrous buildings and brutal scale today; this is a process that rewards, rather than prohibits, creeping gigantism. Call it a giveaway, call it exploitation, call it clever legal sophistry, or just call it the failure of good intentions. Call it absurd, obscure, and dangerous, and eventually lethal. But don't call it zoning.

July 13,
December 14, 1980

*The Royal Plaza,
South Bronx, New
York, 1929*

*From Art Deco to
total devastation, a
story of negative
planning impact*

The Royal Plaza, South Bronx, New York, 1929

From Art Deco to total devastation, a story of negative planning impact

THE SUBWAY AND THE SOUTH BRONX

It is fair to say that the New York subway system and the South
Bronx will be with us for a long time. Their relationship is
umbilical and historical, and both have entered serious phases
of decline. An exhibition about the subway system called "Artists and Architects of the New York Subway" was mounted by
the New-York Historical Society, with the cooperation of the
MTA, to honor the system's Diamond Jubilee, and another
exhibition called "Devastation/Resurrection: The South
Bronx" was put on by the Bronx Museum of the Arts. Such
shows come and go, but the South Bronx display has produced
an important and enduring catalogue that should be reviewed
periodically.

126

The subway show was meant to commemorate the day in 1904 when top-hatted officials pulled a silver handle made by Tiffany to start the first train from City Hall. Seventy-five years of this particular century is a long time in technological and aesthetic terms. The marvel is that the city's subways, decrepit, deteriorated, and discredited as they are today, still work as well as they do. But the real marvel is that they were originally built to such high design and engineering standards. The architects in charge were the illustrious firm of Heins and La Farge, who were more accustomed to working on cathedrals than on underground train stations. Tiled Guastavino vaults were used to roof over spaces decorated with colorful mosaics and ornate brass trim. The City Hall station (closed in 1945) was described at its opening as "a cool little vaulted city of cream and green earthenware like a German beer stein." The New York *Sun* editorialized that the system was "the finest, handsomest, and most complete and best equipped underground railroad in the world." It reached the point where August Belmont, president of the IRT, had to veto a $10,000 solid oak escalator for the 125th Street Station as a bit much even for an undertaking of this standard. It was a little "silly," he said, to have woodwork fit for a ballroom.

The price of all this was $35 million, a sum publicized at the time as "the single largest contract in the History of Civilization." The entire process, from contract signing to tunnel digging and dedication, was recorded in photographs; it would seem that every step of the way was noted or celebrated by formally attired and heavily bearded gentlemen in seated or standing groups, with a little something run up for the occasion by Tiffany. These bibelots range from a huge silver tray engraved with scenes of the excavation and a map of the subway to an ornate presentation cup for August Belmont of a gadrooned and festooned opulence that must have made his own equine trophies seem piffling by comparison. Perhaps most fascinating as objects of history and technology, or even just as "found art," is the early engineering equipment, including transformers, motors, and signaling and switching gear of tremendous technological presence. The archaic, abstract dignity of their shining black paint and gleaming brass and copper makes the intervening seventy-five years seem more like 7,500. Never have art, technology, and society traveled so far, so fast.

What the subway and the South Bronx have conspicuously in common now is their deteriorated state; more important historically, however, is that the subway opened the Bronx for intensive development earlier in this century. The big difference today is that the subway still functions after a fashion, and an infamous part of the South Bronx does not.

As Robert Jensen writes in the introduction to *Devastation/ Resurrection: The South Bronx,* the South Bronx is not only the name of a place, but a name for despair. It is a term that began to be used in the context of fires, destruction, and endless vistas of rubble in the late 1960's. Today, the South Bronx is used to denote everything south of Fordham Road between the Bronx and Harlem rivers—a community of more than twenty neighborhoods and about 600,000 people—as many as live within Boston's city limits.

The publication tries to answer the question that everyone asks, "How did it happen, and why?" And while there are no complete answers, there is a lot to be learned from this material. The South Bronx is an absolutely gruesome history of what might be called negative planning impact. It is a demonstration of how federal policies—aimed at other objectives—can interact with city politics and social, economic, and demographic changes in a vulnerable, older city neighborhood, for an urban disaster of epic proportions. The litany of those federal actions that dealt older cities a body blow includes bulldozer urban renewal and its community disruption, the building of highways, in particular, those carved out of poor inner-city neighborhoods, and the low-cost FHA loans that not only created the suburbs but offered the option of escape to white populations. If the package had been calculated to do a job on such marginal older areas, it could not have succeeded better. And nothing was helped by local housing policies. In addition, the area's instability was accelerated by the city's continuing loss of entry-level jobs and small businesses and industries, coupled with the large Puerto Rican immigration and shifting black neighborhoods. Poverty became entrenched, and mobility became flight.

The decline of building stock through deterioration and abandonment to rubble-strewn lots is explained and summarized in two of the catalogue's most compelling and disturbing pages. But the most nightmarish reading of all is the unbelievable, and not untypical, case history of the destruction of Roosevelt Gardens, one of the Grand Concourse's finest housing complexes of the 1920's. This factual account details the most unscrupulous and inhuman kind of real estate exploitation, from deliberate neglect to dummy transfers to avoid taxes and outright nonpayment of taxes, with deliberate rapid tenant turnover in favor of the city's finder's fees and higher rent payments for welfare clients, many of whom had severe social pathologies. One even learns a common South Bronx phrase, applied to the final purchasers who give such a building its *coup de grâce.* They strip out and sell anything left of marketable value before the arsonists come—if owners as attractive in their management as the owners of Roosevelt Gardens have not brought in the arsonists first. They are called the "finishers."

Unfortunately, the lessons of the South Bronx seem to have been lost on City Hall. No one has connected cause and effect, or faced the enduring physical and human effects of policy decisions. In the end, the politicians are the finishers.

January 13, 1980

BATTERY PARK CITY

Anyone who has been around long enough to have lived through the saga of Battery Park City can view the world with Panglossian optimism. Nothing could have started worse, taken longer, or had so many strikes against it than this stop-and-go (mostly stop), large-scale urban dream. With the New York State Urban Development Corporation's completed architectural designs for 6 million square feet of commercial space in a cluster of new skyscrapers for the long-vacant waterfront landfill just west of the World Trade Center, the happy ending finally seems in sight. An apparently hopeless situation, which included near-default on Battery Park City bonds, has been turned around. If all goes according to schedule, New York will get a coordinated and architecturally first-rate urban complex of the standard, significance, and size of Rockefeller Center, that will add a spectacular new drama to the New York skyline.

In this city, of course, to speak of happy endings is to cross one's fingers against disaster—such as the possibility that Manhattan's commercial building boom might suddenly go bust, as it did in the late 1960's, or some occurrence that could unhinge the developer's plans. Barring unexpected catastrophies, the Canadian firm of Olympia and York has an optimistic schedule for completion by 1987.

This centrally located commercial complex will cover four-teen of Battery Park City's ninety-two acres. It includes four very large office towers, thirty-three to fifty stories high, with floor areas averaging 40,000 square feet; these are immense buildings, even measured by the adjacent World Trade Center. They are to be faced in a combination of granite and reflective glass, with the proportion of stone to glass greatest at the bottom. As the towers rise, the stone grid will become more delicate and the glass more dominant; at the top, they will be glittering shafts. The buildings will be capped by simple geometric crowns of varying profiles, lighted at night.

Two lower, domed, octagonal structures, only nine stories high, will mark the main entrance at Liberty Street. They will be linked to create both a portal to the river and a gateway to the city. A second structure is planned as an arched glass "winter garden" or indoor public room, with an interior as large as the concourse of Grand Central Station. All of the buildings will be joined by a three-acre tree-shaded plaza, with a formal terrace stepped down to the river's edge and a mile-long water-front esplanade. Bridges across West Street will provide access and connections to Lower Manhattan at Liberty and Vesey streets.

The scheme is an outstanding one in the annals of New York development in several ways; some of its most remarkable features are far less visible than its tall buildings. This development is not the result of the usual buccaneering New York investment-building pattern; it is the combined effort of state and city management and private investment, working together in a mutually profitable partnership. The process began with an unusual act by a public agency: right after UDC absorbed the Battery Park City Authority in 1979, Richard Kahan, the head of UDC, asked Cooper-Eckstut Associates to prepare a master plan and urban design guidelines for the area, even before developers were invited to bid. This scheme replaced earlier master plans, which had ranged from daunting complexity to humdrum banality, but all of which had proved equally unbuildable.

The Cooper-Eckstut plan defined street patterns, the location and massing of buildings, public and private space, water-

Cesar Pelli

*Model of World
Financial Center,
New York,
1981–86*

*An upbeat ending
to the sad, stumbling
saga of Battery
Park City*

Kenneth Champlin

front treatment, connections and circulation, and physical and visual relationships to Lower Manhattan—based on careful economic and market analysis. It set superior, knowledgeable standards of urban design. Within this specified framework, the architectural options were left open. But one of the stipulations that UDC made to developers was that these guidelines had to be followed.

Olympia and York was designated as the builder by competitive bidding; then the development firm selected its architect. Cesar Pelli, the designer of the Museum of Modern Art condominium tower, was chosen from an array of stellar possibilities.

Pelli called the guidelines both useful and appropriate. He found that they also speeded the job. It is important to note, however, that he did much more than follow them. The criteria were made the framework of a suave, elegant, stylish, and original solution that is the product of the architect's own considerable talents and highly sophisticated urban sensibilities. Pelli devised a kind of "synthesis" skyscraper style that is boldly modern and yet evocative of earlier New York skyscrapers in its departure from the "box" and its delight in special effects of surface and form. But the shape of the towers comes directly from the planners' guidelines. These specified that the buildings were to be set back at the third, ninth, and twenty-fourth floors, to relate physically and symbolically to the predominant heights of Lower Manhattan buildings. The three-story section parallels the area's remaining early-nineteenth-century structures, and in keeping with tradition, is treated essentially as a masonry wall. This level also provides the scale and surface experienced by the pedestrian. The ninth- and twenty-fourth-story setbacks reflect the size and style of later downtown buildings, with more glass and less stone. The top stories, soaring to today's heights, are largely glass. The buildings' caps, or crowns, suggest the classical or Art Deco towers of the 1920's and 30's without nostalgia or whimsy.

The style might be called romantic rationalism. There are none of the gimmicks or borrowings applied as the heavy witticisms or lightweight historicism being passed off as a "new" architecture today. These towers go far beyond conventional speculative construction, or the one-of-a-kind "prima donna" designs currently favored by New York's developers. The conscious attempt being made to relate these huge structures to the fine-grained, smaller-scaled, older part of the city is called contexualism today. But it is also an imaginative and refined solution for buildings that could be brutally defiant and isolated in their boldness and size.

There is another unusual factor involved that makes this thoughtful unified scheme possible. UDC and Cooper-Eckstut had broken up the plan into six development packages, assuming that builders, as is customary in New York, would be equipped to do only part at a time. To everyone's considerable surprise, the large Canadian company wanted to do the whole project at once. This is a scale of real estate investment unfamiliar to New York, where developers have traditionally preferred monumental penny-ante operations. It requires enough faith in the market to justify very big dollars "up front," with the promise of very large profits in return, as well as a large cash flow. This approach also makes the rest of the Battery Park City land more desirable, more quickly, than piecemeal construction would, for residential and other uses. (A group of apartment houses built by the Lefrak organization adjacent to the planned commercial core was the first, and only, construction on the landfill until the adoption of this scheme.)

In retrospect, I suppose one could call the story of Battery Park City a cliff-hanger if it were possible to hang on to a cliff for so many years. The original idea sprang straight from the head of Governor Nelson Rockefeller in 1966, as from the brow of Jove, with Albany taking New York by surprise. It came complete with a tear-off-on-the-dotted-line plan provided by Harrison and Abramovitz, the architects who were also to give us the dropped-by-Buck-Rogers-spaceship Albany Mall. The city, which had been developing its own waterfront plan at the time, had not been consulted, but a fast political truce was arranged between the governor and then-Mayor John Lindsay so that they could make the announcement together.

From then on, the history of Battery Park City was a series of monumental fumbles. One plan followed another, as the city tried to keep control of the independent Battery Park City Authority. But the authority seemed jinxed by bad luck and

Opposite page:
East 62nd Street,
New York

Manhattan's
elegant side streets
are always under
siege

Fred Conrad/*New York*
Times

worse design. When a glut in office construction coincided with a scheme that was meant to support the entire undertaking with three huge office towers at the landfill's southern tip, the bottom fell out of the project. Since the authority's lack of clairvoyance was matched only by its lack of urban vision, that was not all bad. But it was very bad for the bondholders, and faced with actual default in 1979, the state-city rescue operation was mounted that put UDC in charge.

Battery Park City is a bold and spectacular addition to New York. It has the urban sophistication, the architectural standards, the financial and critical mass to put it over the top. For those of us who see this as a landmark extension of the city's skyline drama, and a significant step in skyscraper design, the prospect is exhilarating. But out of habit and inclination, I keep my fingers crossed.

May 24, 1981

Note: The story is different for Times Square, a similar city-state plan. There the UDC guidelines were largely ignored by the developer, George Klein, and his architects, John Burgee with Philip Johnson for a lackluster, urbanistically inappropriate design.

THE SIDE STREET SAGA: EAST SIXTY-SECOND STREET

This is a script we've played before. The title is Side Street Sabotage. A little suspense-and-disaster music, please. Somehow, this drama is always being performed on East Sixty-second Street, between Fifth and Madison avenues.

As we wrote back in 1968, when Syracuse University acquired the houses at Numbers 12, 14, 16, and 18 with a speculative look in its eye, this block is an almost intact example of the rows of richly detailed, five-story town houses built in the French Renaissance or Beaux Arts style of the early years of this century. Their landmark quality is enhanced by the

completeness of the block. Nothing like them will ever be built again. Same words, same tune.

Side streets like this one, with their minipalaces and brownstones, are not only enclaves of architectural excellence; they are quintessentially New York. They are the other side of the skyscraper coin, the glamorous milieu its upwardly mobile inhabitants aspire to, its most polished, elegant, and worldly face. Any erosion of these blocks diminishes the whole city. Nor is the loss only sentimental or aesthetic; it is the irreversible hard-core destruction of the superior architectural and environmental character that makes New York not just a big-business town, but a cosmopolitan world capital as well.

East Sixty-second Street should have been "landmarked," to use that awful bastard verb, from park to river, a long time ago. Except for a few intrusions, its homogeneous residential scale and character continues over many blocks, with a rich and diverse architectural heritage and a high quota of beauty and charm. Designation is badly overdue for many of these uptown East Side streets, in whole or in part. But this is one that I go out of my way to walk on because it restores the spirit and rewards the eye. A few violins, please, and pan the south side from Numbers 4 to 18, east of the Knickerbocker Club at the corner of Fifth, to the Carlton House on Madison.

Now enter the real estate developer—in this case, George Klein, who has looked at Sixty-second Street and found it good. Because it is beautiful and fashionable, he wants to construct a luxury apartment building on the site of two of the town houses—Numbers 4 and 6—for a distance of seventy-nine feet along the street and a height of twenty-five stories, located a hundred feet from the Fifth Avenue corner. There are, of course, taller and broader buildings in New York, just as there were deeper and wider wounds than Mercutio's, but none that could more effectively spoil the block by chopping into its character and shooting skyward. This one is quite big enough to do the job.

Just around the corner at Sixty-first Street and Fifth Avenue is a large, new luxury apartment house, 800 Fifth, that stands on the site of the Dodge House. It is relevant to our story.

Eight hundred Fifth is a dreadful building, if so forthright a description can fit anything that combines so much banality and hypocrisy, the result of some of the most tortuous and complicated games ever played with the city's zoning law in order to put it on that spot. In fact, this structure was spot-zoned if anything ever was. But since it was the only construction game in town at a time of dire financial need, there was a lot of pressure to waive the rules to get it built. That extremely dangerous precedent has now come home to roost.

Eight hundred Fifth has one of the city's most sought-after addresses, at whopping prices. It also has a false front that makes bows or pratfalls to the cornice height of the Knickerbocker Club, and facades that curtsy obliquely to the views from the windows of Fifth Avenue neighbors to the north. This monstrosity is a money-maker, and so it must be emulated. If there is no more Fifth Avenue frontage in the immediate vicinity for another of these beauties, why not slide one down Sixty-second Street instead?

Why not, indeed. Just a few special permits from the City Planning Commission will do it, plus some virtuous talk about saving the Knickerbocker Club, which is apparently suffering from terminal gentility and could be restored to life by selling its air rights to the project.

Unfortunately, the air rights can be used only if the new building is allowed to break the existing zoning, which is designed to protect the small scale and low density of those side streets. Because the city's planners were wise enough to value their quality, they undertook to preserve them. The midblocks in the Sixties and above are therefore zoned lower, at R-8, than the avenues or major cross streets, where larger R-10 buildings are permitted. On Fifth Avenue opposite Central Park a special Park Improvement District redistributes the permitted bulk of the avenue structures from very tall towers to squatter, twenty-five-story or three hundred–foot-high buildings. The trade-off for extra square footage for the builder, in this case, is not the customary open plaza, but a cash contribution to the upkeep of Central Park.

Surrounded by larger buildings, the midblocks are protected for the increasingly rare human scale that serves as necessary relief for the bulk and density of the avenues. It cannot be stressed strongly enough how essential this zoning is to New York's quality and livability, or how prescient the planning vision was that saw the streets and buildings as unique assets in the larger urban context. But it must also be stressed that although this zoning protects from overdevelopment, it does not save the existing buildings; they can still be replaced by moderate-size ones. Only landmark designation can do that.

Klein's plan is based on an option to purchase Numbers 4 and 6 East Sixty-second Street, which have been the York Club buildings, plus the air rights of the Knickerbocker Club, demolishing 4 and 6 to build his tower. The problem is that twenty-five feet of this property lies in the R-10 Park Improvement District, while the major part, fifty-four feet, is in the R-8 district. Klein and his architect, Emery Roth and Sons, want to put up an R-10 building in the R-8 district. Since they do not have an R-10 site, the size is based on the use of the Knickerbocker Club's R-10 air rights, which they hope to transfer down the block.

This trick will not be done with mirrors; it is to be executed by going to the City Planning Commission or the Board of Standards and Appeals to ask for permits or variances to allow the maneuver. These changes are necessary because the scheme is not only illegal without them but it is also clearly against the intentions of the zoning ordinance.

The argument being made for the proposal, ironically, is based on the virtues of preservation, or the saving of the Knickerbocker Club through the purchase of its air rights. Provided, of course, that the zoning rules are changed, or bent, to allow the twenty-five-story building on the side street where it doesn't belong. The argument is also made that what can be constructed there legally now is a fourteen-story building, and the proposal would "only" be eleven stories higher. Strawman alternatives of the horrors that could be built "as of right" are being hoisted by the developer. (Actually, the legal "split" building, by breaking down the bulk, looks better.)

There is also a lot of familiar nonsense about relating the

base treatment to the cornice lines of the older buildings and the promise of token limestone and a design "reminiscent" of the 1920's, with parts "addressing" themselves to Central Park and a "crown gradually penetrating the sky." That would take Houdini, not an architect. The rendering suggests that a better building could be pulled out of a hat.

In sum, this is bad preservation, bad urbanism, and bad architecture. And it is not, as presented, a question of the future of the Knickerbocker Club versus two houses and the spoiling of one block. If the club is saved by this kind of illegal transfer, the precedent has been set for the destruction of entire groups and streets of buildings of landmark quality that have far more impact on the city's character and style than a single structure. The threat is to all R-8 midblocks, and the danger is not just from the Fifth Avenue side, where sites are limited, but from the Madison Avenue side, which is far more vulnerable to this kind of treatment. Watch them go down like dominoes if this one is built. And don't think other developers aren't waiting to see what happens here.

That is not the only dangerous precedent that would be set. Beginning with the construction of 800 Fifth Avenue at Sixty-first Street, the line is being erased, or smudged, between the densities allowed in the central business district and in residentially zoned areas. If the line moves from Sixty-first to Sixty-second Street, can Sixty-third, Sixty-fourth, or any others be far behind?

There is also the matter of the cash contribution to the upkeep of Central Park, which sounds as pious as saving the Knickerbocker Club. Under the Park Improvement District legislation, the figure was set at $7.20 per square foot of bonus floor area. The munificent check that Klein would write comes to about $150,000. This is a pittance for the park and a bonanza for the builder, because it is so far below what that added space is worth at today's land and market values; it should be listed in *New York* magazine's Best Buys.

Any kind of negotiated settlement by the Planning Commission that sanctions this building can be seen only as a giveaway or default. And any variance granted by the Board of Standards and Appeals—hardship is scarcely a factor with the returns assured by this location—guarantees the rapid loss of some of the city's most valuable environmental and economic assets. Either way, it is side street sabotage. Fade out, New York.

December 10, 1978

Note: The Upper East Side Historic District was designated in 1981 to protect its streets, including Sixty-second Street, from uncontrolled speculative development. The vogue for condo conversions saved some of the handsomer town houses in 1984–85. The builder, George Klein, moved on to much bigger prizes, including designation as the developer of the Times Square project.

WESTWAY: LAST OR LOST CHANCE?

The West Side Highway is not exactly a majestic ruin. It is still operative above Forty-sixth Street, and the cars it carried until the demise of its downtown segment have not gone away. The traffic and pollution have simply moved to other roads. The decaying and largely unused piers have a certain surreal charm, of course, cherished by those who have been able to capitalize on its peaceful desertion and spectacular views, suggesting what New Yorkers, if they lived anywhere else, might reasonably expect in the way of a public waterfront amenity.

The proposed replacement for this part of the West Side Highway was Westway; probably no project in the history of cities was more lengthily debated, more highly controversial, or more violently opposed. As this 1977 commentary on Westway is being prepared for this collection of essays in 1985, the news has come that Westway is dead—finally and irreversibly dead, after a decade of confrontation and litigation. It is ostensibly dead because of its potential effect on the Hudson River's striped bass, a point that narrows large issues down to lunacy, with the coup de grâce administered by the traditional enemy,

New Jersey, but it really doesn't matter anymore. Even those of us who started out for Westway ended up against it, feeling as betrayed as the striped bass. Never was a plan more promising for a city's future, and never was a promise more totally betrayed by the politicians, officials, and professionals who presided over the perversion and abandonment of its principles and the dangers and delinquencies of an openly aborted planning process. Somewhere along the line the chance to link transportation, development, open space, and the use of an irreplaceable waterfront for a rational long-term solution in the public interest lost all visibility and any attention. Watching the planning opportunity of the century turn into the real estate opportunity of the century, subsidized by the government giveaway of the century, made those who care about such things wish as devoutly for Westway's demise as any striped-bass lover. Only it is harder for us, tragic for us, because we knew what was really possible with Westway, and what was lost forever. The fish are not enough. The bass look awfully like red herring.

Perhaps, in New York, such things are simply not meant to be. As one government official remarked a long time ago, New York is the only city in which no higher concerns than real estate profits have dictated its form and functions.

On January 23, 1977, still full of hope and faith, I wrote, as follows, about Westway:

A joint undertaking of the city and the state, Westway is planned as a 4.2-mile, six-lane interstate highway, extending from the Battery to Forty-second Street, of which a large part would be underground in new landfill in the Hudson River. Funding, divided 90–10 by federal and state agencies for interstate highways, provides the road and its facilities with no cost to the city. A later second section of the road would go from Forty-second to Fifty-seventh Street, with a future narrower leg to Seventy-second Street, where all commercial traffic would be dropped, as it met the restricted Henry Hudson Parkway.

Logic says that this is an excellent solution to the demise of the West Side Highway, even with many unanswered questions. But logic means little to New Yorkers. They have been burned too many times—too often lied to and coopted in the name of some greater good. They are partisan, protective, and paranoid. Logic is converted to suicidal illogic while they march their protest banners over the cliff. People, cities, and countryside have been ravaged by expressways, and mother wit and street wisdom say resist—the evil that we have is better than the evil to come. Resist, because we know now about the dislocations and disasters of highway construction, because we fear for our neighborhoods, because we have learned that the status quo is safer than change, because, above all, politicians cannot be trusted. Something happens to their vision of the city with the receipt of their campaign contributions.

The point that has been totally missed or willfully ignored about Westway is that it was never meant to be just a billion-dollar road. It never pretended to be only an answer to transportation needs. There are simpler answers, as opponents have always claimed. Westway was conceived as large-scale, long-term land-use planning for the city's future—a chance to reclaim the mutilated waterfront and the far West Side. It is unique in the city's history as an opportunity to do something extraordinarily constructive and creative. However, planning and development have become bad words for good reasons. The record of both road building and renewal has been catastrophic in human and urban terms.

Westway must not be just a real estate gimmick for developable land; it must be planned, designed, and controlled in the interest of a better city, not of a better tax base. Obviously, with the complexity of the project and the many jurisdictions involved, someone will have to set standards. And those standards will have to be translated into superior and binding legal and architectural solutions. The assumption is that hard lessons have been learned, that the art of planning and urban design is more sensitive and sophisticated, that we have more environmental skills, that cities are more responsive to public concerns and welfare, and that the public will bloody well see to it that they are. This is all true—provided such a creative plan can survive the city's politics and special interests.

Of 181 acres of new riverfront land, only 31 acres would be

used for the road, since much of it would be underground. The waterfront parks would be state-owned and maintained, and New York City would retain the right to zone and control development. The need to zone the new land restrictively and specifically, based on environmental considerations, has yet to be addressed. Housing near Greenwich Village, for example, would have to be low-rise and small-scale. There is understandable concern about the form and impact of development adjoining the West Village, TriBeCa, and Chelsea. The premise is that new construction would be integrated in character with contiguous neighborhoods. View corridors to the water would have to be maintained. But none of this comes about automatically. Other problems the city would face include coordination and management of a vast and lengthy undertaking, as well as specific investment, design, and maintenance decisions. It would be a ten- to twenty-year undertaking to carry out parks and housing in their ultimate form, even under optimum conditions. Above all, superior design talent is required for parks of Olmsted quality, and for housing of suitable scale and style. Design quality is the project's overriding need and the ultimate determinant of the environmental quality of the result. In the heat of battle this has received absolutely no attention.

Most of all, speculation must be controlled, if the creative chance and neighborhood character are not to be lost. Land values will zoom on the West Side, adjacent to new parks and the river and areas of new construction. Zoning restrictions and design review must determine appropriate kinds of building, or nonbuilding, for both the new land and the bordering neighborhoods. These restrictions will be fought by developers, but they must be in place before design begins. Such guidelines were developed successfully for another large development area, Battery Park City. The city must be uncompromisingly responsible. Westway cannot work without conscience and control.

In October 1985, I was content to let the preceding article stand as an appropriate, if ironic, Westway requiem. Herbert Oppenheimer, an architect, has stated the facts of its demise best: in a letter to *The New York Times* he said that Westway was crushed between two powerful forces—the real estate people and their political friends, and the environmentalists and their political friends, and that in the carnage, the essential thoughtful planning work was never done. The requiem should include the information that the idea of Westway began, not in the heart and mind of any real estate entrepreneur, but on the drawing board of one of the most skilled and concerned planners of an earlier generation, Samuel Ratensky, who worked for the city; he died before he could see the mutilation of the dream he had long held for the waterfront, which he believed could be realized through coordinated design and highway funds. The real estate lobby was, predictably, selfishly and self-interestedly wrong; the environmentalists were shortsightedly, uncomprehendingly, and stupidly wrong. Has any lesson been learned? I think not. The striped bass were the only winners.

NEW YORK:
SAVING THE CITY

A LANDMARK DECISION:
GRAND CENTRAL TERMINAL

The announcement in 1978 of the Supreme Court decision in the Grand Central Terminal case in which New
York City was upheld on both the landmark designation
of the terminal and the constitutionality of its landmark law, was
accompanied by sighs of relief from preservationists around the
country and cries of disaster from the real estate community.
Sentimental building buffs would now have carte blanche to
protect everything in sight, stalemating development in older
commercial centers, said the builders. At the very least, we were
told, the decision would set off a rash of ill-considered and
obstructive designations; developers would flee from the center
city to less shackled areas, taking their money with them. Any
new buildings would have to be enormously big to make up for
lost property and profits, the arguments went. At worst, the
decision could destroy the investment economics of cities, and
ailing downtowns would be in greater trouble than ever. The
words and the music are familiar.

That kind of scare talk serves little except the speculators.
Investment is not going to be suddenly choked off in center
cities. Developers are always pushing for bigger buildings; in
Manhattan the city's planners are endlessly strong-armed into

Opposite page:
Warren and
Wetmore, Reed
and Stem

Grand
Central Terminal,
New York,
completed 1913

Neal Boenzi/New York
Times

Below:
A Beaux Arts
landmark crowned
by Jules Coutan's
Mercury clock;
quality and history
upheld by the
Supreme Court

Chester Higgins, Jr./New
York Times

destructive zoning concessions that are hopelessly eroding midtown's side street scale and variety. Overreaching has always been the name of the building game. "They're killing us" is the reprise.

The facts do not support the figures. First, any city that makes irresponsible designations with inadequate criteria is going to find itself right back in the courts again. All designations are subject to judicial review, and capricious or arbitrary selection of landmark structures and sites will no more be upheld by the courts than capricious or arbitrary zoning. By finally equating landmarks preservation with zoning, the Supreme Court no more gave a blank check to preservationists than it did to any other appropriate exercise of the police

power for the general public welfare. What it did was to settle some very basic issues of law that had been uncertain. The highest court accepted the principle that regulation of private property for historical, cultural, and aesthetic values, if it is done in accord with a comprehensive plan that provides benefits to all, is in the public interest.

That equation, in fact, between landmarks law and zoning, is the heart of the matter. Previously, there had been great legislative uncertainty about whether landmarks law could be considered a form of zoning, for which compensation is not required, or whether it was a "taking" of property, in violation of the Fifth and Fourteenth amendments, for which "full compensation" or cash payment for market value was necessary. Obviously, the latter interpretation would bankrupt any city that wanted to protect its heritage and would vastly diminish the means by which landmarks could be saved (purchase of facade easements, for example, a very useful but limited tool). But it was that critical unresolved issue that had landmarks commissions and municipalities hanging on the ropes.

Many, including New York, have been extremely cautious in their designations, for fear that testing their laws in the courts might destroy them. The certainty now is that they are constitutional, provided they are properly constructed. This does not mean that cities will proceed with rashness. Responsible professionals will be as careful as ever, unless a city wants its prime property endlessly tied up in court cases.

The specific question posed by the Grand Central case was whether a city may, as part of a comprehensive program to preserve historic landmarks and districts, place restrictions on the development of individual landmarks without effecting a "taking" requiring the payment of "just compensation."

Penn Central and its developer had proposed that a huge office tower be constructed on top of the terminal, using the air rights over the terminal, which, of course, represent part of the property's value and a great deal of money. The Landmarks Preservation Commission had turned the plan down and Penn Central had sued. New York State's highest court found for Penn Central, and the Supreme Court, on the city's appeal, agreed to review the case. The Supreme Court held that Penn

Central had not been unconstitutionally deprived of its property, because the law's restrictions did not deny the owner a "reasonable return," but only affected the exploitation of the property for its most profitable use. Moreover, the law's restrictions were deemed necessary for the public purpose of protecting landmarks.

The Supreme Court not only accepted the validity of this public purpose, but it also called the railroad's claim that its property had been taken on the basis of the denial of the exploitation of a particular development possibility "simply untenable." One of the most important parts of the decision is the Court's denial of the right to the highest possible return on a property, rather than a reasonable return. The Court also held that interference with the rights of the parcel as a whole must be considered, not just one part alone—in this case, the air rights. It noted, in addition, that the railroad had not been deprived of the building's current use, and that it was assured a reasonable return by the New York law, which also contained machinery and techniques for adjustments to make this possible, as well as providing the greatest latitude for the property's use in keeping with preservation. In this case, the city had gone even further by amending a zoning law that permitted the transfer of air rights from a landmark structure to another site, so that the terminal's development rights would be available to any other Penn Central properties in the area.

Penn Central's use of its terminal air rights, therefore, had not been abrogated, and while the transfer program may be far from ideal and the rights were less than on the terminal site, said the Court, they are still valuable air rights. Their transfer might not qualify as "just compensation" if a "taking" had occurred, but they substantially modified any financial burden the law had imposed. In addition, the Court observed that the Landmarks Preservation Commission had not foreclosed the possibility of a more modest and more appropriate addition to the terminal; it had only refused the railroad's specific submission.

As for the financial burden that Penn Central still had to bear, the decision pointed out that legislation designed to promote the general welfare commonly burdens some more than others, and that these laws have not been held invalid on that account. The railroad's contention that selection of the terminal was arbitrary, and therefore similar to discriminatory zoning, was rejected because the designation was part of a comprehensive city plan for landmark protection under which some four hundred buildings had been listed. The related argument that "the decision to designate a landmark is arbitrary or subjective because it is basically a matter of taste" was also denied. Judicial review is available for any Landmarks Commission decision, the judges said, and the courts will have no more difficulty identifying arbitrary or discriminatory action than in the context of classic zoning.

Obviously, the Court recognized the problems of landmark legislation and tried to deal with them fairly. The word "reasonable" appears repeatedly both as a modifier for economic exploitation of property and to set limits to individual economic burdens. Still another word that occurs to the reader of the decision is "maturity"—this is a country that is finally recognizing its urban assets and the need to protect them for livable cities.

July 9, 1978

THE TEMPTATION OF ST. BARTHOLOMEW'S

If Faust exchanged his soul for immortality, the temptation of St. Bartholomew's is a more pragmatic lure: financial security being offered by a most appropriate modern devil, New York real estate. The testing of moral fiber against sensory gratification or material gain is as old as biblical history, and this time the tempter came in the form of a "prestigious corporation" offering $100 million for the church's prime Park Avenue property as the site for a new office tower. In these days of shrinking congregations and growing deficits, $100 million is an attractive sum. The trials of conscience that have sent saints into poverty and the desert have delivered St. Bart's into the hands of the real estate brokers and developers.

152

Or a part of St. Bart's, since the agreement now rests on a compromise; the rector and the vestry believe that they have found a way to keep the church and turn a profit, too. This revelation was apparently arrived at through divine guidance. The announcement was made, "after weeks of prayerful consideration," that the church is not for sale. What is for sale, or lease, instead, is only a portion of the land, which will destroy only part of the building complex. St. Bartholomew's is considering disposing of its community house and garden, or about one third of the site. At the least, the buyer will get a coveted Park Avenue address and room enough to build a substantial and enormously profitable structure. Actually, that $100 million offer was peanuts.

The forces of darkness are persistent; a second offer evidently followed the first. Not surprisingly, church officials have voted to put the negotiations into the hands of "outside consultants" professionally adept at flushing out the highest bidder. The availability of this choice corner site at Fiftieth Street, virtually the only open space left on an almost solidly corporate

Bertram Goodhue

*St. Bartholomew's,
New York, 1913–30*

*A modern
conflict of God
and Mammon*

Fred R. Conrad/*New
York Times*

Park Avenue in midtown, is sending orgasmic tremors through New York's real estate community. The church sees no loss of spiritual values in its decision. Temptation comes complete with convenient, if confused, rationalizations about people and buildings, missions and mortar. Brick and stone are called secondary to human needs; it is said that cash will serve society better than beauty. And solvency has a beauty of its own.

That the beauty of the St. Bartholomew block contributes to the welfare of the city and all of its inhabitants are not part of the reckoning. The close link between the spirit and the environment is denied. False and irrelevant equations are made between dealing in real estate and dealing with poverty. Although the quality of the church's art and architecture is well known, the serenity and public availability of its sun-filled and flowering garden in the congested commercial heart of the city are a less acknowledged contribution to all the people of New York. Only in a culture where commercial values have vanquished spiritual values would such a church and its setting not be considered a legacy beyond price from the past to the present and the future.

Equally disturbing is the church's odd illusion that it is engaged in an act of preservation. "We have agreed that we will accept no offer, however big, that would harm in any way our magnificent church building . . . ," says the official statement. To which the only possible response is amen. The harm that will be done to the landmark church by this decision will be irreparable. Perhaps it is time for church officials to take a walk outside and use their eyes instead of their calculators.

The architecture of St. Bartholomew's consists of a church building and a community house that form an integrated L-shaped whole. Functionally, the structures are separate, but visually, all the parts are unified. The church was built to the design of Bertram Grosvenor Goodhue in 1918, incorporating a 1903 porch by McKim, Mead and White from an earlier building. The community house was added in the 1920's by Goodhue's firm, after his death. The familiar flat dome of the Byzantine-inspired complex was completed in 1930. Handmade salmon-colored brick and Indiana limestone were used throughout, enriched by skilled carving, rare marbles, and fine details; the church contains numerous works of art. With all the exterior elements meticulously matched in scale and style, the complex is meant to look like one building, and it does.

This two-part construction wraps around the garden, embracing and sheltering it with an architecture of agreeable human dimensions, against the backdrop of skyscrapers beyond. The planting acts not only as a frame and setting for the church, but also buffers it from the street and the impact of the larger buildings. The destruction of the garden, which protects and enhances the church at the same time that it opens the corner to the street, is a loss all too easy to understand and deplore. However, it would do more than remove rare open space of great beauty and amenity; it would destroy an essential part of the architectural composition, leaving the truncated church like a jewel without a setting.

The quality and relationships of the buildings and landscaping have been recognized and respected by the architects of neighboring structures. Both the Art Deco General Electric building, designed by Cross and Cross in 1931, and the otherwise standard new commercial offices behind the church and community house, demonstrate the considerable care taken to find a sympathetic match to the color of St. Bartholomew's brick. Fortunately, their location on the Lexington Avenue side also makes them background buildings. The entire block works extremely well as one of the city's better examples of urban design.

To understand what the changes would be like, it is necessary to look at the church complex from the street. First, imagine one arm of the garden enclosure lopped off. Next, mentally wipe out the garden. Then try to see the church minus the planting to the south that frames the building and insulates it against the march of encroaching blockbusters. Next, visualize an immense tower filling most of the space now occupied by the community house and the garden. Give or take the questionable amenity of a windswept and sterile plaza or arcade with some token planting at its base—features that permit a builder to add more height—the bulk of this tower, no matter how designed, will overwhelm the church beside it; at worst, it will wall up the corner. Consider the truly destructive scale and jarring impact of this construction. Think really big: the kind of building that can, and will, be put up under the present zoning, combining the permitted avenue size and bonuses and the church's air rights, is monstrous. Why else would anyone offer that kind of money?

But a bargain is a bargain, and this brutally disfiguring transformation comes along with the cash. Has anyone really thought about it in these terms, prayerfully or otherwise? Is this irreversible sell-off of art and urbanity something the church should knowingly sanction? Is this kind of destruction just too difficult for the nonvisual nonspecialist in urban design to "see" or imagine? Is no one able to understand what will happen before it actually takes place? Can it really be a matter of equating the beauty of a building with idolatry, an incredibly warped interpretation of the role of architecture in the physical and spiritual life of centuries of civilization which moves the church back to a position so small that there is barely room for the spirit at all? Or is the temptation just too great? The threats to the integrity and even to the survival of the city's art and history today are as devastating as any posed by the bulldozer; they are just wrapped in real estate clothing. Can the church no longer understand or afford the gift of urban grace?

October 26, 1980

Note: After public hearings, the Landmarks Preservation Commission of New York denied the church a Certificate of Appropriateness for the construction of the tower. The church then reapplied on the grounds of economic hardship, which was also denied after exhaustive study of records, reports, and documents. After this decision, in the spring of 1986, the church announced its plans to sue the city on constitutional grounds.

SELLING OUT THE
SOUTH STREET SEAPORT

The saga of the South Street Seaport makes the Perils of Pauline look pale. Since the 1960's, when the objective was to set up a maritime museum in the Schermerhorn Row and restore some of the area's nineteenth-century buildings, the story has been a series of crises dealing with the seaport's struggle to stay alive. But with the signing of a contract with the Rouse Corporation—the celebrated developers of Boston's enormously successful Faneuil Hall Marketplace in the restored and remodeled Greek Revival Quincy Market buildings of the 1820's—salvation seemed to be at hand. With the help of the Boston architectural firm that did the Quincy Market renovations, Benjamin Thompson Associates, the seaport is to be transformed into a similar preservation-merchandising complex, its museum operations shifted to Burling Slip, adjacent to its pier and ships. Only a few spoilsport nonbelievers in this marriage of convenience between history and commerce have qualms.

In phase one of the project, a $250,000 study by the Rouse organization, funded by the Astor Foundation, it was determined that the commercial development of the seaport was feasible; phase two involved the preparation of plans for adapting the old buildings and designing new ones. What the Rouse people consider necessary for the success of this kind of venture is 200,000 to 250,000 square feet of contiguous retail space, achieved here through the creation of a shopping "corridor" on Fulton Street. This requires turning the first two floors of Schermerhorn Row to commercial uses, constructing a new building opposite on the empty site of the old Fulton Market, meant to recall the old structure, and the completion of the corridor with a new pier-platform over the water at the river end.

This complex has been advertised as promising a yield of a percentage of the profits for the seaport of about $1 million the first year, with rising expectations after that. Beyond the money, the advantages and appeal of the plan are obvious. We are told that it will "save" the seaport, will "recycle" the old buildings to a useful end, and, as in Boston, add profit and pleasure downtown, where both are needed.

How can one quarrel with both salvation and success? I am less than happy with some of the details of the Faneuil Hall Marketplace transformation, but I can only commend the genuine concern for the past with which the job has been done. The fact remains, however, that Boston's Quincy Market complex—which consists of unified, axially composed, powerfully handsome, block-long structures by a single architect, Alexander Parris, focused on Parris's equally strong, domed Greek Revival market building in the center—can hold its own architecturally and urbanistically against the overwhelming paraphernalia of a chic and trendy shopping center. That is an essential balance that will be very hard to establish in the more modest seaport buildings, which have a scattered impact and an intimate, evanescent charm.

Can one really create 200,000 square feet of contiguous shopping in such a random group of small, frail, nineteenth-century buildings without essentially destroying them? I do not believe that it can be done. To make the necessary selling space, will they all be "restored back" to neat and sanitary stylistic uniformity as was done in Boston by the Redevelopment Authority? Is it possible to avoid an inevitable metamorphosis of the area? At what point does maritime history drown in upscale consumerism and does destruction by any other name smell sweeter because it also smells of money and popular success?

What Rouse and Thompson have pioneered in Boston is the creation of a carefully controlled shopping environment that is a highly civilized advance on the banality of the suburban shopping mall. It beats the boring boxes when you can coopt architectural history. It has also been a brilliant way of reviving downtown. The results are being universally imitated, and a number of good old buildings are being saved here and there. But the approach is becoming a formula, with all of the standardization and exploitation that this implies.

I have very mixed feelings for the seaport. I guess that what I am really doing is saying goodbye. What will surely be lost is the spirit and identity of the area as it has survived over centuries—something that may be important only to those of us who have really known and loved the small shabby streets and buildings redolent of time and fish and the shadows of ships, or shared the cold sunlight of a quiet winter Sunday morning on the waterfront with the Fulton Market cats, when the nineteenth century still seemed very much alive.

The project is now all-too-appropriately called the Seaport Development. In the process of saving the seaport from an uncertain future, it is certain that it will be turned into something else. This is not preservation. There are a lot worse things, of course, if we are only honest about what we are doing and what we are destroying. But it is a little hard for some of us to accept the reality that what is at the end of the preservation rainbow is the shopping center. Even if it is called a Festival Marketplace.

As this is edited for publication in 1985, it would seem that these doubts have been well founded. The seaport appears to have sold its soul for a tastefully designed mess of yuppie pottage. Its share of the pass-through profits, so far, have been much below the promised level, and a degree of disillusion seems to have set in for some of the trustees and staff. The local community has cried "foul" about the amount of public waterfront provided by the developer as part of the deal; "a matter of interpretation" says the city. Through processes far too complicated to detail, meant to encourage both preservation and development, which includes the manipulation of air rights and other economic esoterica, there is now enormous, overbearing commercial construction bordering the seaport, after a required gavotte took place about the "suitability" of its design.

As preservation, this gets curiouser and curiouser. When such places do survive, by proper planning or by inadvertence, they give a city the irreplaceable enriching references of history and style. They provide the touchstones of the original residual fabric, the patina of time and change, that make authentic reference to the way it was, with room for ghosts to feel at home. I still feel pain for the loss of Peck's Slip, an even older intact group that stood opposite Schermerhorn Row until the 1950's, and for the superb stand of Greek Revival

warehouses on Water Street, demolished for street widening, and the splendid nineteenth-century mix of Brooklyn Bridge Southwest pulverized by the urban renewal bulldozer. Vandalism comes in many guises. The city was the villain in all of these wanton acts, and a subtle and more invidious kind of destruc-

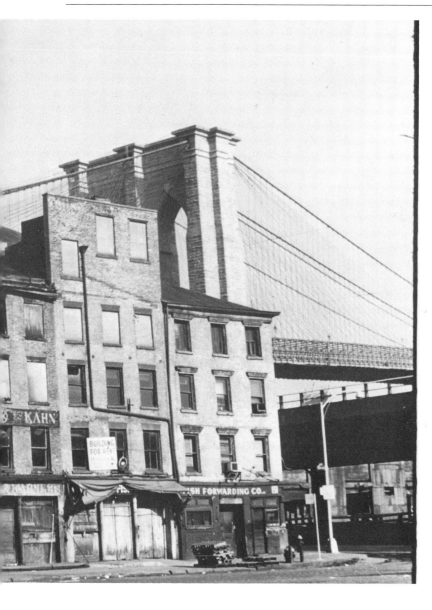

Peck's Slip, New York; built c. 1800, demolished 1960's

Greek Revival remnants destroyed, gentrified or replaced by trendy upscale marketing

Garth Huxtable

tion is continuing the process now. The seaport's stylish transformation is finishing the job. What is lost forever is the real thing.

February 25, 1979
updated October 1985

BLOWING IT IN
BOSTON

When the invitation came to be "credentialed" for Boston's "Great Cities of the World" conference—the grand windup event of the city's 350th birthday celebration in 1980—I knew that I could not go. I did not want to be "credentialed" by anyone for anything; beyond my dismay at the word and the process, I was intimidated. I might not earn my badge. And if I did, the idea of being tagged and slotted was depressing. The affront was double—to one's professional personhood and to the language of Emerson and Lowell that was being replaced by communispeak.

Things got no better with the "media advisory" that arrived from Boston's City Hall. The press was promised a clambake and a boat ride, "photo opportunities" with visiting mayors from around the world against the Boston skyline, human interest features such as barbecues in Boston backyards, and ample opportunity to listen to and take pictures of Boston's Mayor Kevin White. One proferred plum was the unique experience of seeing guests dine on the stage of Symphony Hall while Boston Symphony musicians serenaded them from a box, a feature advertised as a novelty which the fourth estate, uninvited for dinner, was offered the first few minutes of the meal to record. All these were unabashed media events—those sublimely puerile and tasteless nonevents created solely for publicity purposes.

As for the working sessions of the conference, press attendance was not guaranteed because of restricted space; so much for the business on hand. Only the promotional hoopla was as big as all outdoors. Although the meeting was billed as "the first major urban affairs conference ever sponsored by an American city," it seemed surprisingly short on urban affairs and long on political hurrah. Whatever was missing in serious content was apparently to be made up for by the latest in "computer conferencing"—also known as "teleconferencing" —which eventually will substitute communication by computer terminal for old-fashioned speeches and panel discussions. The medium is the message and it does not truck with the niceties of nouns and verbs.

Boston was referred to in the releases as a "world-class" city (put that overworked term on the verbal hit list with credentialing and conferencing), but official tours of the world-class city were minimal. There was a boat trip around the harbor, which offers a spectacular example of impressive waterfront renewal. Boston's mix of the marvelous old and the striking new, the richness of its restored and recycled landmarks of solid eighteenth- and nineteenth-century brick and granite and the dramatic twentieth-century development of the adjacent Government Center and business community, sets a high level of civilized continuity. It is unlikely, however, that anyone pointed out how close this exemplary and delicate balance is to being destroyed by success and a formularized gloss and the city's infatuation with real estate deals and development.

A walk was planned for the rather unexceptional downtown retail district and its predictable pedestrian paraphernalia. The clambake was to take place in the historic Charlestown Navy Yard, which is the site of a redevelopment program. Almost everything that makes Boston unique was conspicuously missing. In a city so blessed with architectural and urban history and sophisticated students of its style, the accent was overwhelmingly and blatantly Chamber of Commerce. Maybe that is what world-class means. Instead of seeing Boston as an urban and cultural whole, with its successes and failures, mayors and planning officials from abroad were taken to visit appropriate "ethnic" neighborhoods; wind up a politician and he runs to ethnic neighborhoods. But neighborhoods, as such, and some of Boston's are conspicuously troubled, were not on the agenda. "They don't have them in other parts of the world," a spokesperson explained.

What may have saved the week, and the conference, were the programs contributed by the educational institutions across the river in Cambridge—the Massachusetts Institute of Technology, Harvard's Kennedy School of Government, and a joint conference held by the Institute of Urban Design and the Graduate School of Design at Harvard. Where City Hall's idea of serious sessions consisted of those weary, cosmic, meaningless subjects that no one can come to grips with and that can always be relied on to produce platitudinous and soporific generalities, like "The City in the Year 2000," the Harvard program took up the hard issues—the role of public investment in development and change, for example, and specific guidelines for relating the historic city to new needs.

That everything is not necessarily peachy in Boston was acknowledged in Mayor White's high-flying opening address, which referred to "the challenge of pavement and pollution, of ambition and angst" and confirmed the presence of "suffering humanity," as well as of an aggressively alliterative speech writer. It was a stunning rhetorical performance that touched all political bases. But the opportunity was lost—if it had ever been considered—for a genuine international forum in which the problems and programs of cities could have been usefully addressed. Boston was the ideal setting for such a dialogue; the city's physical rebirth is remarkable in both economic and aesthetic terms. It provides valuable lessons, from the bulldozer destruction of the West End, which taught cities what not to do with their neighborhoods, to the overwhelmingly popular Faneuil Hall Marketplace, which taught cities how to capitalize commercially on their landmarks, a success that has been relentlessly cloned. But how a revitalized downtown can be plugged into the larger social and economic welfare is something no one has begun to solve, in Boston or anywhere else. Many of the visiting dignitaries offered little more than glamorous travelogues and upbeat statistics.

Everyone was shortchanged by this exercise in mutual boosterism. The Boston *Globe* was generous in its reportage, but to its credit, the paper passed up most of the "media opportunities," although it did go in rather heavily for visiting celebrity interviews with canned background material. One lively exchange between Jane Jacobs, author of *The Death and Life of Great American Cities* and champion of neighborhoods and incremental growth, and James Rouse, the developer responsible for the Faneuil Hall Marketplace, may survive. Arguing the virtues of big plans versus little plans, Rouse, a big planner, recalled Daniel Burnham's famous exhortation to make no little plans that fail to stir men's minds, and came out for big plans as the "new, compelling, rational images of what a city could be." Jacobs didn't find the image particularly compelling. She thought that "piecemeal" should be made a respectable word again. "Life is an ad hoc affair," she said, "and has to be improvised all the time." Jacobs's observation that "cities would never be humanized by conceiving urban models at Harvard" got her the conference's standing ovation.

The concern expressed by Ian Menzies, the *Globe*'s urban affairs columnist, that Boston should be a pacesetter in the discussion of "gut issues" of violence, racism, and the quality of urban life went unheeded. Great cities, he wrote, "are the conscience of mankind." By the end of the conference it was clear that greatness takes more than hype from City Hall.

October 12, 1980

LONDON STYLES

To visit London a dozen different times is to see a dozen different cities, as if a spotlight were being moved from place to period. It is a city so infinitely rich in so many kinds of architecture that the eye cannot encompass them all. And so one sees the city selectively, with a constantly shifting perception. But what one sees is focused through specific expectations, and those expectations conform to a prevailing taste. There are changes in the fashion of seeing—and looking at architecture is shaped as much by fashion as any other human endeavor.

On my first trip to London I found the city of Christopher Wren, a black-and-white landscape of Portland stone anchored by Wren's elegant churches. On other visits I discovered a planner's world of serene green squares, or a Piranesian world of alleys and viaducts in which accident had triumphed over art. The pursuit of Hawksmoor led to a powerful, perversely baroque London that I had not known before.

There is a London of High Victorian streets in endless rows of gabled and orieled red brick, and another London of turn-of-the-century banks and business buildings trimmed with classical colonnades and boxes of blooming flowers, where the world of affairs has tailored its impressive image to an elegant eclectic cut. But we tend to see the thing that it is popular to see at the moment, the style and the image that are currently in favor with those who deal in scholarship and taste.

The landmarks remain, but the city's centers of gravity shift. Neighborhoods go through adjustments in function and character, or their style is dramatically altered by the juxtaposition of new and old. The removal of the Covent Garden Market from the West End has created an area where shabbiness is being replaced by upscale chic. Some of London's best mixed uses in these modest eighteenth- and nineteenth-century streets are being transformed into expensive homogenized bars and boutiques.

That most volatile center of fashion, the business of fashion itself, has moved relentlessly—from Carnaby Street, where it once swung, to Kings Road, where it was mod, and on to South Moulton Street, a trendy stretch of shops on a pedestrianized block that is disappointingly small-town in both size and standards. Many of the better Bond Street stores have moved, in turn, to Sloane Street in Knightsbridge, which has the air of a moneyed provincial town.

The best London style is still its architectural style. In the city, streets with names like Milk and Poultry, Cornhill and Threadneedle, hold an ever-denser nexus of prestige headquarters and status corporations in which every other building seems to be a bank. Structures of solid stone and marble with superb detailing and solemn sculpture have created a style to parallel the institutional grandeur of the British Empire in its prime.

From the old Leadenhall Market, with its vibrant food, sights, sounds, and colors under a glass-roofed street, it is a short distance to the London of the newest corporate skyscrapers. Large office blocks are dropped down without any thought of context; these are the same prepackaged clichés that are delivered to any city in the world. Inevitably, they include the standard bare, bland plaza; impersonal token art does nothing to lessen the brutalization of the existing urban fabric. Whole blocks of the old city are being breached and ruptured in this fashion by these sterile symbols of corporate style. They leave churches with exposed flanks as if they were caught undressed in a public place. They break open handsome "street walls" of buildings that offer a splendid ensemble of facades. And they ignore the lessons of the passages and inner courts that thread the area for the change of pace and scale that is such a specific contribution to London's varied, intimate and unexpected pleasures.

In the face of these multinational spoilers, it gets easier all the time to love the design assurance and respect for tradition of the academic architecture that has existed in an uneasy critical limbo for most of this century. This was the city celebrated in "London, 1900," an exhibition devoted to its turn-of-the-century architecture, held at the headquarters of the Royal Institute of British Architects in 1978. Coming out for Tradition with a capital **T** ranks as radical in some circles. But this show was one of the more solid exercises in cultural reexamination and architectural revisionism. Still, its mixed bag of exuberant eclecticism, so long out of favor, opened an absolute Pandora's box about what makes good and bad architecture, with all kinds of reputations turned inside out and upside down.

Architectural Design, the English magazine that prides itself on its forward stance in the profession, devoted a double issue to the exhibition, under the guest editorship of Gavin Stamp, the show's organizer. There is no question that Stamp's essay makes a serious contribution to architectural scholarship. There should be no controversy about this work at all, Stamp explains to us, like a patient parent to a slightly slow child, except for those so hopelessly steeped in the "dogma" of modernism that they are unable to perceive the quality or value of a period and kind of practice that modernism rejected —an age not only of monumental building and profligate eclecticism, but of symbolic image-making and a consistently grand urban ideal.

Its architectural leaders were in unashamed pursuit of classical nobility, as well as of all kinds of interpretations of the respected past, from Italianate to "Pont Street Dutch." Such establishment practitioners as Edwin Lutyens, who denied modernism out of hand, have become the new cult figures for a postmodernist generation. Lutyens's particular talent was to combine whatever technology he wanted with whatever form of classical vocabulary he fancied, for an ordered, rational solution and ingenious, erudite devices with which he manipulated plan and space with virtuoso skill. He was an architect of exemplary urbanity. The Midland Bank headquarters on Poultry Street, carried out in three stages from 1924 to 1937, in association with other architects, is frankly a monument "far more splendid than it needed to be." These are buildings with an enduring, built-in snob appeal.

Names like Aston Webb, E. A. Rickards, John Belcher, and Reginald Blomfield, who dealt in everything from classical and baroque to fashionable Mannerism and such specialties as "Champs Elysées French," are commanding new respect. Stamp puts them just slightly higher in the pantheon of English architecture than the previously enshrined "proto-modernists," Norman Shaw, W. R. Lethaby and Philip Webb, as men who understood what city-building was truly about. They ruffled no conservative or aristocratic sensibilities; they offended only the modernists, which is no longer a sin.

There is no doubt that these men built very, very well. As for style, the show clearly asked whether it was either possible or necessary to create a "new style" at that time, and whether style is not properly a slow organic development of tradition and lessons from the past. It can be counterargued, of course, that at best, this is a selective, partial, and deficient definition. But what was most disturbing about the show is that there was so little consistency in the work—in the sense that the outstanding creative periods in the arts have produced strong aesthetic unities. This, alone, causes some discomfort and a reluctance to swallow Stamp's thesis whole. Critical judgment will undoubtedly be hoisted by the avant-garde's own petard of "pluralism." However, it is this inconsistency, and the lack of a unifying and illuminating aesthetic whole, in spite of the high individual quality of much of the work, that is the most serious argument for calling this a period of high competence rather than of greatness.

It was also a period of enormous building activity that produced much of London as we know it now. Aston Webb's

Richard Seifert

*Westminster Bank
Tower, London, 1979*

Garth Huxtable

*Opposite page:
Edwin Lutyens*

*Midland Bank,
London, 1924–37*

Garth Huxtable

*Suave classical
solidity to flashy
skyscraper modern
in London's styles*

classical refacing of Buckingham Palace in 1912–13, and his creation of the Admiralty Arch for a formal processional axis to the Strand, are pivotal to the city's character. The large-scale erection of new business palaces like Lloyd's Registry of Ships, in the "Arts and Crafts Baroque" of T. E. Collcutt of 1900–1, or Lutyens's suave Georgian models, do much to define London's image. In addition to great numbers of public and private buildings, there were the new museums, libraries and educational buildings, and commercial construction, including department stores and factories, as well as hotels, theaters, and flats. Those solid structures, confident and conservative, are a large part of the essential London—beyond the genius of Wren and Hawksmoor and the familiar Victorian monuments. In this sense, there is indeed a London "style" unremarked in textbooks and guidebooks, but powerfully present on its streets.

If Gavin Stamp is right that the argument of the "goodies" versus the "baddies" no longer applies, then his work redresses many wrongs. "Are we to dismiss the architects who did most to embellish London in those years?" he asks. "Do we dismiss the buildings that give form and symbolic shape to the city as tedious shams?" According to the standard interpretations, he explains, "all went well in the 1890's, but round about 1900 English architecture took a lurch in the wrong direction and the torch of Artistic Progress was passed to Germany, to the delicate, eager hands of Herren Behrens and Gropius."

He is clearly unconvinced, and that is not very delicate irony. Those were talented hands, belonging to men of vision and concern. These architects could not believe that traditional ways were always best, or even good enough. As Robert Venturi has said, we do not need to kick our fathers to honor our grandfathers. But honor them Gavin Stamp does, and that recognition is overdue. Through these architects the line leads back to Wren again; in London splendor is the constant theme.

July 2, 23, 1978

THE SIEGE OF DUBLIN

D ublin is a city in a continuous state of siege. In a war
between the promoters of speculative construction
and the protectors of the city's heritage, battles are
fought on both sides of the Liffey, from Hume Street to Mountjoy Square, with skirmishes in the most fashionable neighborhoods. The battle scars are the broken fanlights and windows
of wrecked rows of eighteenth-century houses, and boarded-
up and deteriorating historic buildings on otherwise sound
blocks. Derelict new construction, started but never finished,
has left gaping wounds in streets of uniformly classical beauty,
and rubble-strewn lots are like bombed-out ruins.

The cause of the destruction, and the conflict, is Dublin's
economic growth, a badly needed prosperity that passed this
city by in the nineteenth century, leaving it virtually intact as
one of the great Georgian cities of the world. The result of the
recent boom is a precipitous rise in land values and a wave of
new business construction competing for addresses in the best
and most historic parts of town—a condition that attracts
speculators like the proverbial honey.

Land-price records are broken regularly. Because profits for
the conversion of residential to commercial property in the

Fitzwilliam Square, Dublin

This Georgian stand remains while speculation has made other streets bombed-out ruins.

Garth Huxtable

center of Dublin can be five to ten times what the present land use would yield, the incentive for eviction, demolition, and new construction is far greater than for rehabilitation or preservation. In addition to the deterioration being encouraged by purchasers in a gamble with percentages, the city is now pockmarked with so many new projects begun and then abandoned when funds ran out that an inventory of those eyesores was called for by the Dublin City Council.

But even with the accelerating destruction, Dublin remains a city of special charms. Although much of this appeal has been associated with its literary character, Dublin has unique architectural qualities. Continuous rows of homogeneous Georgian construction maintain an intimate human scale marked by singular style and grace. There are long streets of four-story, handmade brick structures with arched colonnaded doorways and delicate fanlight tracery surrounding doors in a rainbow of colors. The interiors vie in the elegance of their Adam-style plaster details.

These eighteenth- and early nineteenth-century buildings often make up entire neighborhoods or border landscaped squares, with vistas unmarred by twentieth-century intrusions. Merrion and Fitzwilliam squares, on the fashionable south side, remain much as they were, the houses now converted to professional offices prized by doctors, lawyers, architects, and small specialized businesses such as advertising agencies. Across O'Connell Bridge on the north side, identical streets, dingy and unrestored, accommodate rooming houses and marginal commercial uses. Mountjoy Square, one of the most beautiful examples of this eighteenth-century urban genre, has been restored on one side and is in ruins on the other, where preservationists were unable to save a particularly distinguished stand of houses.

These battles are fought, and often lost, by private organizations that include the Irish Georgian Society, the National Trust for Ireland, and a local association called the Dublin Civic Group. Looked on as elitist groups led by either a moneyed or an intellectual aristocracy—Desmond Guinness is the crusading head of the Irish Georgian Society, and a passionately articulate history professor, Kevin Nowlan, leads the Dublin Civic Group—the preservationists have been unable to command popular support. The traditional Irish mistrust of wealth and privilege, born of centuries of poverty, has been carried over to a lack of interest in historic properties that originally served both. With no effective landmarks legislation for threatened structures, that antipathy has played right into the hands of the speculators.

The streets around St. Stephen's Green, one of the choicest Dublin areas, have been under concentrated attack. The east side of the green represents the outcome of an earlier struggle with the forces of destruction, which led to a compromise that has turned out to be one possible answer to the problem of new building. After a donnybrook with the developer, citizen groups succeeded in getting a preservation-minded architect involved with his plans, and instead of the proposed demolition, restoration and some discreetly faked infill have kept the Georgian street front almost as it was. An entrance through the block leads to new office construction behind it.

The south side of the square was not so fortunate. The old buildings were bulldozed and a row of new banks and offices were erected to the old cornice height, as a sop to traditionalists, in the bland faceless mode common to all cities today. Somehow this is more offensive in Dublin, where the uniform character and quality of the old city make their dissident banality seem particularly out of place.

On the west side of the square the speculative process has clearly been at work. First, short-term leases that brought in the purveyors of fringe chic and other obviously temporary uses undermined the area's stability. Maintenance stopped and floors emptied out above transient ground-floor stores. One section was pulled down for parking. At the corner of the green, in an outstanding gesture of civic insensitivity, the street was widened to create a traffic island, destroying the former serene sense of closure. The corner was further eroded by the unexpected demolition of one of Dublin's best hotels, the Russell, with no replacement on the site. That action precipitated the area's downward slide.

The disease spread to Harcourt Street, another fine Georgian row just beyond the green. The rape of Harcourt Street includes boarded-up buildings next to the open rubble of the corner, followed by a well-kept stretch flanked by a gaping hole and a silent crane left from an aborted construction project. On the opposite side of the street the rusting steel and shabby concrete of an ill-conceived and unfinished shopping center break the row. Periodically, signs are posted on buildings being allowed to decay that announce them as future development sites.

No protective action has been taken by the city to prevent the destruction of Dublin's unique urban fabric. Beyond the "listing" of historic buildings, their protection is largely unenforceable. There are two listed categories: the first gives full protection to a limited number of landmarks; the second permits demolition or alteration under certain circumstances. Plans must be filed with the city, but change or razing is allowed with predictable regularity, often because the damage is already irreversible. The only deterrent is something called a third-party appeal, in which an individual or group may register an objection and ask for a hearing. After the hearing the plan can be refused, granted, or modified, but this procedure is understandably pressured by forces for development that government is reluctant to discourage.

At present the process is producing a curious compromise

that preservationists consider an ingenious architectural and political cop-out. Demolition permission is granted with the proviso that the new construction be "in keeping" with the neighbors left standing on the mutilated block. This usually takes the form of a fake Georgian facade to replace the real Georgian buildings being razed, thereby permitting the construction of greater interior commercial space. More acceptable to urban critics is the practice of restoring the original buildings and constructing the new space behind them, as has been done successfully in some places. But conservation or recycling are rarely perceived as desirable or profitable activities, and the city has established no incentives to make them so. The facades that have been called the most elegant in the British Isles continue to be cannibalized. And the traditional addresses that are now in such demand for corporate letterheads are increasingly unrecognizable on Dublin's streets.

July 3, 1978

Emile Aillaud

Housing,
La Défense,
Paris, 1978

Art or outrage,
depending on the
viewer or user

Garth Huxtable

PARIS: GROWTH, GRANDEUR, AND DRAWING-BOARD STYLE

I t is ten minutes from the heart of Paris to La Défense and
a few thousand light-years from the French architectural
tradition of measure, restraint, and homogeneous quality.
This Manhattanized section on the outskirts of the city, which
reared its first towers in the 1960's, continues to grow extrava
gantly. Think, for size, of Pittsburgh's entire downtown—the
rebuilt Golden Triangle. The difference here, and it is of pivotal importance, is that what would be the central business
district anywhere else has been pushed beyond the city's historic heart. Given unusual freedom from Paris' traditional controls, the developers of these bank towers, corporate
headquarters, and luxury apartments deliberately seek new
images. And except for those who live and work in these
structures—the expensive apartments have filled surprisingly
quickly, while the sleek offices rent more slowly, in a reversal
of speculative expectations—La Défense is almost universally
considered an architectural disaster.

But what La Défense really represents is a *coup de style:* this
is the outrageous and provocative creation in Paris of a new
style of urban environment that has only been suggested, or
threatened, elsewhere. La Défense is the Houston of Paris,

with considerably more architectural license; anyone who loves Houston can love La Défense. In contrast to Houston, however, which celebrates its own chaos, this materials manufacturers' showcase and designers' Day-Glo dream has not come about through unplanned growth. Its look and form are the result of the intervention of planners, and it is that planning framework that lifts it from the accidental and ordinary to the cosmically unreal. The new towers are raised on platforms and connected by ramps and walkways, with landscaping of artificial hillocks and artful piles of stones, all of which seem to have come straight from the modelmaker's shop. The developers' taste for blockbusters is equaled only by their liking for tutti-frutti colors. The familiar Parisian street life, measured by the shopfront, the café, and the consistent scale of streets and buildings—the profound pleasures of observation and social intercourse only a few miles away—might as well be on another planet.

The difference, again, is one of style, in its deepest and most universal sense. In Paris style is everything. That is traditionally understood. Every street, every structure, every shopgirl has style. The style of Parisian architecture has been proved and refined by at least three centuries of academic dictates and highly developed taste. There are few violations of this taste, and there is exemplary architectural consistency. Paris has defined the aesthetics of a sophisticated urban culture.

The style of La Défense is drawing-board architecture. It is the kind of stuff that designers fool around with on paper. There are knockoffs and caricatures of everything going: crisp mirror-glass towers flank acrobatic concrete next to wildly articulated space frames and severely flat slabs. The result is a stage set by someone designing a city out of cardboard and plastic and product manufacturers' catalogues.

One is grateful at least for the impulse, and the planning, that have pushed most of this new construction to the city's edges, unlike London and New York. La Défense, Front de Seine, Place d'Italie, and other high-rise clusters that ring the city have grown out of the recognition of the need to bring Paris into the twentieth century. It is as essential to Paris' continuing vitality to accommodate multinational business on the scale to which it has become accustomed, and to provide more housing, as it is to protect the city's historic heritage.

But even on older streets under conventional controls, the buildings inserted into the city's "tissue," or fabric, are grossly incompatible. Wherever it is, the new French architecture is either depressingly ordinary or aggressively trendy—which is more depressing still. It is not just that the new buildings are different than the old ones; so were the radical additions of Hector Guimard and Auguste Perret earlier in this century. Those buildings succeeded by offering innovation with grace.

Surprisingly, when it gets worse, it sometimes gets better, or at least more interesting. The housing at the far edge of La Défense has entered a kind of architectural cloud-cuckooland; it leaves commercial formulas behind to move into another kind of art, or outrage, depending on the viewer. These particular buildings easily evoke Magritte in their poetic surrealism and colorful hard-edged abstraction. One group of apartment ziggurats defines its stepped pyramiding shapes with bold red, blue, green, and orange stripes. Another group, by Émile Aillaud, an architect who has always marched to a different drummer, is a series of round free-form or petal-shaped towers with random round or eye-shaped windows. The walls are "camouflaged" with stylized cloud patterns in white, sky-blue, and violet. In an abstract and otherworldly way, these are surprisingly beautiful buildings, although in a more worldly way, their livability for the low-income families for whom they have been planned is questionable. It is difficult to equate this work with a city always known for the rigor, propriety, and sophistication of its aesthetic standards. From the Place Vendôme to La Défense, it is culture shock all the way.

But perhaps more striking than the architecture is the attitude of planners and Parisians toward the city, and who chooses, or is encouraged, to live there. In the United States, a country that has traditionally looked down on its cities and celebrated an agrarian and rural ideal, the reward of the American dream is the escape to the suburbs. Many of the privileged and most of the middle class have fled the cities, leaving behind the poor, as well as the problems. In Paris, by contrast, the poor are increasingly housed in the suburbs, because it is government policy to build subsidized housing in the outlying areas and new towns. And the city itself continues to attract not only the rich but also the middle class (what city with this incredible elegance and vitality would not?) as part of a tradition in which city dwelling has always been the cosmopolitan choice. This is true to such an extent that older sections and former slums, such as the seventeenth-century Marais, have been reclaimed as fashionable historic districts, with that curious side effect, "gentrification," or the driving out of the poor and working class for an influx of affluent, chic residents and pricey restaurants and boutiques. It is not necessary to take a demographic survey; it is easier to count the Mercedeses and Alfa-Romeos jammed along the narrow streets.

Considering Paris' beauty, this preference for the city is not unusual; what is surprising is its translation into official planning policy. For hundreds of years, kings and emperors spent princely sums for which they accounted to no one, for their own and Paris' greater glory. Today, handsome sums are still being spent, but the money and power are now being directed at both the inner city and the outlying regions, including large outlays for transportation and new towns. The new towns are showcases of the most incredible styles, with civic centers striped like zebras, undulating-patterned plazas, and apartment towers resembling giant artichokes. But the French, like just about everybody else, are estranged and alienated by unfamiliar architecture, by the strident clash between the nineteenth and twentieth centuries, by conspicuous environmental failures. For those who can afford it, Paris still offers the timeless gratification of the most cultivated sensibilities of the mind and eye.

June 6, 11, 1978

LES HALLES:
THE DEATH OF
THE HEART

The city, Paul Valéry wrote in his *Théorie Poétique et Es-thétique,* is virtually all of civilization. This is not a hard idea to support in Paris. The unabashed and splendid elitism of the city's glorious buildings and spaces, its unapologetic elegance and grandeur, are as pervasive as the marvelous limpid light. Surely, one thinks, these traditions and standards will always be part of the Parisian consciousness. Here are history and art made manifest by architecture.

Well, one thinks wrong. Take the whole sad affair of Les Halles—the infamous case of the destruction of Paris' central food market and the vicissitudes of the plans for this important site in the heart of the city. The first mistake, and it was a bad one, was to tear down the "iron umbrellas" built for the market by Victor Baltard in the nineteenth century, when the operation was moved to Rungis in the 1960's. The handsome and historic glass and iron pavilions would have been as susceptible to reuse—and every bit as successful—as Boston's Quincy Market buildings, which, as the Faneuil Hall Marketplace, offers a phenomenal demonstration of the imaginative commercial recycling of a distinctive place. There are close similarities in location, scale, and use.

Pencreac'h and
Vasconi

The Forum, Paris

On the site of Les
Halles, a super
shopping center
of redundant
familiarity

Garth Huxtable

Once the pavilions were demolished, however, the future of the "hole" in the heart of Paris, as it became known internationally, was a matter of general speculation. What followed were countless inept, unsuitable, or controversial schemes over a period of more than ten years. Fortunately, none were built. Meanwhile, the hole's lower levels were filled with a subway and suburban rail line complex. (Mass transit is one of the areas in which the French have invested substantial resources with outstanding success.) The one constant component that survived from the earliest commercial development proposals was a large shopping center for part of the site, called the Forum. For the rest of the site, the plan that was finally adopted specified an amorphous open green space and plaza, usually described as an ambitious combination of Paris's formal parks and the Campo di Siena. The Forum is finished and operating, and is supposed to be Paris' Number 2 wonder after the Beaubourg. The park plan will, presumably, go ahead. But while government officials like the result, much of the architecture profession does not.

The Forum is the work of Pencreac'h and Vasconi, a French

firm responsible for a good deal of building in the new town of Cergy-Pontoise. It is a super shopping center of redundant familiarity; the only novelty for the American visitor is the switch to French fast food, although we are catching up rapidly in the croissants department. This largely underground mall consists of four cleverly disposed levels of stores and services surrounding a depressed open plaza that celebrates nothing. An escalator slashes diagonally through the plaza from its top level to the ground, for a kind of spurious and totally pointless high drama. Around this plaza, which offered some extraordinarily banal sculpture when I was there in 1980, apparently subject to change, are entrances; they seem to be the least used of many. An arched, double-level, metal-framed, clear plastic enclosure creates an eye-catching container for the commercial space. This striking design feature also admits daylight into the lower ranges, and that anticlimax is just about the high point of the plan.

The Forum has room for two hundred shops, from the enormous facilities on two levels of FNAC, that remarkable dispenser of books, electronic equipment and sporting gear, to the familiar, brand-name couturier boutiques that appear automatically in new construction everywhere and that look, and are, the same all over the world. Twelve restaurants and assorted bars dispense everything from *haute cuisine* to stand-up snacks. A series of new-old street signs mark underground corridors that seem to be named after streets demolished above, a cute gimmick appearing in other rebuilt parts of the city, more suggestive of loss than of gain.

Like all shopping centers, this is a standardized nonplace. Inside, everything is carried out at a high level of boring competence. The details are conventionally expert and often quite cheap; unattractive exposed ceiling services, for example, are camouflaged by open high-tech metal grids. There is pricey consumerism to the point of overkill. But there is no real architecture or urbanism here at all; it is merchandising, pure and simple. It is hard to prefer this flashy, empty, replicable, and ultimately ordinary formula to the eccentric charms of the streets above. Yet, this is what the official communiqués have described as the "renaissance of the heart of Paris."

The results of an architect-sponsored competition for an alternative proposal, held partly in protest and partly as a quest for a more inspired solution for the rest of the razed area, were all equally bad. It would be polite to say merely that the designs were disappointing, but the truth is that they brutally betrayed the Candide-like belief of the sponsors that good faith and intentions would produce something better than the official plan. The international submissions ranged from the bizarre to the boffo. It is not the French, alone, who have failed. There are the usual cult figures and their imitators, with their trademarks simplistically and narcissistically superimposed on central Paris. There are pretentious private languages of metaphors, symbols, and typologies. A pastiche of neo-Haussmann nothingness puts down what it is supposed to emulate. Above all, the real challenge of how to create a distinctive and sympathetic intervention in the historic fabric of Paris has not been met. What this generally curious and frightful array of "solutions" demonstrated is that a lot of today's architects are arrogant, isolated, or out of touch, interested only in scoring polemical points. There is a place where they must touch base with the real world, and the failure to do so was particularly striking here. The irony is that a number of the presentations were quite beautiful; they will look great in a volume of visionary designs.

Something is clearly awry—and not in France alone. The breach between architectural performance and public needs and expectations has never been so great. There are calls for a dialogue between architecture and the public, but this kind of demonstration makes me feel that architecture should just shut up. If the city is civilization, I weep for history.

March 20, 1980

HOUSING WEST BERLIN

The wall, of course, is the immutable reality in West Berlin; its acceptance is a demonstration of how the surreal and the awful become ordinary if you live with them long enough, and after twenty years Berliners treat the wall as a fact of the local geography, like the forests and waterways that make the city such a special place. The line on the map that cuts the city apart at its heart, the Brandenburg Gate, dismembering the axis of Unter den Linden, is a shocking act of urban amputation. As one stands looking east and west, at the two Berlins, the bland brutality of the division is as disturbing as the actual concrete barricade with its sinister baggage of alarms, mines, and guards. No work of art can ever aspire to memorialize this presence and its meanings. The wall is its own best monument.

But the city of West Berlin is divided in its own way and the issue is housing; riots and demonstrations have called international attention to a continuing shortage of housing, particularly of affordable housing, in a city that glitters with good living. The situation is aggravated by geography—West Berlin is an island in East Germany with no place for normal outward expansion—and by a population which is 30 percent aging

Berliners and 30 percent young people, many of whom are sitting out the draft years because of an exemption given to West Berliners in an attempt to stem the city's declining numbers. An immigrant Turkish community that accounts for another 10 percent of Berlin's residents has crowded into the older quarters. This concentration of the young poor, the old poor, and the minority poor has created the classic constituency for housing problems.

Housing in West Berlin is, therefore, both a very real crisis and a radicalized cause. The issue is highly political, and the government steps around it with extreme caution. The situation has been brought about, in part, by the city's earlier housing policies. In general, construction in the 1960's was concentrated in peripheral areas, in the all-new decentralized developments that were preferred in international planning at the time. The inner city, in common with inner cities almost everywhere, deteriorated badly, compounding the war damage. Urban renewal meant demolition and rebuilding, and large segments of older sections were earmarked for this treatment. Buildings stood empty for years.

What really lit the fuse was the situation in the spring of 1981: 10,000 "condemned" apartments were unoccupied, while 80,000 Berliners were looking for a place to live. Rents and "key money" reached outrageous levels. In protest, people simply moved into the empty buildings. Frustration turned into violence. But the confrontations have done more than dramatize the need; they seem to have changed the city's policies from bulldozer clearance to rehabilitation of old neighborhoods and existing housing stock—a trend that is already well established in American and other European cities.

Unfortunately, another building issue was drawn into the controversy: the Internationale Bauausstellung, or International Building Exposition, planned as a showcase of new architecture and ways of dealing with the city. The housing crisis split Berlin into two camps—those who backed the exposition as a demonstration of specially commissioned, creative new solutions for the inner city, and those who wanted its government funding diverted completely to immediate rehabilitation and conventional new housing. IBA, as the exposition was called in its German acronym, found itself under serious attack. It provoked heated accusations of favoring "abstract interventions," or textbook projects, over "reality" and highly visible needs. Its opponents turned the debate into a confrontation between urgent social programs and esoteric art.

IBA's program, in fact, was meant to include both conservation and new construction. Its director, Josef Paul Kleihues, is a leading German architect of international reputation and sophisticated design skills. Its co-director, Hardt Walther Hämer, a champion of rehabilitation, had previously rebuilt two pilot blocks in Charlottenburg and Kreuzburg—the latter the site of some of the housing demonstrations. Hämer talks with feeling about people and neighborhoods; he sounds like the populist "advocacy" architects of the politicized 1960's. But he, too, designs with sophisticated skills, and a visit to his Kreuzburg housing reveals aesthetic as well as social preoccupations. The political polarities were falsely drawn.

The traditional purpose of an international building exposition is to demonstrate the latest state of the art in housing and urban design in the highest and most advanced architectural terms. Today, that covers a wide range of techniques, and the approaches used in Berlin would be as varied as the participants' styles. Through competitions, IBA has assigned some of the world's most talented practitioners to specific parts of the city. Among the stellar names with projects scheduled for completion in the late 1980's are James Stirling, Charles Moore, Raimund Abraham, Rob and Leon Krier, Oriel Bohigas, and Ralph Erskine; other projects are the work of Peter Eisenman, Arata Isozaki, Aldo Rossi, Oswald Ungers, Mario Botta, and Gottfried Böhm. A number of these architects, while widely admired, have been more publicized than built; others have major construction to their credit. All are on the leading edge of architectural design.

It seems certain that some badly needed "social housing," as government-sponsored and -funded housing is called here, will be built in Berlin under public programs with or without IBA's "interventions." What the controversy comes down to is whether the city wants housing with, or without, architecture —or at least, architecture in its more innovative aspects. And

Opposite page:
Hardt-Waltherr
Hämer

Houses, West
Berlin

Rehabilitation in
the Kreuzberg area

Garth Huxtable

what that, surprisingly, turns out to be is something that everyone thought was laid to rest a long time ago—the eternal and consistently false struggle of the avant-garde against the philistines and the traditionalists. All of the objections, including the urgent social issues, are redolent with the echoes of the old debate.

Much of this was explored in 1981 at a conference on "Berlin and Its Architecture," sponsored by the Aspen Institute, Berlin, which brought together a group of German and foreign professionals for an international look at the situation. The energy of the talks reflected the turbulent ideas that are changing the vision and practice of architecture and planning throughout the world. This is a time of transition—of controversial developments and charged interchanges—in a creative climate not unlike that of the equally turbulent 1920's. At that time there was a rejection of the past for a future that was supposed to solve all human problems, including housing, in a totally new way. Now we are in the process of painful readjustment to the pragmatic present and the perception of the possible.

What has been forgotten in the controversy is that Berlin has a long, impressive, and signally important history of architectural innovation in this century. That history includes a series of international building expositions that have given Germany a unique place in the building of our time. Held in Berlin and other German cities, they have included the classic examples and prototypes of Walter Gropius, Mies van der Rohe, Le Corbusier, J.J.P. Oud, Bruno Taut, Ernst May, and other revolutionary modernist practitioners. The Weissenhofsiedlung of 1927 in Stuttgart is a housing landmark, and people are still living in it; Mies's model housing in the Berlin Building Exposition of 1931 had immense and lasting impact. Berlin's 1957 Interbau, which reconstructed the Hansaviertel, was less successful as planning than as star performances, but its housing is still considered a prime place to live. A visit to the Siemenstadt site confirms the enduring excellence of those experiments of 1929–31. These avant-garde exercises have not only produced enormously influential housing; they have also been

responsible for a considerable part of the history of modern architecture.

The chief difference between the earlier expositions and IBA is that they were based on tabula rasa planning—a unified, cleared site was turned over to the architects to design the world, or neighborhood, of the future. Today's efforts are sadder, wiser, and considerably more limited and complex. Now we try to mend the existing city; to understand it as "a place with a memory" in Professor Kleihues's words; to work sympathetically within its culture and conditions. That is why the choice this time is not a monolithic demonstration in a single location, but a series of scattered sites that need sympathetic reconstruction or new "infill" building. The words used for planning today are "contextual," "fragmentary," "incremental," and "inclusive," as opposed to the Olympian, homogeneous, controlling idea of the earlier master plan. The aim is always the same—better housing and better living. But the problem is being approached today in a radically new context of urban perceptions and beliefs. The one idea that is not new is the belief that art can serve social needs.

Meeting the challenge at this level would be in the best Berlin tradition. If programs and costs can be satisfied, an array of techniques of urban rebuilding and 30,000 additional apartments could result. If an aggressive program of neighborhood rehabilitation is carried out as well—and this should be a high government priority—there will not only be more housing, but the city's architectural character will also be saved and strengthened.

There is the possibility of an extraordinary constellation of new buildings in Berlin, in the city's best tradition. Some of today's best architects are being given a chance to build in that tradition, just as earlier "radical" architects were given the controversial commissions of the 1920's and 30's. The rest, as they say, is history—and art.

October 18, 1981

BUILDINGS

MONUMENTS

WASHINGTON'S STILLBORN BEHEMOTH

After thirty-two years of planning, twenty years of design, and nine years of construction by a consortium of three architectural firms under the direction of two Librarians of Congress, two Architects of the Capitol, three chairmen of the Senate Office Building Committee, four chairmen of the House Office Building Committee, and seven chairmen of the Joint Committee on the Library, and after one abortive takeover attempt by the space-hungry House of Representatives, the James Madison Memorial Building, the new addition to the Library of Congress, was finally dedicated and turned over to the cultural and informational service of the nation in 1980.

The ceremony marking the official transfer of the completed building from the federal government to the library was held on the anniversary of the signing of the original Library of Congress legislation by President John Adams in 1800. The new Madison Memorial Library is colossal; it is the second largest building on Capitol Hill, just after the elephantine Rayburn Building. This is big even for official Washington, which specializes in Brobdingnagian scale. It is less ludicrous and more efficient than the Rayburn Building, and it is the last

of the solid marble bombs in the long line willed to the nation
by the late Architect of the Capitol, J. George Stewart. Stylistically, this one has not quite caught up with Moscow's Palace
of Congresses, or the Soviet avant-garde of the 1960's. But any
attempt to fit this born-dead behemoth into postmodern classical rethink would do a disservice to twenty-five centuries of the
Western classical tradition. It is too big for camp, and lacks the
leavening of corn.

Built at a cost of $130 million, it occupies the superblock
bounded by Independence Avenue, C Street, and First and
Second streets, just across from the main Library of Congress
Building, a Beaux Arts monument of notable grandeur completed in 1897. The new building is 514 feet long and 414 feet
deep, has nine stories, and contains 2.1 million square feet of
space and enough computerized and mechanized library
equipment to put Gutenberg into shock. Among its features
are a James Madison Memorial Hall with a life-size statue of
Madison surrounded by marble, travertine, and teak (the memorial was incorporated into the library in 1965 in a marriage
of conspicuous political expediency), a two-story exhibition
gallery that one might categorize as flashily *retardataire,* an
interior garden court that, in common with much of the staff,
will never see the light of day, and 1.56 million square feet of
usable working space.

Let us immediately state the best and the worst of this new
building. It is both desperately needed and totally ordinary. So
much ordinariness becomes almost extraordinary. The interiors that are to be devoted to the display and dissemination of
the world's art and culture are pure catalogue commercial; the
executive offices are unadulterated corporate cliché, from the
sliding-wall conference rooms to the relentlessly overcon-
trived lighting. The whole is clothed in enough Georgia marble to sink a Ship of State.

But the building was long overdue for an institution bursting at every seam, with personnel tucked into nooks and corners of balconies and hallways and offices carved out of
corridors and triple-decked under thirty-foot ceilings. The library and its staff are grateful for every undistinguished inch.
The present Architect of the Capitol, George White, who

inherited the project, has managed to upgrade its execution. And the space is being very well used by the library's rather awesomely named planning unit, the Environmental Resources Office, under James Trew, to put in effect a total reorganization plan that has been conceived by the present Librarian of Congress, the historian Daniel Boorstin.

This reorganization involves the Main Building, the Thomas Jefferson Building (an extension largely for storage built in the 1930's), and the Madison Building. Collections will be shifted to form "halls of knowledge" of related artifacts and research materials devoted to Western and Eastern civilizations, the arts and sciences, language and literature, philosophy and religion, maps and geography, manuscripts, law and bibliography, and library science. The result will create a kind of "multimedia encyclopedia" for easier access and use.

The additional space that makes this rational rearrangement possible is the new building's chief virtue. But there is another conspicuous and very important benefit: the spectacular Main Building will now be released from the pressure of overuse for restoration. As the index to all of the collections, this historic structure will remain the library's centerpiece. Since this splendid building suggests a cultivated richness of mind and spirit, thank heavens for that.

It can be stated without reservation that the turn-of-the-century Library of Congress Building is one of the most magnificent works of its time in this country, representing a period and style, a quality of workmanship and material, a richness of color, detail and decoration, that will never be seen again. It is the work of a Washington architectural firm, Smithmeyer and Pelz, collaborating with sculptors, muralists, and artisans in an earnest pursuit of the muses that produced splendor at its least, and art at its best. The interiors show a masterful use of ceremonial and symbolic public space that is still inadequately understood, and in this case, almost unequaled in American architecture. This building is one of the capital's few real gems. I am thinking, in particular, of the Great Hall with its stairs, colonnades and balconies, of an architecture so sophisticated and skilled in its manipulation of levels, planes and light, and so lavish in its use of decorative arts, that it recalls

the Grand Foyer of the Paris Opéra; this is only a little less extravagantly baroque, but no less successful. The huge, domed, circular main reading room is one of the most impressive interiors in the United States.

I am thinking also of parts of the building that cannot be seen, which are increasingly visible through gaps and holes as "temporary" offices are dismantled. Four glorious corner pavilions, connected by two-block-long vaulted and coffered corridors or galleries that completely encircle the building's perimeter, have been hidden for decades by partitions, false ceilings, screen walls, and assorted interior crimes and atrocities. One could not even guess at their existence except for the presence of floating capitals and giant column segments sandwiched between wallboard and ceiling panels.

Fortunately, little was destroyed. These changes were rea-

Library of Congress

The entrance hall of 1897 and the Madison Memorial Hall of 1980 are a study in the decline and fall of public architecture.

Library of Congress

sonably careful acts of spatial desperation by a growing staff dealing with burgeoning collections; such incursions can be easily removed to reveal the building's original splendor. Restoration is now a top concern and priority of both the Librarian of Congress and the Architect of the Capitol. Does one need to remind the Congress that this is its library as well as the national collection?

The ceremony, symbolism, and art of the older structure are the qualities most obviously lacking in the new building; there is no indication that this is a place that contains and celebrates the treasures of civilization. Nothing here suggests that architecture traditionally gives expression to such values. This is any speculative office building behind a Mussolini-modern facade. In the Madison Memorial Hall, the standard nine-foot, three-inch ceiling is pushed to two stories and the walls and columns are buttered up with wood and travertine for a result that is merely vacuous, not noble. The garden court behind the entrance is another exercise in punching up the space, three stories this time, in response to early protests about the building's lack of beauty and amenity. Because the court is topped not by sky, but by six more stories, and surrounded by standard dark glass, curtain-walled offices, a battery of artificial lights must mimic sun for ficus trees (that most durable of species) buttressed in granite. Only 6 percent of the building's surface is windowed; the set-back top floor, with a glass wall offering views from the staff dining rooms and executive offices, is like a release from limbo. There is no excuse for this at all.

One could simply file this building under the heading of the decline and fall of public architecture, but it is considerably more complex than that. The architects selected in a typical bureaucratic shotgun wedding—Roscoe DeWitt of Texas, Alfred Easton Poor and Homer Swanke of New York, and A. P. Almond and Jesse Shelton of Atlanta—were in the rear guard, rather than the vanguard, of architecture. They produced a dated and lackluster design that embodied a program that also became obsolete as the long bureaucratic process of appropriation, approval, and construction proceeded over twenty years.

In those years, a revolution in computerized library technology took place; as recently as a year and a half before completion the power capacity of the building had to be restudied and upgraded. The flexibility that was supposed to be built into the plan has proved to be more theoretical than practical in spite of modular design; the movable partitions weigh two hundred pounds. Twenty years ago libraries and museums avoided destructive natural light like the plague. But even at that time, the new filtering and reflective glass that has created a radical and agreeable change in their architecture was being developed. Today the idea of the windowless behemoth is dead. Two of the architects who started with the project are also dead, and most of the others are retired. The Madison Library, in fact, could be called dead on arrival.

There are no easy answers to technological revolutions or congressional tastes. But even the most superficial research indicates that other countries are building national libraries in less time that relate better to the state of architecture and technology. It would be worth finding out how it is done. Washington is running out of room for these stillborn federal blockbusters, and it has long since run out of art.

May 4, 1980

THE PROBLEM OF THE PRESIDENTIAL LIBRARY

The presidential library is a curious phenomenon. Intended originally as the repository for a president's papers and related documents, it was brought into existence by a federal law which stipulated that a museum be included with the archives. Scholars and political innocents, anxious to see consistent and reliable provisions made for the preservation and use of presidential papers, were willing to go along with what they visualized as a few discreet display cases, or perhaps an accessory gallery, containing historical objects and memorabilia. It seemed like a small concession in exchange for federal guarantees of maintenance and operating costs for these libraries. The buildings were to be constructed with publicly raised private funds, and then the General Services Administration was to take over their expenses and upkeep, running them as part of the National Archives.

What has happened, of course, is that the union of library and museum has gone unexpectedly askew; it has turned into a Catch-22 shotgun marriage in which the museum function has expanded to the point where it has taken over more and more overtly from the archives. The result is an odd architectural couple, with the library serving as an excuse for the museum, which has turned into a popular tourist attraction. The presidential library, in this cart-before-the-horse version, has become the biggest draw since Disneyland. Its combination of history, sentiment, politics and patriotism, its glimpses of power and personalities, all suavely orchestrated and slickly manipulated by the most expert commercial display techniques, have proved to be an irresistible lure for the American public and the ideal destination for the family vacation tour. It is an exercise in heroic hype peculiar to our time.

The John Fitzgerald Kennedy Library in Boston is the latest, but far from the last, in a growing line of these inadvertent and highly competitive presidential monuments. Devised by family, friends and associates, designed with varying degrees of ambition or opulence, these monuments will continue to be built until the end of presidential, or republican, time. Their increasing number, at increasing cost, on a scale never envisioned, will be maintained by the federal government, or taxpayer, in perpetuity. And since the politician or statesman does not exist who could resist the temptation to write his own history in his own way, in a setting of commensurate dignity or grandeur, these undertakings will instruct, persuade, inform, and propagandize, cleverly or crudely, depending on the talents employed. Increasingly, the presidential library is being designed and constructed as an immensely impressive and skillful exercise in selective immortality.

Having said this, let it also be said that the Kennedy Library, which has come out of fifteen years of fund-raising, controversy, site-switching, and reprogramming, is the best of the bunch so far, given the questionable assumptions. For what it is meant to be, the design by I. M. Pei and Partners is very good—architecturally, symbolically, and in the use of the arts of display. Measured against its predecessors for Truman, Eisenhower, and Johnson, it is a giant step forward in its level of design sophistication for this peculiarly American alliance of art and politics. At this point, however, the tail totally wags the dog; the museum function is completely dominant and engrossing. In addition, this building is clearly designed as a memorial. That was inevitable, given the short life and tragic death of this president, and the mystique that has surrounded the man and his administration.

If you look for the archives, they are more or less tucked into the roof. The presidential and other papers are literally housed in two tightly compressed floors at the very top of the structure with audiovisual material in a kind of ceiling plenum of the main ceremonial hall. Only one of the nonmuseum floors that wrap around this hall is devoted to public use of the archives; the rest are administration offices of which the greatest part, and most of the staff, are for the museum operation.

The building, understood as a monument, is starkly effective, consisting of three intersecting geometric forms of monolithic, if somewhat uncommunicative simplicity. A 125-foot-high, nine-story white concrete tower, housing offices and archives, and a low circular section containing two theaters are connected by a truss-walled, gray glass pavilion that rises a full 115 feet to form the ceremonial heart of the structure. The imposing interior space, light filled, latticed by the huge steel members, is referred to as a "contemplation pavilion," but barring that rather unfortunate terminology, it is the most effective part of the building. In combination with the almost scaleless exterior, the result is a sense of monumentality beyond the building's actual size. Finishes and details are neither luxurious nor special; standard components have kept the cost to $20.8 million raised from public gifts and the Kennedy family.

The true function of this austere architectural drama is to enclose a circulation system to accommodate a sequence of spaces and experiences through which 6,000 visitors a day can be "processed." That means moving people through the museum's exhibits with maximum efficiency while imparting a message that stresses information and orchestrates emotional impact. This objective has been carried out with great expertise by the exhibition designers Chermayeff and Geismar Associates; the work has been reviewed by historian-advisers and an assiduously attentive Kennedy family. The exhibits are a sophisticated blend of the historical and the sentimental, worth studying both for their documentation and their subtly manipulative theatrical drama—a unique feature of these displays that has now been developed to a high art.

The site, of course, is not Harvard, as originally planned. After much bitter controversy with the Cambridge community over the prospect of a tourist invasion, plans for the library-museum were relocated to 9.5 acres of a desolate promontory on the "wrong" side of Boston harbor called Columbia Point, at the far edge of the University of Massachusetts campus. The project for the Harvard location was for a much larger, three-part complex that was to include the library-museum, the John F. Kennedy School of Government, and an Institute of Politics. The size of the complex would have been imperial, but only the School of Government has been built at Harvard. The research material is not with the school, where a library would normally be expected, but with the memorial at Columbia Point—one of the more disturbing side effects of the presidential library-museum syndrome. Another uncalculated side effect is that the expenses of the ever-expanding museum facilities have to be borne by the National Archives.

Getting there, for the Harvard or other scholar, is not exactly half the fun. Public transit is available, but for those who wish to go by car, there is the choice of a circuitous route around Boston on expressways, getting tangled up with bridge and tunnel traffic and through-state and Cape-bound cars, or inching through South Boston traffic in what looks like the bombed-out ruins of Berlin. It is no small design feat that Pei has maximized the site's best features—the view of the harbor and the surrounding open space—to turn a windswept liability into a spectacular asset. The building, poised at the edge of the land, not only looks out over the water for magnificent views of the harbor islands and the Boston skyline, but the design focuses the view in a way that makes it an absolutely integral part of the structure and even imbues it with a symbolic aspect.

This concentration on the harbor is reinforced by the landscaping, carried out by Rachel Lambert Mellon and Dan Kiley, which raises a bank against the rather grim view of the university buildings on the peninsula side and provides a walk along the water. On what was once a dump, there are dune grass and Cape Cod roses.

Scholars and museum-goers, like oil and water, will not mix; separation of tourists and students is necessary because of the anticipated numbers. Tourists enter a lobby through which they see the great hall and view of the harbor beyond, but they are moved directly into one of the two 250-seat theaters for a half-hour film on John Kennedy. They exit on to a lower level of 18,000 square feet of exhibition space arranged around a central gallery containing a copy of the president's desk (the real one remains in Washington) flanked by the most popular presidential artifact of all, the Kennedy rocking chair. The story does not end with his death, however; it continues with Bobby Kennedy's career. All this is presented within the larger context of the Kennedy family, beginning with a huge group photograph at the entrance. The course of Kennedy empire is made clear by a "history line" that runs around the top of the galleries in which epochal world events are paired with parallel Kennedy family events: Lincoln issued the Emancipation Proclamation and John F. Fitzgerald was born in Boston's North End; Queen Elizabeth II succeeded to the British throne and John F. Kennedy announced for the Senate. Personal history becomes cosmic history. There is no fudging of pantheistic intent.

In display cases below, there are objects of enormous and instant appeal—a Kennedy christening dress, Jack Kennedy's desk at Choate, Rose Kennedy's file box of her children's lives, the torn flag and navy jacket of the heroic PT boat rescue, as well as books, letters, and manuscripts. Documents and memorabilia are reinforced by the most sophisticated display techniques—audio and video tracks, animated fiber optics for the presidential campaign, rear-projection slides, and moving photo montages. A final room contains what has become the customary presidential sideshow, the gifts and curiosities that "the public expects," in the words of the designers.

Wall-size photo murals of the two Kennedy brothers—the

president in the Oval Office with his young children, Bobby embraced by civil rights workers—have an intense, poignant impact. As one exits into the great hall, reeling from the two tragic assassinations, mourning lost youth and leadership, there is the almost unbearable knockout punch—an eighteen-foot-long image of a smiling Jack Kennedy walking through dune grass in the Cape Cod sunlight. Then, seen through the glass wall beyond, in carefully planted dune grass, is the master stroke—his sailboat, invoking lost life and pleasure, an epitaph played against the harbor view and the void of the soaring memorial space. No music here. Only a huge American flag. This is consummate drama, art and politics.

I think it is fair to say that given the phenomenon of the presidential library and the phenomenon of the Kennedy family, this building is a remarkable synthesis of the two. But it is clearer than ever that the archives are misplaced as part of the museum; the marriage of convenience has turned into an awkward and costly relationship. What this building demonstrates conclusively is that architecture is a powerful instrument of symbolism and an extremely effective shaper of the environment and emotional responses. The Kennedy Library succeeds magnificently in the presentation and promotion of a particular presidential image through an unavoidably subjective kind of history and superb polemical design. But it makes unanswered questions of cost, logic, and purpose more pressing than ever. This is not the definition of library to be found in any lexicon.

October 28, 1979

Note: Attendance has never reached the expected level; figures have dropped at all presidential libraries in recent years—a trend that may or may not be permanent or significant. The problem of the continuing and escalating maintenance costs of these increasingly extravagant monuments has finally been addressed by proposed congressional legislation that would mandate a maintenance endowment as part of the privately funded construction package. The bill has been held up by the insistence of the Reagan administration that the Reagan Library be exempted from this requirement.

MUSEUMS

LESSONS FOR THE EIGHTIES

The museum explosion of the 1980's is making the museum building boom of the 60's look like a practice run. In some ways this new museum wave is producing much more interesting buildings; they are far more revealing about the arts, including architecture, than most of the earlier structures. Many of today's most prestigious commissions are going to the architects of what used to be called the avant-garde—a sure indication that new styles, and new ways of thinking about the arts, are being adopted by the establishment.

The trend is international. There are James Stirling's Staatsgalerie building in Stuttgart and extensions for the Fogg Museum in Cambridge, Massachusetts, and the Tate Gallery in London. Richard Meier has designed museums for Frankfurt and Atlanta. Arata Isozaki is responsible for the new Museum of Contemporary Art in Los Angeles, and Michael Graves has received the commission for the addition to the Whitney Museum in New York. All of these architects are redefining a "modern" building type that was born in classicism and the Beaux Arts in the nineteenth century.

The twenty years between these cultural building booms have made a tremendous difference. With a few notable exceptions, the museums of the 1960's leaned heavily toward windowless warehousing, or more correctly, their directors did. Frustrated by older monumental structures with enormous architectural presence requiring constant installation battles, curators demanded total control of the presentation of their collections. They asked for, and got, anonymous all-purpose spaces in blind bland boxes. The vagaries of daylight were eliminated for sophisticated artificial lighting systems. In essence, nothing was supposed to interfere with the art itself—least of all the architect, who was often a troublesome fellow.

The results, which should have been ideal, were disappointing. The buildings were not just neutral, they were dispiritingly characterless. The scientifically controlled lighting lacked life. The museum was reduced to containerized art, curiously static and one-dimensional. Most surprising of all, the works of art actually seemed diminished, rather than liberated, by their ordinary setting. Since then, the return to daylit galleries and specially designed spaces has been gradual, but steady, and the return of architecture as the supplier of context and measure for the other arts is quite overwhelmingly evident.

There were three particularly important exceptions to this 1960's trend—the Centre Pompidou in Paris, the East Wing of the National Gallery in Washington, and the National Gallery in West Berlin. All three are national museums, and each was meant to establish a national cultural image. All opted consciously for architecture.

The Centre Pompidou, known as the Beaubourg, was the product of an international competition won by the firm of Piano and Rogers. The design sought to create a distinctly new kind of building for a radically conceived museum function intended to restore leadership and vitality to Paris as an artistic world capital. The East Wing of Washington's National Gallery, by I. M. Pei and Partners, had to meet special criteria of site, status, and suitability. The National Gallery in West Berlin, which was the last major work of Mies van der Rohe, was the summation of that master's painstaking investigations of structure, space, and style—a work of art in its own right that was to house the national collections.

How have these museums fared? The results are distinctly mixed. None has been problem-free. Each director has wrestled with his particular devil, or architect, a process complicated by changing exhibition ideas, styles, and functions in the 1970's and 80's. These have ranged from the all-star supershows to increasingly didactic displays reinforced by historical and literary references.

But the successes and failures of these buildings are instructive. The Beaubourg has turned out to be a winner, after a rocky and uncertain start. The National Gallery in West Berlin is a loser, for reasons that have less to do with design than with unsympathetic use that ranges from bad housekeeping to calculated insult. The National Gallery's East Wing in Washington is an uneasy draw, depending entirely on the nature and scale of what is on display.

How much of this can be attributed to the architecture? Saying that "a building doesn't work" covers a multitude of sins and sinners. No building is flawless; its uses are too complex. Even the most careful program can be out of date by the time the structure is finished. No all-purpose space works equally well for all purposes. "Flexibility" puts even more creative strain on the abilities of those who use the spaces than on the original designer. Using any building well means working with, not against, its visions and intentions. Some buildings present more obstacles than others. But there are clear cases of overt hostility to a building by a client or user, and the result is always a disaster. Whether the hostility is conscious or not, insensitivity to the architecture can lead to sabotage. This seems to be the case with Mies's National Gallery in West Berlin. The misunderstanding of its aesthetic and the mishandling of its space, the unfeeling destruction of this subtle, elegant, and highly vulnerable structure—the visual and conceptual damage—makes one's heart ache.

To begin with the ludicrous, this is probably the only building in West Berlin—or perhaps even in Germany, a country where cleanliness counts—with dirty, unwashed windows. For a Mies building, that means grimy glass walls. The crystalline quality so essential to these transparent glass planes and their visual interaction is smudged by a dull nasty film.

Mies's typical, perfectly calibrated, steel-framed enclosure stands on a stone platform in a hostile, unsympathetic setting

Mies van der Rohe

*National Gallery,
West Berlin,
1962–65*

*A superb
twentieth-century
monument of
stringent aesthetic
restrictions, ill
treated as a
museum*

Garth Huxtable

as amorphous and ill scaled as any dismal scene out of standard American urban renewal. Obviously, we have no monopoly on this kind of environmental mutilation. By dint of its sheer design strength, however, the building manages to make a self-contained statement. The land on which it stands slopes sharply to the rear so that the plaza becomes a podium, with galleries for the permanent collection and a sculpture garden at the lower levels. From the street, one enters a huge open room. This single, superb, unified and unashamedly "univalent" space is the basis of the classic Miesian aesthetic. The

making of such a grand space is a timeless architectural preoccupation; in this case, it is defined and enriched by a full range
of subtle adjustments of structure to skin, closed to open, the
whole to the parts, of details, materials, and finishes. The resolution of these elements, in this building, occupied Mies
wholly in the last years of his life.

All of this care is canceled out by abusive misuse and abys-
mal maintenance. In the tradition begun with Mies's 1929
Barcelona Pavilion, this room is a singular twentieth-century
setting for the selective display of the best twentieth-century

art. It brooks nothing "unsuitable" and nothing second rate. The building demands its own standards and fealty to its own, or a sympathetic style. (So does Lou Kahn's revered Kimbell Museum in Fort Worth, Texas—a consideration wholly respected by its director and reflected in its collection and the building's overwhelmingly favorable reception.) Admittedly, that is a sublimely restrictive principle. But for anyone truly interested in the arts of our time, this unity has a valid rationale: the unique integration of art and architecture represents both a challenge and an achievement at the highest expressive level.

What the room contained when I saw it were some badly related paintings documenting some of the more unattractive trends of the last two decades, all better represented elsewhere. They could not have been more willfully selected for unsuitability or sabotage. To add injury to insult, a clumsy and unfeeling installation had ham-handedly amputated the green marble columns meant to soar from floor to roof. The kind of sculpture that is made of random old rags and boards was dropped, like discarded trash, on the far-from-clean floor. The hallmarks of the Miesian aesthetic—precision, elegance, rigor and refinement, the perfection of placement and detail—were conspicuously lacking. But what was also lacking was the indispensable "eye"—that elemental visual sensibility of which good art museums are made.

It is clear that this structure is not without serious problems. One can only think of the curatorial battles with Frank Lloyd Wright's Guggenheim Museum spiral that sent at least one great director, James Johnson Sweeney, flying off in frustration. At the same time, successful installations there, such as the grand sweep and glow of Mark Rothko's luminous canvases, are unforgettable; the whole is even greater than the sum of its parts. Container and contained, art and architecture, can make an enormously powerful statement working together.

The Berlin museum's restricted plan obviously shortchanges administrative and curatorial space. Its strong aesthetic also dictates the use of carefully chosen scales and styles. It is here that everything breaks down; every change, every choice, is wrong. Every attempted solution is a jarring intrusion, from signs to coffee shop. Whether this mishandling stems from unawareness, ineptness or hostility, or, as is sometimes suggested, from the Marxist rejection of a formalist modern work that is a popular response in certain ideological circles, is really beside the point. What is evident is an administration out of step with everything the building is, and should be, and the result is its virtual destruction.

The success of the Beaubourg, on the other hand, shows how a talented and determined staff came to terms with equally problematic architecture. This structure promised the impossible: both the competition program and the design solution made visionary claims of multipurpose space and multimedia arts. Faced with installing much of the same old modern art and more or less conventional exhibitions, the staff found that the stylish plumbing, which enclosed and served the "flexible all-purpose" space, kept getting in the way. The building insisted on celebrating its own technology over everything else. With the Paris–New York and Paris–Moscow shows, however, the most serious of the installation problems were brought under control, and content overrode novelty. These spectacular and scholarly exhibitions not only combined theme, contents, and setting to stunning effect, they also set equally noteworthy standards of scholarship and display. They were landmark art events. The irony, of course, is that this building is not working the way it was supposed to—as a kinetic laboratory of the arts that would leave the rest of the world behind—but it is working well. It has certainly achieved its basic objective of putting Paris back into the mainstream of the modern art world.

At the East Wing of the National Gallery in Washington the monumental atrium does what the National Gallery in Berlin was meant to do—it creates a strong visual statement about the twentieth-century relationship of the arts, and by extension, about the total modernist aesthetic. It achieves the synthesis through a total environmental experience. Mies's building would have done this with consummate subtle artistry, but that point, alas, is moot. Washington's is a bolder and more popular (democratic?) approach in which art and engineering meet with changing light and cloud patterns in a series of public spaces alive with crowds and movement. It is art as act, as social and activist rather than as contemplative experience. The trouble with the East Wing comes with the transition to smaller spaces and more intimate exhibits. When the scale of the exhibits is small—like miniature Impressionist paintings or royal European treasures, or when they make a discreet, stylistically related entity, as with the David Smith sculpture or Matisse cutouts—these galleries can be an exquisite and quite personal delight.

But the big show of Rodin sculpture, for example, was a powerhouse that writhed and twisted explosively through the rooms and could barely be contained in those spaces and the transitions between them were impossible; the plunge down the small spiral stair of an intimate corner gallery to the Sturm und Drang of Rodin's monumental "Gates of Hell" below, was an architectural absurdity. There was a basic incompatibility here that the architecture could not seem to handle. The bathetic extravaganza of the sculpture seemed all the more exaggerated against Pei's controlled and gentlemanly geometry, but the difficulty was one of relationships of space, scale, and circulation. These are real problems, and ones that the National Gallery will continue to face.

When a museum and its contents come together as an integrated aesthetic whole, however, something very special happens. The art is enlarged and exalted, and so is the experience of the viewer. Creating that revealing and enriching synthesis of art and setting is the challenge that still faces architects and directors. It is also the secret of a great museum.

November 29, 1981

PEI IN BOSTON

What does an architect do after he's designed the East Wing of the National Gallery in Washington? If you are I. M. Pei, you design the West Wing of the Museum of Fine Arts in Boston, adding one more museum to the distinguished list completed by the firm of I. M. Pei and Partners in recent years. Boston's West Wing is a $22-million, three-story structure that provides 80,000 square feet of dramatic space. It is part of a five-year master plan being carried out under the guidance of the museum's director, Jan Fontein, and associate director, Ross W. Farrar, that is rearranging collections, renovating facilities, and providing new galleries and public spaces for the 111-year-old arts institution.

The East Wing of Washington's National Gallery, with its no-holds-or-costs-barred approach to magnificence in the modern manner, is a hard act to follow. Boston's building completes the formal, sedate 1909 monument designed by Guy Lowell, one of the better examples of the Beaux Arts structures that defined the art and cultural ambitions of American cities at the turn of the century. That, too, is a hard act to follow.

The East Wing brought the integrated experience of modern art and architecture to the nation's capital. It also established today's museum as a spatial and pedestrian phenomenon at the social and spectator level, rather than just as a place to see art. That bothers some people, who feel that display and viewing have become subordinated to circulation in something resembling the atrium of a shopping mall. They will probably feel the same way about Boston. They are not all wrong, of course, but what they fail to note is the logical and not unreasonable connection between the consumerism of culture and commerce. Those who have campaigned to make art accessible and agreeable to everyone have ignored the most obvious and legitimate way that this is actually occurring. It is in these handsome spaces, as much or more than the supershows they serve, that the message is understood and has its greatest impact. This unity of art and environment is basic to the best art of our time. What matters is the level and quality of the experience provided, and the way in which it is controlled by the architect and the museum staff to determine its meaning and value.

It is the rare visitor to the National Gallery's East Wing, for example, who does not at least sense that some kind of total aesthetic has been offered beyond the special exhibition that he may have come to see. I first sensed this a number of years ago

in Pei's Everson Museum in Syracuse, New York, where it was possible to feel that one was part of a kind of art that included the building, the Morris Louis on the wall, and the view of trees through a strategically placed window, all orchestrated by space and light and a sensibility particular to our time. This is also true in Boston, although the program and needs are quite different from either Washington or Syracuse. All of these new museums tell us a great deal about the ideas that are shaping both museums and architecture today.

The Boston building offers a full measure of elegance, dignity, and delight. A white-walled space, approximately two hundred twenty-five feet long, is topped by a soaring glass barrel vault fifty-two feet high through which changing daylight streams; the word "galleria" has been abused and misused, but this is the real thing. This spectacular three-story-high interior forms a circulation spine between new exhibition galleries and a bookstore, restaurant, and cafeteria, with classrooms and auditorium on the lowest level and offices at the top. The walls are a surprising combination of lacquered white panels on one side and smoothly crafted concrete on the other. It is the suaveness of both finishes that unites them, while creating surface interest for the long narrow passage between them.

Part of the new space was quite literally carved out of an earlier addition, which was stripped of its facade and incorporated into the plan. Given a new glass wall, this section now houses a bookstore and restaurant that are visible from the central corridor and also open one side of the galleria. The problem of matching new and old columns has been stylishly resolved. A delicate aluminum frame makes a sunscreen for the vaulted glass roof. The wing offers direct axial connections to the old building, with views to the handsome classical rotunda and glimpses of the park outside. New and old sections merge without confusion or jarring transitions. And daylight is triumphantly present everywhere, in the galleries and public spaces —a return of natural light to museums after years of darkness that should be a cause for universal rejoicing. The look is restrained, pristine high tech, tempered by Pei's familiar, superbly finished boardmarked concrete.

Alas, it is impossible to read this interesting interior from the

Opposite page:
I. M. Pei and Partners

West Wing, Museum of Fine Arts, Boston, 1980–81

A building that celebrates and accommodates museum going as a social experience

Garth Huxtable

outside. The barrel vault projects slightly above the roofline of a virtually unrelieved horizontal box broken only by glass openings held flat and flush with the surface. This nice but dull exterior, perfectly and painstakingly detailed in the same Maine granite used for the original structure, is both bland and unrevealing. That is unfortunate, because the new facade will become the main entrance, adjacent to parking. Guy Lowell's Huntington Avenue facade still wins, hands down, because it is so rich in what might be called the "received" assets of tradition. Columns, stairs, cornices, and moldings and all of the details, paraphernalia, and conventions of the Beaux Arts vocabulary automatically assure scale, proportion, and contrast. These are the freebies of the classical style.

But the new wing has a particular interest, beyond its obvious purpose of adding space and the admirable one of freeing the collection for reassessment and rearrangement. Its design virtually defines the museum's changing role today and offers an exemplary solution to the growing problem of active versus passive pleasure, of experiencing art in crowds or through quiet contemplation. This building focuses on other than art-viewing functions, and organizes them all in one place. An area where one can eat and socialize, an enlarged bookstore and sales shop, the museum's education department, seminar and lecture facilities—all the things that serve group activities are located here. And so are the special galleries, with their daylit coffered skylights, which will accommodate those record-breaking, crowd-pleasing, transient supershows that seem to have become a way of museum life.

This building celebrates the new museum-going; it emphasizes circulation and shared activity; it is predicated on the social pleasure and communal experience of being there. And by collecting all this in one place, it becomes possible to return the rest of the museum to its fundamental purpose: scholarship and the private, personal contemplative communication that is the essential response to great art. This basic function of the museum has been all but destroyed in escalating head counts. The design of the new wing is a shrewd and suave trade-off. The recognition of this new social and cultural role has figured prominently in the museum's planning. But there is also a shrewd awareness of how to capitalize on this programming as a financial resource. The West Wing is bound to be one of Boston's most attractive and inviting places to go; it can be open when the rest of the building is closed. The marble tables under the trees in the galleria, with views of some of the museum's more spectacular works of art, will undoubtedly create a permanent traffic jam—but that is hardly a serious matter, and has its own appeal.

Pei's High Modern Style evident here and in the National Gallery, is considered by many of the younger generation to be somewhat old hat. But what few seem to be noticing is that these recent buildings have been moving into some of the areas that have been staked out by postmodernism. Architecture today has advanced beyond the simple open plan, or direct progression from one space to another. New buildings like this one have more in common with those marvelous sixteenth- and seventeenth-century drawings of stage sets where stairs and ramps give on to platforms and balconies glimpsed through arches and balustrades, for spaces seen and experienced at the same time. There is a rediscovery of that misunderstood feature "waste space," with a carefully choreographed arrangement of related levels and vistas. Movement is an essential component. The intricate relationships are both real and implied, and their definition by light and geometry is as important as their perception through structure and space. Today, no one does this better than Richard Meier; these effects often become the building's organizing principle. But they are also present in more conservative structures like Boston's West Wing. This kind of architectural event is a significant part of what the new museum offers to the consumer of culture. In fact, it is where art and architecture are going today —together.

July 12, 1981

MOMA IN NEW YORK

If it is impossible to imagine New York without the Museum of Modern Art, many of us are finding it almost as hard to imagine a new version. The $35.6-million expansion of its present building and site on Fifty-third Street that will double the museum's size is an extremely controversial undertaking— as controversial in its way, and for its time, as the original building completed in 1939. The controversy then was about the radical modernism of its architecture; now it is about the nature of the project, which conspicuously incorporates an income-producing condominium tower. The issues are the more complex ones of urban design, or how to build in a city, and money and patronage, or how to keep an arts institution alive. The marriage of culture and commerce raises a host of uncomfortable questions for our time.

In current development language, the building will be a mixed-use structure. A new six-floor wing of about the same size as the existing museum will be built just to the west of it; the two will be joined, with substantial revisions of the original, to increase the gallery space from about 40,500 to 80,650 square feet. The fifty-six-story apartment tower will be incorporated directly into the complex, but with no direct physical connection.

That the museum needs both money and space is beyond argument. Consider, for example, that the permanent collection (or what can normally be displayed of it) had to be completely removed to accommodate the Picasso display that was the last in the old building. And consider that those who cannot walk upstairs have always had to wait for what seems like a week for one of two wretchedly inadequate elevators. Once in the galleries, there is never space enough to see the pictures, except on an off, off hour. Large purposeful groups descend on the building like hordes from outer space, guaranteeing close encounters of the wrong kind. Restrooms are few, unreachable and unspeakable, and to get through this chaos requires the skill and stamina of a running back. The building is an aesthetic slum.

To want the Museum of Modern Art to stay the way it is forever can only be put down to *nostalgie de la boue.* More kindly, this attachment to the status quo can be attributed to remembrance of things past. The museum is a hotbed of sentimental recall for its aficionados. Scratch any real New Yorker and the memories and milestones of this remarkable institution come pouring out. For half a century, the Museum of Modern Art has been both an international force and a uniquely local phenomenon, an essential part of this city's life and style.

The new design disarms its critics because Cesar Pelli's solution has both ingenuity and elegance. The problems of transitions, the utilization of awkward areas, are resolved in a creative synthesis of plan and circulation that could be a handsome as well as a functional achievement. There are, by necessity, many compromises. But there will also be some very accommodating spaces for the museum's next fifty years, now that it has celebrated its first half-century.

If the tower is the dominant element of the design, that is not without a certain ironic symbolism. Through a complex legal device called the Trust for Cultural Resources, the apartment tower will provide the money to take care of the costs of expansion and the museum's dangerously mounting deficits. The museum's future rides on that commercial tower, for better or worse. It is probably the most artful real estate deal ever devised. This entry into the real estate business is held at very careful, legal arm's length so that the museum's tax-exempt status will not be affected. Through the trust, the museum has sold its air rights, or the unused space over its small building that could have been filled with construction under the city's zoning, to private developers for $17 million. This provides immediate cash-in-hand. The trust will also be used to transfer annual payments from the tower to the museum equivalent to the real estate taxes that the owners would normally pay to the city. The city will get the taxes that it receives now, as if there had been no development at all. And the museum will have a guaranteed income, if all goes well.

The controversy surrounding the museum project has centered on the tower and the trust. There were questions about the legality of the trust, and the condemnation powers given to it, and there was a court fight, which the museum won. But what bothered most people—and still does—was the destruction of the special nature of Fifty-third Street that the expansion entailed. This has been one of midtown Manhattan's most attractive and cosmopolitan side streets, with its varied uses and styles and small-scale older buildings, its brownstones and town houses converted to shops, galleries, and restaurants in a fine architectural, commercial, and cultural mix. Sparked by the museum and related to it, these activities gave the street a special New York character.

What disturbs those concerned with more technical matters of zoning and development is the increasing evidence that these special features can be destroyed so easily, and the fact that a tower of this size and bulk can be built, completely legally, on a narrow side street where smaller buildings are more environmentally sound. The museum complex, with all of its sensitivities, cannot be anything but a large monolithic structure. The midblock tower becomes an irreversibly destructive act.

The trade-off, according to the museum—and it is a hard argument to answer—was survival. Through this legal and financial maneuver, it was able to convert its greatest economic asset, aside from its collection—that valuable midtown site—into money needed for its future. The gamble, and it is one, may well pay off. Other cultural institutions with air rights are either watching carefully or involved in similar plans of their own. But the alliance between speculation and survival raises all kinds of cloudy issues, including the manipulation of the city's zoning for undesirable midblock towers.

It has been no small job, and it has taken no small team, to translate this complex and conflicting program into a coherent work of architecture. The anguish of the process was clearly visible in the early studies. But the style and success of the design solution that has evolved must be credited to the museum's architect, Cesar Pelli, who has had the job of coordinating the entire project. The tower has been through two developers and two versions. Changes in the program resulted in a noticeable improvement. The new developer hired the firm of Edward Durell Stone for the apartment layouts, and

Gruen Associates is handling the working drawings and super-
vising construction for the museum. But Pelli's fine Argen-
tinian hand is everywhere, from the tower's corner living
rooms to the subtly detailed, sleek glass skin tying the whole
complex together that has become his recognizable trademark.

By electing to stay on the site, the museum faced some
enormous design problems; it would have been far easier to sell
out at a handsome price and start from scratch somewhere else.
But that would have erased the institution's historic identity, so
closely allied with the city and the art of our time, and meant the
loss of its central, fashionable midtown site. It would also have
ensured the destruction of the garden designed by Philip Johnson that is one of New York's great amenities. In this scheme,
the garden is kept virtually intact, a fact that forces the expanded
museum into a long narrow structure along the street. This
elongated shape not only makes planning difficult, it also makes
provisions for adequate circulation almost impossible.

Pelli's answer is a circulation system that will become the
museum's most dramatic new feature: a greenhouse-type enclosure added to the rear, or garden side, of the building will
rise to the structure's full height to form an enclosure for
escalators. His design removes the present back wall and re-
places it with glass, which projects about eighteen feet into the
garden to create the necessary extra room. The loss will be
compensated for by the visual unification of the garden and the
building and the inclusion of stunning city vistas. The glass can
be truly transparent because the north exposure permits it to
be clear and untinted; reflective glass tends to become an
opaque wall. This functional solution suggests a spectacular
aesthetic addition. There will be views of the garden and galleries on every level. And while it is not exactly Beaubourg,
there is an interesting kinship in making the glassed-in ride as
much of an experience as the art itself. Still, one remembers
with particular nostalgia the ritualistic ascent by the old stairs
to the collections on the second floor.

The raised eastern end of the garden will also be lost, replaced by a two-story pavilion that will house the public and
members' restaurants. By moving the restaurant from its present location, however, part of the garden is regained at the

western end. And by resisting the temptation to make the pavilion higher, its smaller bulk relates to the open space. There are many real gains. There will be more and larger galleries for the permanent collections, and temporary exhibition galleries with room for several shows at once. Not only will each department just about double its display space, but each will have a publicly accessible study center as well. The lobby will be one-third again as large, and gallery visitors, office visitors, and organized groups will be accommodated separately. The library will be moved and enlarged, and there will be an additional auditorium. Mechanical systems will be overhauled completely.

But the most difficult design decision, because it has so little to do with either function or reason, has been the question of what to do about the original museum facade. The interiors behind it will be completely changed, and the old building will cease to exist as an independent entity. Designed by Philip L. Goodwin and Edward Durell Stone (before Stone renounced modernism for his harem-classical style, and long before such renunciation became fashionable in the name of postmodernism), the Museum of Modern Art is a genuine landmark. It has become as symbolic an image of early modernism as Duchamp's "Nude Descending a Staircase" and the famous fur-lined teacup. To destroy it is to destroy the touchstone of an era and a milestone in the history of art.

Early studies for the new building showed the International Style facade eliminated for a uniform treatment of the enlarged Fifty-third Street front. There were some intellectualized rationalizations about "integrated architectural treatment" and the abstract "recall" of the original motifs. Fortunately, the museum has decided not to cannibalize its architectural past. The old facade will be cleaned and restored, rather than resurfaced. The size of the original glass panels is being used as a module for the design of the new glass skin, which will be in shades of warm gray; the same module, with variations dictated by function, will make up the tower. The abstract patterns that result are like a glistening tapestry. Although the old facade is flush and continuous with the new one, its white marble framing will set it apart from the rest as a discrete architectural and historic event. It will serve as illusion and allusion, as artifact and metaphor. And it will also suggest a more intimate scale for the street.

But is anything really preserved with gestures and metaphors? So much has changed in fifty years. If the original Museum of Modern Art was an act of architectural daring, the new building is an act of consummate accommodation. If the museum of the 1930's was defining a new "truth" and engaging in a special mission, the museum of the 1980's envisions no radical statements, programs, or policies. Its aims are continuity, flexibility, and enough space to make its unique contributions clear. Neither truth nor art is quite as simple as it seemed half a century ago.

June 29, 1980

Note: It is hard to find the "old" Modern in the "new" Modern, except in those galleries for the collection that consciously replicate the original size and scale. Not only are the museum, the street, and the neighborhood transformed by the Modern's real estate venture, but so, also and alas, is the Modern itself, far beyond its increased size. The museum's relationship to its public, once so personal and idiosyncratic, is now coolly institutional. Physical gains are offset by losses of spirit and style as large as the condo tower.

AMERICANA AT THE MET

The new $18 million American Wing of the Metropolitan Museum of Art is a 130,000-square-foot structure six times the size of the old American Wing. It contains, as its focal point, a spectacular, glass-enclosed seventy-foot-high garden court that is one of the city's most beautiful and important spaces. This is the third and best of the skylit courts that are a repeated theme of the museum's ambitious remodeling and reconstruction. The first of these, for the Lehman Wing, was small and charming, but as dubious an addition as the wing itself; much too much was made, architecturally, of an uneven collection wrongheadedly installed in a pointless imitation of its original quarters. The second court was the overscaled and barren gymnasium that upstages the tiny Temple of Dendur.

The American Wing court is the first of the glassed-in spaces that was supposed to create a transitional structure between park and building; it is also, and primarily, a handsome indoor-outdoor room. That room is significantly enriched by the artifacts it contains. Taken as a whole, however, the architecture of the new wing, like that of the other additions, is disruptively strong, with a tendency to overshadow the old Beaux Arts building and the exhibits alike. The new construction is aggressively stylish and coldly monumental; it has produced impressive amounts of space and a creeping corporate veneer. It is also proving distressingly insensitive to the job at hand, the integration of new and old in the appropriate service of the arts. For better or worse, it is a style that seems to suit the imperial place that the Metropolitan has become.

The three new floors that have been wrapped around the old American Wing on its north and west sides make it possible to display almost all of the museum's comprehensive collection of American painting, sculpture, furniture, silver, ceramics, glass, textiles, and decorative arts for the first time, in everything from evocative room settings and more academic permanent and temporary exhibitions to study-storage areas. Also for the first time, the painting and sculpture collections have their own galleries. Nine new galleries contain the paintings familiar to every student of Americana: the sharply observed Copley portraits, the huge romantic landscapes of Church and Bierstadt, Bingham's fur traders becalmed on a glassy Mississippi. The fine-arts collection ranges from 1700 to the end of the nineteenth century. The ever-popular period rooms, closed during the five years of construction, have been reinstalled according to the latest scholarly standards. Full-size architectural elements that could never be shown before now have stellar space in the huge garden court. The result is a theatrically handsome art and architectural blend.

On the north side of the garden court, the entrance to the galleries is through one of the architectural displays: the re-erected facade of the 1822–24 Branch Bank of the United States, or Assay Building, by Martin E. Thompson that stood on Wall Street until 1915. Some time after it was torn down, in 1924, the front wall was moved to the "back yard" of the museum at the rear of the first American Wing, where it was barely visible for years. Now the mellow creamy marble (snow-white when it was new), with its domestic classical details, has the drama of an architectural stage set within the concrete and steel-framed glass and limestone courtyard. The new space and construction are immensely enriched by these relationships of new and old style and scale. One wishes only that the bank facade were not quite so paper-flat; it would have been better if it had projected beyond the containing walls for more of a sense of its original architectural quality.

It is a poignant footnote to art and architectural history that the artifacts on display, which have been so beautifully integrated with their new setting, are here almost without exception by courtesy of the bulldozer. (Period rooms, of course, are cultural tokens often rescued from similar vandalism.) Built into the court's south wall is the flower-columned loggia from Louis Comfort Tiffany's own home in Oyster Bay, Laurelton Hall, built from 1903 to 1908, with his superb landscape window of wisteria-framed sky and water in jewel-toned glass. A pair of ornate bronze and iron stairs by Louis Sullivan that once graced the 1893 Adler and Sullivan Stock Exchange Building in Chicago lead to a balcony level. The east wall of the court contains a Tiffany mosaic fountain of about 1905–15, and a majestic entrance hall mantel from George B. Post's house for Cornelius Vanderbilt 2d, with caryatids representing Peace and Love supporting an entablature and mosaic, designed and executed about 1880 by Augustus St. Gaudens and John La Farge. Also incorporated are additional Tiffany and La Farge works in stained glass, and Frank Lloyd Wright's windows for the Coonley Playhouse of 1912.

In addition to these architectural elements, the court contains a selection of the museum's American sculpture collection, long assigned to oblivion and still troubling to the experts. Arranged enchantingly among trees and greenery, virtuous Victorian maidens, and anecdotal and allegorical

groups, stronger on nostalgia than on aesthetics, have an un-
deniable sylvan charm. A pool and fountain and nineteenth-
century American garden furniture complete the setting. The
parkland used for the court is no longer open public space; it
has become a part of the museum. There is supposed to be an
entrance from the park when the landscaping is approved,
funded, and completed. (On a 1986 visit, the doors were not
only locked, but heavily chained; security has obviously taken
precedence over promises.)

The 12,000-square-foot garden court, in common with all of
the elements of the museum's master plan, is the work of the
architectural firm of Kevin Roche, John Dinkeloo and Associates, working with Arthur Rosenblatt, the museum's vice president for architecture and planning, who has been the on-site
overseer of the entire operation. The court has been landscaped by Innocenti and Webel. In line with the growing
practice of crediting the source of construction funds that is
producing a kind of Almanac de Donor, this is the Charles
Engelhard Court, and the paintings are housed in the Joan
Whitney Payson Galleries, with special exhibitions in the Erv-
ing and Joyce Wolf Gallery. The new and old American galleries are intricately connected on several levels. The old rooms,
unfortunately, have lost their windows on the park; they now
look out on artificially lighted, painted backdrops of views
meant to suggest the original settings of the departed houses.
They may have acquired accuracy, but they have lost life. This
trade-off gains the spacious set of new display spaces surrounding the old ones, which are simply and elegantly detailed with
oak trim.

The painting galleries, which have been installed by John K.
Howat, curator of American paintings and sculpture, are on
the park side of the building and are flooded with natural light.
There was no American department, as such, until 1949, although the museum had routinely acquired American work.
The emphasis now is on a full representation from Colonial
painting and primitive and folk art, through the Hudson River
and American landscape schools, to American Impressionism.

It comes as something of a surprise to realize that the original American Wing opened more than fifty years ago, in 1924.

Designed by Grosvenor Atterbury, the building was a meticulous "period" construction that coincided with a fashionable rise of interest in English-influenced American furnishings of the seventeenth through the early nineteenth centuries. The view of the American past that the museum espoused was a limited one—culturally narrow and qualitatively high, with an arbitrary cutoff point for what was not deemed to merit serious respect. The re-created rooms were an instant and lasting success and one of the museum's most popular features.

With the hindsight of half a century, the limitations that were set then seem highly questionable. The original displays reflected as much of the taste of the 1920's as they did of the architects and artisans of the early Republic. A bit of fudged plasterwork here, a fashionable Chinese wallpaper there, or the use of wing chairs to suit twentieth-century ideas of comfort and style gave the rooms additional appeal and immense influence in the revivals that were sweeping the home furnishings field. One question that faced Berry B. Tracy, curator in charge of American decorative arts, and his staff, was how much to undo in the redoing. The line that has been walked in the process of reinstallation is a curious and delicate one, but the rooms have been furnished more accurately this time around, using original inventories and new scientific knowledge about colors and finishes.

Not all of the 1920's has been removed. It is acknowledged that this taste, too, now has its place in history. The taste of the 1980's—cooler, more austere, and possibly more reliable—overlays the taste of the 20's, resulting in a palimpsest of art-historical revivals. There is more informed guesswork and less willful "correctness" now; acknowledged uncertainty rather than doctrinaire tastemaking. It is only during the last twenty years, in fact, that the museum has acquired examples of American architecture and the decorative arts from 1825 to 1915, extending the collection to include Gothic Revival and Victorian examples, as well as a room from a demolished Frank Lloyd Wright house.

The new wing comes at a time when the American heritage has been fully released from the limitations set by earlier generations. It is now recognized as a broad, eclectic, and almost unlimited source of creative vitality to which no single yard-stick of taste can apply. Much of what was aesthetically reprehensible has become respectable. Those changing attitudes are made visual and pleasurable in the new American Wing.

May 25, 1980

HOUSING

LONDON MEGASTRUCTURE

The Camden Borough Council of London has produced a megastructure, under the design leadership of architect Naeve Brown—a radical architectural concept that has intrigued practitioners and theorists for the past two decades, and like most radical architectural concepts is going rapidly out of style. In this case the concept has been translated into council housing, the British version of public housing, which has had as checkered and controversial a history there as in the United States.

Essentially, a megastructure is what it sounds like: a big building of many parts. In the case of the housing complex on Alexandra Road, it is a thousand continuous feet of low-rise, high-density, terraced apartments, built on a slight curve, which creates its own pedestrian street and "village" atmosphere.

What makes megastructure different from conventional big building, or from the row houses of the past, and what made it so attractive to the radicals of the 1960's, is an idea of infinite flexibility and extensibility; it was to be a free, liberated architecture capable of open-ended change and adjustment to match the popular and permissive ideas of those who were "restruc-

turing" society at that time. But it also fitted the architect's eternal utopian search for a kind of physical order that could be imposed by design on the chaos of living. Both notions invite skepticism.

The concept was embraced by the architectural avant-garde in the 1960's and adopted by the establishment in the 70's, and declared officially dead in 1976 by the critic and historian Reyner Banham in his succinctly titled book *Megastructure—*

232

Naeve Brown

Camden Borough Council Housing, London, 1978

Public housing as megastructure and instant village

Martin Charles

Urban Futures of the Recent Past. Obviously, this was an idea whose time came and went with astonishing rapidity.

Which makes it all the more remarkable is that the Alexandra Road housing is both handsome as architecture and promising as urban design, and like many handsome and promising housing solutions before it, has no guarantees of success. But allowing for those sociological imponderables that turn some housing efforts into cozy homes and others into urban night-

233

mares, it shows signs of settling in as part of the London scene. The design is thoughtfully related to earlier housing on the site and to the scale of its surroundings. Basically, it follows the megastructure formula that calls for a large, continuous structural framework that can accommodate smaller units, such as rooms, apartments, or houses. It can also include commercial units, administrative and other facilities, and public space, as it does here.

The idea is a rational one, as expandable as the kind of building it envisions. The cost of this unconventional construction is high, however, which must be figured into any final evaluation. It always turns out to be one-off rather than replicable construction, with a custom price tag. (One British firm, somewhat carried away at the height of the concept's popularity, proposed a visionary urban megastructure across the entire United States.) The best-known executed example of the genre is probably Moshe Safdie's Habitat at Montreal's Expo '67, a housing megastructure that demonstrated both the strengths and the weaknesses of the concept in terms of design, production, and costs. (In 1986, the tenants of Habitat bought it from the Canadian government. It has been successful and popular housing.)

In the field of public housing, however, Alexandra Road may be the beginning, and the end, of the line. Quite aside from its theoretical aspects, it strikes the visitor as a sensible and attractive solution to accommodating a lot of people on a difficult site; it is smack against a railyard, on one of those leftover bits of appallingly problematic land invariably given to council housing in English cities. The scheme is organized as terrace housing on a pedestrian street. A continuous row of five six-story blocks, joined by glass-enclosed elevator shafts, lines one side of the street, with three five-story blocks on the other side. The larger row forms a wall against the railyard at the northern edge, acting as a baffle for the noise. Between this street and a three-block row of town houses there is a park and recreation area. The site also contains community buildings. Garages and access roads on a level below the terraced housing keep pedestrian and vehicular traffic separate.

Within this unusual street and structural framework is some

well-planned housing. The apartments are very small, compact duplexes, with balconied living rooms above the bedrooms. Interiors have clean simple finishes and attractive, superior design details, such as ceramic tile countertops and natural wood cabinets in the kitchens. The amenities of rather stringent architectural design can easily roll with the punches of tenant taste.

Construction is poured-in-place concrete, with a few precast parts. This, too, is a custom-made megastructure—it was actually cheaper to "hand make" it on the site—rather than the industrialized product that theoreticians have envisioned. Mass production still remains a visionary ideal. But the massive monolith is less forbidding than would be expected for something so overbuilt; this much heavy concrete can be intimidating. The great length of the continuous structure is ameliorated by the curve of the street and the buildings—a deflection from the straight line that manages to suggest intimacy rather than infinity.

The architect has also accepted the challenge to provide high-density housing in low structures—an approach currently favored among housing experts. Towers, or point blocks, as they are called in Britain, have been as notorious breeders of social problems as high-rise projects in the United States. They are the buildings that everyone loves to hate. But the feature that succeeds most dramatically in breaking this housing mass down to an acceptable scale is the stepped balconies of the street facade. These balconies, softened by greens and flowers in the planting troughs that are part of the design, are set back on each floor as they rise from street level. This feature guarantees some light and privacy and a human dimension.

If anything, that human dimension may prove to be a little close and crowded as the entire curving structure is occupied; the prospect could be either for jolly Neapolitan street life or local gang wars. But this will never be an impersonal environment. Alienated, perhaps, or even destroyed, as is so common in these troubled times. But a heroic effort has been made to create a distinctive community instead of just packaging a specified number of dwelling units in no particular context. To do it this well has required a decade of perseverance on the part

Opposite page:
Gwathmey-Siegel

*Student housing
and Heyman
Humanities Center,
Columbia
University, New
York, 1981*

*High art versus
maximum security*

Richard Payne

of the architect, amounting almost to obsession. If megastructure has failed to deliver the city of the future, it has produced some dramatic and provocative housing on Alexandra Road.

December 3, 1978

COLUMBIA DORMITORY

Consider a building that has to be vandal-proof, constructed of maintenance-free materials with every surface resistant to neglect and abuse, where violation of design and function must be an anticipated fact, along with defacement and petty thievery—a place where surveillance is a necessity and population is transient. A description of a maximum security prison? Not at all. This is a dormitory at Columbia University.

Although it sounds as if even Michelangelo might have trouble getting out of this kind of architectural straitjacket, the firm of Gwathmey, Siegel and Associates has transcended the grim requirements to produce a serious work of architecture that makes some impressive contributions to the design of housing and the treatment of urban space. If parts of the buildings are too bleakly institutional, it is easy to see how an austerely simple aesthetic can be brought down to this dispiriting level very quickly when the practical requirements for building survival require a quasi-penal solution. The effect is helped along considerably by missing light covers in the halls and littered lobbies.

That these structures display a high level of ingenuity and imagination and a consistently superior level of design is, therefore, no small achievement, even for architects with the good track record of Charles Gwathmey and Robert Siegel, who are responsible for some of today's most refined and precise neomodernist buildings. (If there is postmodernism, then neomodernism must follow, for the work of those who are maintaining, or reviving, the modernist vocabulary rather than rushing to the history books.) The firm's best-known work is a series of widely acclaimed, suavely spectacular, costly

custom houses of the kind that both the architectural and home magazines love.

The $28.7 million Columbia project is the largest to come from the Gwathmey, Siegel office to date. The transition to the new scale and complexity is handled well, although the solution conspicuously lacks the luxurious finishes and details that have characterized the houses. The 360,000 square feet of the East Campus complex includes two dormitories, one a twenty-three-story tower and the other a four-story block, that face each other on the east and west sides of a court meant to suggest a "cloister," or a quad, in coolly contemporary terms. The north side of the court is formed by the three-story Heyman Humanities Center, which contains office, study, conference, and exhibition space for staff and fellows; the south side is enclosed by a large faculty-student lounge. Accommodations for three hundred fifty students in walk-up "town houses" and split-level duplexes occupy the low building and the lower part of the tower. The walk-ups in the tower are capped by fourteen floors containing four hundred duplexes and flats reached by skip-stop elevators. The typical dormitory unit has four single rooms with a living-dining room and kitchen above them. Cantilevered from the narrow south side of the slablike tower are double-height lounges with spectacular city and river views in three directions.

This self-contained residential, academic, and community complex supplies some of the best current architecture on the Columbia campus, which started in a blaze of McKim, Mead and White glory at the end of the last century and then went steadily downhill. Pretentiousness has been mixed with shoddiness until the nadir was reached in the Uris Business Building of the 1960's. Recently, the university rediscovered architecture, and the 70's produced Mitchell-Giurgola's Life Sciences Building and Alexander Kouzmanoff's discreet underground extension of Avery Library. There is a good chance that more will come. The new construction even manages to repair some of the environmental (but not the visual) damage done by the banal pomposity of the adjacent Schools of Law and International Affairs. Their raised platform base—a planning idea destined for obsolescence, sterility, and abandonment—has been connected to a new access plaza that also ties in other previously isolated buildings. The overbearing Law and International Affairs buildings alone could have alienated a few generations of students who have busied themselves attacking the structures that shelter and serve them. But since the bad seems to get it with the good, no architectural judgments are apparently involved.

For the new dormitories, the architects worked with the students to be sure that they got what they wanted. They did, but not in quite the way that was anticipated. Most of the furnishings have been removed from the lounges to student rooms. Chairs, tables, and bulletin boards have all been "liberated." Unable to use the marble, stone, brick, or wood that have traditionally graced campus architecture because they are defaced too easily, the architects have drawn on far less vulnerable materials. Whether by coincidence or irony, the selection of this particular firm was fortuitous, because the high-tech vocabulary of hard-surfaced unembellished finishes has always been central to their work. What they have done is to make a kind of a silk purse out of ceramic tile. Two colors of this tile are used, red and tan, to face the reinforced concrete construction with the addition of clear glass and glass block, aluminum windows, and trim. The result is a "modern" style drawn from history and memory and postgraduate pilgrimages to the European works of Le Corbusier and the early-twentieth-century masters. It is full of flat surfaces, smooth curves, and sophisticated nostalgia. These neomodernist buildings often bear a remarkable resemblance to some of the pictorial images of the classic black-and-white photographs of the revolutionary structures of the 1920's and 30's. Today, art imitates art.

There is at least one striking image in this vein in the Columbia buildings. The court is flanked on either side of its sixty-foot city-street width by sentinel rows of curved stair towers, faced in glass block, that provide the entrances to the walk-up units. The "look" of these repeated cylinders is of a formal, rather handsomely eerie city landscape, rigidly neorational in style, with shades of Le Corbusier's Salvation Army period in Paris, Russian Constructivism, Italian rationalism of the 1930's, and a suggestion of the surreal symmetries of Aldo

Rossi. But these towers are used to create more than a lasting visual impression. They are also a circulation device that permits entry to the dormitories on several levels while allowing natural light to penetrate to recreation spaces below the plaza.

Color is used to recall the material and scale of earlier Columbia buildings. The Morningside Drive facade of the tower is divided horizontally, with red tile on the lower section, to the height of its brick neighbors, and tan tile above. This attempt to relate to other construction and to de-emphasize the tower's size (a doomed effort) is repeated on its west, or court, side, and the theme is carried out by the low red building opposite. The only surface pattern is provided by the fenestration, which clearly reflects the interior layout—wide bands of glass for the living quarters, small paired windows for the bedrooms. There are plans for stores on the street-side ground floor.

All this is thoughtful and competent design. But perhaps the complex's most skilled and unusual feature is the corner entrance—an essentially awkward and unceremonious approach that was dictated by the tightness of the site and the surrounding construction. This entrance is reached by either crossing the Law School platform or coming through a 116th Street passageway that has been turned into a relatively pleasant, cloistered enclosure. At this point, the south end of the low dormitory block has been raised to a greater height than the rest of the building, to significantly alter the scale. This end is opened for a full three stories, with a massive corner column played off against a recessed undulating wall. The device is strong enough to be read as a formal entrance and it also succeeds in visually reducing the tower behind it to a backdrop. That is architectural legerdemain of a very high order.

The refinement of the design of these buildings is marred by ordinary construction and small bad touches like plaques placed conspicuously in the wrong places. In spite of campus and community fears of the brutality of high-rise density, a unified concept of housing and urbanism within a stringently elegant aesthetic manages to comes through. The Heyman Center for the Humanities and these badly needed dormitories are a superior addition to the Columbia campus. One can only look at the fresh-faced, clean-cut young graduate students who occupy the new buildings and try to guess who threw the paint in the courtyard, and why they tried to pry the floor-stop number plates off the elevators. One wonders what kind of humanists they can be.

October 4, 1981

DESIGN DILEMMAS

WISHFUL THINKING
ON FIFTH AVENUE

The subject is Pyrrhic victories, or, to mix mythology and metaphor, the Architectural Pathetic Fallacy.

The Architectural Pathetic Fallacy is more literal than literary; it is a sad kind of self-delusion in design, full of good intentions and bad results. This particular fallacy operates on the principle that if you are going to put an out-of-scale, out-of-context, discordant structure into a setting where it will be damaging or destructive, you can make it less so by "recalling," or "extracting" the essence or details of the surrounding older architecture. Borrowing from the existing for the new is supposed to make the two incompatible structures compatible.

In actual practice, this is almost always hogwash, with results ranging from well-intentioned bungling to pious hypocrisy. The Architectural Pathetic Fallacy is most frequently invoked to get a bad building put in the wrong place. But it has some obvious attractions. There is the "sensible" feature of compromise, which appeals to reason and intellect, and is particularly desirable in situations that are fraught with controversy. Because such a "solution" partakes of new and old, champions of both are mollified. One can point to the compromise and say that two buildings "go together" because they share a common cornice line, or related material and color. One is supposed to admire the way the addition "picks up" themes or motifs from its neighbors, no matter how it violates them in its totality. This kind of design usually gets high marks from those protecting the integrity of a landmark or the scale and character of a neighborhood. But answers meant to satisfy all camps seldom do, and compromise in architecture can be compared to the work of the committee assigned to design a horse that comes up with a camel.

As design philosophy, then, the Architectural Pathetic Fallacy turns out to be classic false reasoning. As design practice, it is usually a pitiful cop-out that falls between two stools with more of a thud than a crash. I suppose I should make the necessary disclaimer here by saying that it sometimes works; top talent can generate excellence from almost any set of givens. But more often it doesn't, and the reasons are manifold: blockbusting scale and bulk cannot be corrected or much ameliorated by decorative trim; the use of a traditional vocabulary does little more than reveal its current impoverishment; and an illusory approach based on wishful thinking cuts off more creative solutions.

This brings us to the case histories of two large buildings on Fifth Avenue that were faced with a monumental problem of compatibility in a design and urban context shaped by earlier zoning and a classical Beaux Arts taste. These are both apartment houses, one at 800 Fifth, at the corner of Sixty-first Street, where the Dodge Mansion stood; and the other at 1001 Fifth, between Eighty-first and Eighty-second streets on the site of two demolished town houses across from the Metropolitan Museum.

Because both buildings planned to breach the avenue's scale and style—a disruption permitted by the city's zoning—they were highly controversial from the start. Both were designed originally as perfectly routine Philip Birnbaum luxury specials, efficiently laid out to the builders' customary bottom line of marble-trimmed plasterboard inside and brick and glass outside. In each case a "prestige" firm was called on to transform the speculative duckling into a "suitable" swan—Ulrich Franzen and Associates for 800 Fifth, and Philip Johnson and

*Ulrich Franzen
and Associates*

*800 Fifth Avenue,
New York*

*The pastiche road
to the past . . .*

Marianne Barcellona

John Burgee for 1001 Fifth. Each resorted, ultimately, to the Architectural Pathetic Fallacy.

Here a little historical digression is necessary. The relationship of past and present has been an architectural dilemma for

Johnson, Burgee

1001 Fifth Avenue, New York

. . . is the contextual pathetic fallacy.

Marianne Barcellona

most of this century. Architects, generally, ignored it, intent on the modernist revolution and doing their own thing. In principle, the modernists rejected all revivals, or copies, of older styles. Compatibility, when considered, was to be achieved only through pure modernist design, the relationships restricted to adjustments in scale or selection of material.

Sometimes this was done very well—the Italians, in particular, treated the new structure as a complementary contrast to the old, rather than as a copy of it, in terms of sophisticated oppositions, such as glass against marble, carried out with great dramatic and aesthetic skill. But the Italian sensibility is not universal and too often the results have been jarring juxtapositions. Today, with all the modernist rules being broken in a counterrevolution reputed to be "beyond modernism," the past has become respectable and usable again. A kind of historical eclecticism, or pastiche modernism, is presently in vogue.

Ulrich Franzen didn't go the easy way with 800 Fifth. His first revised design was full of references to the surroundings so abstract that only the architect could know for sure. The building came out as something far jazzier than Philip Birnbaum's simple pragmatism—an approach, incidentally, that is far from being without its own virtues.

The next version was pure Architectural Pathetic Fallacy. It could also be said that the completed building was negotiated to death by the city and the community. The result is a pitiful compendium of watered-down mannerisms that are supposed to maintain the integrity of the avenue and relate to adjacent buildings, but speak more clearly of the inflation of costs and impoverishment of crafts in our own time. (See the Hotel Pierre's urn-topped carved balustrades, and the "balustrade" of holes in the stone with metal rods that are supposed to recall it at 800 Fifth, or the all-cut-stone facade versus weak stone trim at the corners.) If there is any achievement here, it is the dubious one of making the bland grotesque.

The "honest" gesture of leaving the false front clearly visible for what it is simply misfires; it is appalling from the side approaches and would have been considerably better if it had been "honestly" faked. If the neighboring Knickerbocker Club, whose cornice height set the measure of the new building's base, should not survive, anyone would be left wondering what this ambiguous mediocrity was all about. Thus are fallacies compounded.

Johnson, on the other hand, jumped into historical recall

with both feet. Taking his cue from the McKim, Mead and White apartment house on the south, he trimmed his tower with a series of "classical" moldings (which do not relate to the house on the north) in delighted defiance of "modernism," and topped it with a slanted roof that is mansard in front and bare behind. But the dark gray bay windows and their connecting metal spandrels form strong vertical elements that totally negate these horizontal strips. And the "honest," or tongue-in-cheek, gesture of stopping the moldings short of the sides of the building may be amusing for those in the know, but their use just seems unresolved. It does not help that the moldings look like sliced-off Tootsie Rolls.

The entrance, however, has the elegant Johnson touch. Designed originally as a Sullivanesque arch—a feature that was abandoned—it has turned out to be the least "reminiscent" feature and the best part of the building. Simple rectangles of intersecting stone and void suggest solidity and openness at once, a currently popular kind of ambiguity that is richly resolved in a much more "modern" treatment than anything else in the building, whatever the source. Actually, it looks as if Johnson were really designing.

For contrast, farther up Fifth Avenue at Eighty-sixth Street, there is a glass-fronted apartment house built considerably more than a decade ago. No masterpiece, it would probably make Mies blanch, but it has worn extremely well. A facade of double planes of transparent windows and balconies, neatly detailed, continues to please. Moreover, it is nicely compatible with the landmark Carrère and Hastings house at the corner. The lesson is that it "recalls" nothing. There are no sight gags from Banister Fletcher; no instant entrapment in the decline and fall of traditional forms. The building speaks quietly of contemporaneity, continuity, the virtues of a restrained and refined resolution, and the cultural context of which architecture is a prime indicator. The modernists may have been on the right track after all, even with their hands tied behind their backs.

February 11, 1979

PLACES AND
PLEASURES

GARDENS OF DELIGHT

The delights were endless in the Cooper-Hewitt Museum exhibition called "Gardens of Delight." That is not surprising, since every artful interpretation of the natural world was considered eligible for display from the Garden of Eden on, and nature has been a source for artists and artisans of talent and sensibility throughout history. Architects have dealt as thoughtfully with landscapes as with bricks and mortar. You might say that the subject is as big as all outdoors.

This preoccupation with natural beauty, from its simple replication to the most exotic translations, alternating between romantic "naturalism" and an intellectually imposed classical order, has left us with some of the loveliest objects in the history of art and design. The Cooper-Hewitt, the Smithsonian Institution's National Museum of Design, seems to possess a remarkable number of choice examples. What it does not have was supplemented for this show by the generosity of other museums and institutions, which have filled the gaps with such things as a superb millefleurs tapestry of a garden with musicians and flowers that hangs in the wood-paneled main hall, and a Japanese Rimpa screen of breathtaking blue morning glories on a dazzling gold ground, in a second-floor gallery, on loan from the Metropolitan Museum.

Edouard Dupérac

Engraving of the Villa d'Este

Gardens as grand, opulent fantasies of splendor and extravagant delight

Cooper-Hewitt Museum/Smithsonian Institution

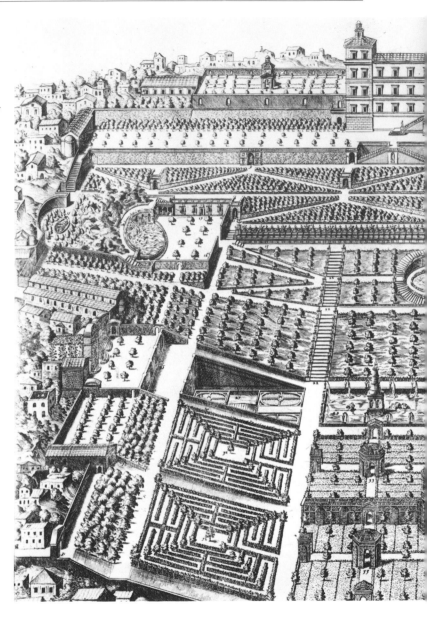

The omnibus subject allowed some understandable license and self-indulgence among those expert staff members who selected and installed the exhibition, and who must have been dizzy with a surfeit of temptations; delight was clearly the

252

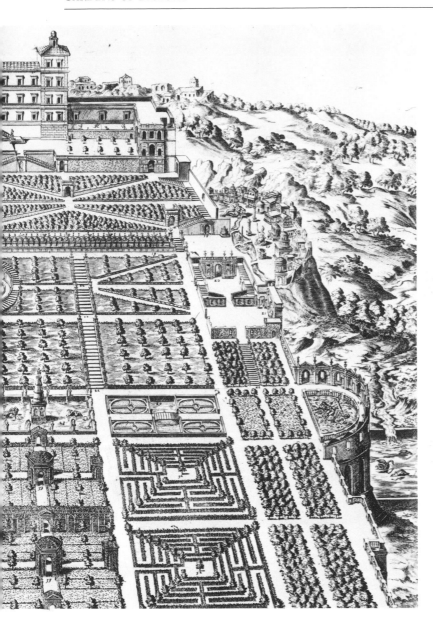

universal and unwavering theme. What better escape from
New York's blistering summer streets than the conservatory
with its gentle splash of water from a borrowed cast-iron fountain that had clearly found its home and ought to stay, sur-

rounded by a generous tangle of flowering plants, courtesy of the Horticultural Society of New York and the Office of Horticulture of the Smithsonian Institution. In galleries on either side of the conservatory, filling the rooms of the second floor, were nearly two hundred architectural drawings and at least three hundred objects in glass, ceramic, silver and other metals, textiles, laces, wallpaper, and jewelry. There were things so delicate and fragile that you held your breath just looking at them, and the kind of enormous exposition pieces that bowled over the Victorians with drop-dead aesthetic bombast.

Because this was a sampling, there were few intellectual demands. There is no reason why summer pleasures should not be easy. If it seems like an indulgence just to enjoy the objects for their own sake, that, after all, is what they were originally intended for—the direct sensory pleasures that creative and beautiful embellishment afford. I, for one, can take Fabergé or leave it alone, but there is an airy Fabergé dandelion puffball, which looks ready to be blown away, that must be the ultimate insouciant jeweled gesture. A complete set of early-nineteenth-century wallpaper panels by Zaber et Cie, still brilliant as a June day, create a summer world of their own. An Art Nouveau *étagère* by Gallé with a cow-and-parsley motif proves that all is art in the hands of the artist. In the clothing section, picture a cabbage leaf hat, slightly wilted by time.

These disparate delights were organized in two parts: gardens and flowers. Obviously, such categories were scarcely confining. "Gardens" included both real and imaginary gardens, empty and peopled, as formal designs or as settings for such appropriate activities as fireworks and amorous dalliance. They ranged from Rigaud's engravings of the elaborate parterres at Versailles to photographs of Gertrude Jekyll's consummate English gardens for Lutyens houses in this century. There were follies and fountains, grottos and gates, and all of the bucolic furnishings that artists and architects have devised.

The section on "Flowers" showed the transformation of natural and botanical motifs into decorative objects and patterns, from a turquoise-glazed Egyptian plate of a stylized lotus garden to an eighteenth-century, floral-embroidered French waistcoat. This is where the Cooper-Hewitt collections shine.

And this was where Dorothy Globus's installation also shone; her delight in juxtaposition was clearly evident. A tin wedding bouquet and a precious brooch of jeweled flowers sat side by side; a translucent, latticed Belleek china tureen with roses and thistles shared surprising references with embroidered laces; the soft glistening poppies of an Art Nouveau vase were echoed in a floral fabric; a room devoted completely to irises and tulips revealed a galaxy of styles. What seemed arbitrary was really a special sense of visual affinities that illuminated the objects on display.

There was also more explicit information for those who wanted it, covering much of the history of garden design and the arts that have recorded it. A set of six marvelously detailed etchings of the gardens created for Francesco de Medici at Pratolino, near Florence, were made by Stefano Della Bella in the seventeenth century. These gardens, designed by the well-named Bernardo Buontalenti, were an artistic and mechanical marvel. They are filled with surprises, including aquatic "jokes," a grotto with mechanical figures, and a dining platform in a huge gnarled oak, reached by a rustic spiral stair. There is a view of Giovanni Bologna's colossal garden sculpture of a giant personifying the Apennine Mountains—one of the few things that survives—crushing a monster from whose mouth water gushes into a pool.

Such gardens were grand, opulent, mysterious, and extravagant fantasies that stagger our smaller imaginations and resources today. The grotto was one of the genre's triumphs; artificial caves and artful rocks, ferns, shells and fish, cooling streams, fountains and water basins, miraculously united with the whole range of classical mythology in sculptured allegory. The aviaries, pergolas, waterworks, and topiary of the formal garden persisted through the centuries. It became a matter of personal choice whether garden architecture should be in the form of Greek temples, Gothic ruins, Chinese pagodas, or "primitive" huts. In England, Capability Brown (called Capability because he always found "capabilities for improvement" in his clients' estates) and Humphrey Repton popularized the new informal landscape—a kind of romantic naturalism achieved at enormous effort.

Elaine Evans Dee, curator of prints and drawings at the Cooper-Hewitt, has pointed out that gardens are fragile and transitory, victims of seasons, weather, and time. Art preserves them for us in paintings, drawings, prints, and photographs. The decorative arts transform their evanescent elements into lasting enrichment for our lives. And the pleasure of these objects is based on evocation and memory as well as the skilled interpretation of natural forms.

Francis Bacon wrote in "Of Gardens" that the flowering landscape "is the purest of human pleasures." Gardens offer repose, the tranquil refreshment of indolence and beauty, and the benign indulgence of the senses. There is very little of any of this in modern life. Today pleasure is defined as a function of activity rather than of thought; the senses are pushed to extremes; passivity is considered a form of defeat. But the secret gardens that once nourished eye and heart can still be recaptured in the arts that recorded them.

July 19, 1981

GETTING
AWAY FROM IT ALL

PALACES FOR THE PEOPLE

I n 1977 an exhibition of resort and vacation architecture at the Cooper-Hewitt Museum called "Palaces for the People" offered a summary of one hundred years of America seriously at play. The photographs, drawings, models, postcards, and "artifacts" (actual table settings, menus, and matchbooks from a galaxy of celebrated and obscure hotels and motels) packed into the small downstairs gallery provided some instant, vicarious resort-hopping. The material, drawn from the collections of such long-term aficionados of the genre as Jeff Limerick and John Margolies (who may be seen around town, when he is not at a motel, sporting his Madonna Inn T-shirt) and from the Library of Congress and National Archives, and the hostelries themselves, was all pulled together in a provocative rewriting of American architectural history by Richard Oliver, curator of architecture and design at the Cooper-Hewitt.

The show could be enjoyed on one fast, easy level as high camp, or it could be considered more carefully (and correctly) as a perceptive documentation of a coherent and continuous architectural phenomenon that expresses much of the American character and taste, as well as changing social rituals and standards. But on any level the material was nostalgic, enlightening, and fun.

Historically, these buildings were on the cutting edge of both fantasy and technology—the first to offer elevators, modern plumbing, electricity and steam heat, at the same time that they were designed as calculated stage sets far removed from the ordinary world. The rituals of flirtation, promenade, social gamesmanship, and ceremonial dining were carried out against an elaborate and exotic backdrop. Today, the season stay of the Victorian belle with forty trunks and a retinue of servants has given way to the overnight motel stop with a car pole of leisure suits. But the most ambitious designs have always invited the vacationer to enjoy an atmosphere where reason and restraint were dispensed with in favor of illusion.

There is, for example, the splendor of the 1888 Hotel del Coronado at San Diego by architects James M. and Merritt Reid, which offered every luxury and diversion, including a vaulted domed ballroom (since remodeled with a dropped ceiling for air-conditioning-by-the-sea) and the earliest hotel electric lighting. At first, there were daily balloon ascents; later there were movie stars. The Greenbriar at White Sulphur Springs, a twentieth-century rebuilding of a nineteenth-century spa devoted to Hygeia and favored by tycoons who came in their own railroad cars, specializes today in a rich refinement rather than theatrical flamboyance. Still, it could seat 1,200 for a gold-plated banquet in its heyday and even now it maintains vermeil dinner services for special events. The now-classic Miami Beach hotels of Morris Lapidus in the 1950's—the Fountainebleau, the Eden Roc, the Americana—the apogee of the gaudily ordinary known as "the architecture of gorgeous" are the dream world of the innocent to whom enough dross is as good as gold. They have also become a kind of aesthetic funk chic for the cognoscenti who dote on architectural malapropism. Equally in favor is the punk Pop of the standard motel. In every case the senses surrender.

Although the myths and anecdotes about these buildings have been well recorded as a kind of social history, their design history is only beginning to be written. Architectural revisionism informs us that this is an important and indigenous art and

building form overlooked by the official chroniclers of taste and style. Exuberant spaces and materials, temporal high fashion, and careful image-making are all meant to please and impress. And the evidence of success is overwhelming.

More than any other kind of construction, resort architecture has been directly responsive to geography and culture. The exhibition reflected this in its three sections devoted to the buildings of the seashore, the wilderness, and the highway. The nineteenth-century worship of nature and the "sublime" landscape was fed by the "scenic wonders" of the new United States—the mountains, lakes, virgin wilderness, and ocean coasts. Postcards are a wonderful inventory of those features: a storm in the Grand Canyon, cacti blooming in the desert, light breaking through the redwoods, sunset on Lake Champlain and in the Everglades, moonlight on Bar Harbor. These magnificent views and spectacular settings determined the lo-

James W. and Merritt Reid

Hotel del Coronado, San Diego, 1888

Luxurious resorts at the cutting edge of fantasy and technology

Cooper-Hewitt Museum/Smithsonian Institution

cation of the hotels. The destination was always fixed. The grandeur and beauty of the accommodations were what counted. Verandas were measured by the mile. Immense "log" beams, rustic furniture, and giant boulder fireplaces set the style of the great National Park Service hotels at Glacier, Yosemite, and Yellowstone. Palatial European references fed the aspirations of Addison Mizner's Palm Beach, where Leonard Schultze's regal Breakers hotel opened in the 1920's. (To point out that many of the best examples, like the Grand Union at Saratoga Springs, are gone, and that others are struggling for survival, is to state the pathetically obvious.)

The big change, of course, came with the automobile, which brought about a twentieth-century resort revolution. It inaugurated the vacation sport of "motoring" and the era of the motel, and the practice of seeing as much as possible en route instead of contemplating a single mountain peak from a porch chair. The postcards began to show views of the roads—the Mohawk Trail, the palm and oleander-lined U.S. Highway 80, the Transcontinental Highway between Colorado and Arizona. But the natural landscape along them was increasingly urbanized and developed. The unprecedented job for the motel builder was to create a sense of place where there was no character or identity at all.

Thus the Madonna Inn at San Luis Obispo—with its one hundred nine incredible "theme" rooms of boulders and round beds and hot pinks and reds, called "Cuernavaca," "Pioneer America" and "Hearts and Flowers," places and images that exist only in the fertile minds of the owners. And the Mount Vernon motels and "Colonial villages" that appear in Daytona Beach, and tepee motels in Cheyenne, Wyoming, and Orlando, Florida. Fantasy transplants its symbols or starts from scratch. Fantasy and escape are still what resort architecture is made of. The tradition is clearly alive in imaginative architectural schemes by Charles Moore, James Righter, Roger Seifter, Robert Stern and Venturi and Rauch. But their calculated art pales beside spontaneous instinct and invention. The unreal thing is a hard act to follow.

July 17, 1977

NO PLACE LIKE HOME

I find that I have to remind myself that New York is the center of the universe after several weeks in a New England town. It is not just that one is seduced by the insidious idea that small is beautiful, or that one builds up a false ideal of small-town virtues that may be largely in the mind, or that one confuses the reality of work with the unreality of vacation—it is that the living is easy. That means that compared to life in New York every minute of the day isn't a hassle. Compared to life in New York, every encounter isn't a joust with survival.

The weather has something to do with it, of course; summer is the time when one sheds one's tensions with one's clothes, and the right kind of day is jeweled balm for the battered spirit. A few of those days and you can become drunk with the belief that all's right with the world.

But the one thing that stands out, and that I do not really understand, is why the house where we spend those weeks is so much more comfortable than the apartment in New York. It is a rented house, to which we have returned for many years, so while we have done some rearranging and added a few personal touches, we had nothing to do with the design and furnishing in the first place. That it seems to work so much better is surprising, because we have devoted a fair amount of time to how our New York place looks and functions. We have selected the furnishings with care and planned layout and storage meticulously.

It is understandable, of course, that we are happier in a house where we can (and do) get up with the first colors of the sunrise and watch the gulls commute morning and evening over a harbor that turns from blue to pearl or steel with the changing weather. Or where one starts the day with a tour of the garden to see which flowers have bloomed or faded overnight.

But chiefly, it is not a house one worries about. It is an easy house that rewards affection and any kind of care. It is full of old things, and comfortable things, and shabby things—objects that have been used and loved or just discarded gently. Some

Cottage by the sea

Where the living and the style are easy, with lessons for "architecture"

Garth Huxtable

of these things are useful and some are not. (Still, I could not spare the framed membership certificate in the Warren G. Harding Memorial Association or the Grover Cleveland plate.) There is wicker, but it is not the kind of wicker that has surfaced fashionably and expensively; it is the kind with irretrievable dust in the crevasses. There are no loveseats or *étagères,* but a collection of old rockers—even one that kicks you when you come downstairs in the dark.

An assortment of tables has no relationship to known styles, periods, or purposes, but there is always one where you need it. The bric-a-brac ranges from Bennington and art glass to vintage Woolworth and early Sunsweet, and it includes whatever you could possibly want at the moment you want it. Beds are high and old-fashioned and easy to make. The flagpole has a view of the ocean and so does the laundry line. There is fresh mint for cutting outside the kitchen door, and friends supply parsley and basil.

The house is full of surprises, even after years of intimate association. This year I found a Thebes stool. I had not noticed it before because it has always been covered with Caruso records or old magazines. It was such a handy place to toss an afghan or sweater, in one of those convenient dark corners that new houses totally lack. The only reason that I know it is a Thebes stool now, or know what a Thebes stool is, must be credited to the Tutankhamen exhibition and an old issue of a British journal, *The Architectural Review*. It seems that a stool called the Thebes stool was in Tutankhamen's tomb and was copied endlessly in the 1920's, at the time the great archeological discovery caused fashion waves in clothing and homes.

The Liberty stool, by Liberty of London, was probably one of the best copies of the type. I am not sure, but there may have been other nineteenth-century versions, dating from those British arts-and-crafts episodes of earnest intellectual nostalgia. The process of reproduction and knockoff is going on again today with the latest Tutankhamen vogue. Our house version was clearly a 1920's product, and after "restoration" with soap and water and scouring powder and the addition of a velvet cushion, it came out of the corner. This was the home furnishings event of the summer.

Every year brings similar projects. In summer houses, the caned seats of chairs constantly break through, and an entire instant decorating scheme can be set in motion by a search for cushions to camouflage them. One table (known as "the gaming table" because of its permanent shaker of alphabet cubes, for tossing on rainy days) listed relentlessly to port; it was a summer's job to break it apart and reglue it at right angles. Considering its dubious provenance, this was clearly a labor of love. Chairs are "upholstered" on impulse with mill ends and pins. Everything is relaxed, undemanding, and inviting. There is nothing new or showy or fashionable. The effect is as far from the British idea of tatty-chintz country-house status as it is from the trendy vacation homes featured in the fancy shelter magazines. I would say that the house has a certain kind of class.

The town has class, too. One of the loveliest sailing harbors in the world is surrounded by a pre-Revolutionary settlement that did much of its building by about 1820. The narrow Massachusetts streets are a casual treasury of Federal and Greek Revival, cheek-by-jowl clapboard houses on rising hills with gardens tucked between. It is all topped by a redbrick Ruskinian Gothic, Victorian Town Hall, which houses that archetypal American painting "The Spirit of '76."

Old Town, as the original section is called, has had its share of buffeting by groupies, and geometrically increasing numbers of cars have made streets all but impassable and unparkable. The buildings are increasingly filled with boutiques. But the place withstands the invasion of twentieth-century lifestyles surprisingly well, and it has also resisted both Williamsburg and Disneyland influences. The blows of change are softened by installing traffic islands, where needed, of solid masses of petunias. Priorities are, properly, the availability of the first corn and the state of the tides, and important events tend to be ice cream socials at the local historical mansion.

If there is anything here of the kind that makes New York go round—and there is a certain infiltration of the super chic, supercostly, overreaching for status—I have managed to steer clear of it. This is a home and lifestyle forever away from stainless steel and black glove leather. I have managed, in fact, to restore heart and soul here for another year's go at the great metropolis. There are country tomatoes and parsley in the city refrigerator. I cannot see the morning sky or the gulls skimming through the open porch (old houses have porches, with and without screens) and the hassle is on from the moment I arise. I think of that house as the single most beautiful thing that I know.

September 29, 1977

AVENUE ALLURE:
MADISON AND WORTH

S hopping centers are a lot like junk food; no matter how opulent the merchandise or spectacular the setting, they are basically the same, blandly familiar and ultimately boring, lacking in any real flavor. Their malls and atriums photograph dramatically, if predictably, and their shops seem to promise exciting goods and experiences. But it all turns out to be more of the same standardized formula, which is why the atriums get higher and the trees and fountains get bigger and the visual impact becomes more striking, to lure the shopping junkies from the old malls to the new ones, where similar stores and merchandise provide the same eventual ennui.

What is missing in this vacuum-packed consumer environment is a little thing called urbanity—the surprises and rewards of the special, the unexpected, the unique and the offbeat, rather than the sterile stereotype; the instructive and entertaining mixture that only a sophisticated culture can offer; the genuine context, the eternally intriguing and self-renewing aspects of a real place.

Give me the magnificent mélange of New York's Madison Avenue every time, and you may have all your Chestnut and Cherry Hills and their successful facsimiles to suburban in-

Opposite page:
Madison Avenue,
New York

A natural mix of
intriguing variety
and appealing scale

Jack Manning/*New*
York Times

finity. And for a change of pace, for sheer escape and nirvana, I will take Palm Beach's Worth Avenue—for a few days, at least—but I will take Madison Avenue for a lifetime.

In fact, I have spent a good deal of my lifetime on or near Madison Avenue, discovering whole different sets of pleasure from childhood to middle age. Unlike even the best of the shopping centers, Madison Avenue never palls. In the roughly fifty blocks stretching from the Forties to the Nineties, its richness is extraordinarily worldly and complex, and its extremes, from humbly utilitarian to grand luxe, make for a variety that never stales. If the prices get more outrageous daily, making me feel like the poor little match girl looking in windows, I still like to know that world of outrageously beautiful things—as opposed to the merely outrageous, which are also well represented—still exists.

I grew up with an awareness of Madison Avenue as a special place, riding the streetcar to Sunday school, enchanted by the view through the windows of second-story shops of shabby gentility or understated elegance (little dressmakers, domestic employment agencies, purveyors of fine linens, repairers of antiques) above the sedately stylish stores that lined the street at ground level. Even more intriguing and memorable were the distinctive details—which I never thought of as having anything to do with architecture until much later—of those upper floors of four- and five-store brownstones, town houses, and early apartment buildings that passed before my eyes. I would look for an oriel or bay window, a bit of tiled roof, some carved Gothic trim, a plant-filled conservatory with curved glass windows at the top of a corner flight of stairs, a snatch of applied half-timber, a dash of Deco, scattered through the constant rhythm of nineteenth-century stone lintels, sills, and cornices. These are the things that created the visual touchstones anchoring me to the avenue to this day. Their survival is no small miracle in an area of fashionable real estate and merchandising.

I enjoy Worth Avenue in Palm Beach in a very different way; I value those four elegant blocks bounded by the ocean and Lake Worth for their complete and masterly artifice and single-minded luxury. For the first twenty-four hours, still full

266

of urban angst, I am turned off by its expensive, elaborate hothouse artificiality, and then, losing touch with the real world, I am totally seduced by its balmy champagne splendor. Window after window contains feathered and sequined chiffon gowns to be worn to the next gala, and the dominant color is pink. I will never have any occasion to buy these or the trinkets to wear with them from Cartier or Van Cleef and Arpels.

What counts for me is that these indulgences are offered in an unparalleled architectural stage set. Because Worth Avenue, like the later shopping centers, was created out of whole cloth, or in this case, Florida mud, in the 1920's by an architect of dramatic inventiveness and a sure sense of theater, Addison Mizner, who knew a few salient things about pleasure and environmental design that modern shopping entrepreneurs have not learned yet. What I find most rewarding are the surprising similarities with Madison Avenue that yield timeless lessons of scale, use, and character.

The difference between the two is, of course, one of design and accident; in New York these features came about naturally and incrementally; in Palm Beach they were artfully and artificially devised. Both have an unbroken pedestrian promenade of intimate scale and rich detail, in which small things keep happening of changing architectural interest, from the charming to the eccentric, and small shops that succeed one another within just a few steps, and for just enough time, for one to savor a continual parade of temptations and visual delights.

On Madison Avenue this happened because city brownstones had twenty-foot fronts, and when they were converted to stores at street level, the same small scale was kept. This led to a mixture of commercial and residential uses. It was an ad hoc process that made every block unique and every part of every block different. Succeeding waves of stylish storefront conversions were contained within the architectural context that established and maintained the street's character. The results are beyond the efforts of even the most skilled planners, accustomed to working in terms of a "well-designed" and unified total shopping concept, or the multiblock scale of the urban environment.

They were beyond any architect, that is, except Addison

Opposite page:
Addison Mizner

Via Mizner, from
Worth Avenue,
Palm Beach

The artful creation
of stylish intimacy

New York Times

Mizner, whose designs were based more on the dreams and desires of the very rich, and those who aspired to be very rich, than on any principles of formal architectural teaching. Palm Beach and Boca Raton, developed during and just after World War I, were virtually his creations. They were a fanciful compendium of pastel picturesque references to Spanish, Creole, Florentine, and other "appropriate" semitropical and classical architecture, relying more on romantic details and evocative trim than on textbook correctness.

Worth Avenue is a superb act of theater and urban design, virtually unchanged after fifty years. A cloistered arcade of shops is broken only by pedestrian walkways called vias, which lead beyond the avenue through picturesque passages and fountain-dotted patios to the next street, or back to the avenue again. The vias have shops upstairs and down, reached by steps and bridges that also lead to apartments and unexpected balconies and towers. Pedestrian, commercial, and residential uses make a lively mix. Mizner described Worth Avenue and the vias in terms of the narrow streets of Granada, but he created a very personal imagery. He described its elements himself: "Light stucco walls in pastel tints, topped with tile roofs and weathered cypress woodwork, and the inevitable coconut tree with its decorative tufted shape and play of light and shade."

Madison Avenue is short on trees, palm or other, but it also has touches of Granada, as well as bits of Merrie England, proper Georgian and Beaux Arts, the Brown Decades, and just plain postwar speculator brick. Except where office buildings have taken over in the Fifties, or large apartment houses have disrupted the blocks above, small intimate and eccentric buildings remain that refute the city's overpowering scale and impersonality. Above all, there is the intriguing change of architectural detail that Mizner understood so well and worked so hard to invent. An important part of Madison Avenue's appeal is its constant and continuing storefront conversions; the shifting, trendy elegance of its merchandising design provides much of the street's stylish vitality. The latest image is the hard-edged chic of the current invasion of pricey European boutiques. But it is the existing architectural context within which this all takes place that really counts on Madison Avenue, that makes its modishness a form of continual renewal rather than something episodic or destructive.

A zoning amendment that requires shops on the street floor of any new construction does not address the problem of how to keep what is above them. It has taken less than a lifetime for Madison Avenue to reach a dangerous tipping point where its successfully delicate environmental and aesthetic balance is threatened. What was an ongoing gentle shift of shops and services within a familiar urbane and humane framework has become a real estate push of gargantuan new buildings in the Fifties, made possible, and inevitable, by the city's overzoning. The Upper East Side Historic District was established in 1981 (after this column was originally written in 1980) to protect the architectural character and scale of the Madison Avenue blocks in the Sixties and Seventies, but there has also been a mass influx of expensive designer boutiques that are the standardized product of designer companies, the same in every city. Since New York continues to make noises about "restudying" the landmarks law and procedures, to the background music of developer discontents, how long Madison Avenue, or any other landmark building or area, is safe, is a matter of political conjecture.

Enough is still left of the native, the offbeat, the exceptional, and the unique, in a special architectural setting, to retain a great deal of the avenue's sunny intimacy, exceptional quality, and cosmopolitan character. Those boutiques and bakeries, drugstores and chocolatiers, restaurants and coffee shops, fine food and wine stores and omnipresent Gristede's, the antique shops and art galleries, delis and designers, all mixed up with the funny and familiar facades that are still within reach of the eye, tell you exactly where you are, better than any street signs. That is what makes this Madison Avenue rather than Third Avenue, where the shops merely trim an anonymous and characterless brick street facade. Madison is one of the great international shopping streets and one of the urban delights of the world. But only because it is vintage New York.

March 13, 1980
updated October 1985

ARCHITECTURAL
DRAWINGS

The interest in architecture on the popular high-art cir-
cuit is relatively new. Architecture is being perceived
and promoted as an art form equal to and intricately
connected with painting and sculpture. It shares with those arts
much of the troubled philosophy and arcane aesthetic of recent
times and represents a creative force with implications deeper
than the obvious aspects of the built environment. Its artifacts
—drawings and models—are being viewed as collectible
items, which buildings are not, except for a handful of corporate Medici. In addition, architectural drawings are proving to
be highly marketable, a development that dealers and some
architects have lost no time in exploiting.

After the impressive exhibition prepared by David Gebhard
and Deborah Nevins of "Two Hundred Years of American
Architectural Drawing" held at the Cooper-Hewitt Museum in
1977, it was hard to understand why the subject had always
had a kind of second-class status. By any definition, this was a
major show, and it was also a superb one, both as a record of
the American building genius and as a moving experience
of a consistently subtle and exquisite art. Many of the drawings shown were breathtaking in their technical mastery and

expressive skills, and their beauty was further enriched by their revelation of conceptual ideals. In such drawings one sees architecture as it comes straight from the mind and the eye and the heart, before the spoilers get to it.

In fact, one thing that architectural drawings make abundantly clear is that the architect worthy of the name is an artist first of all—a creative sensibility involved in the making of art, however wisely or unwisely that art is used and whatever expedient or structural corruptions take place in the practice of it. These drawings present the act of architecture in its most pure form, and on this level they can be enjoyed for their own sake. But the viewer adds to that sensuous pleasure the intellectual pleasure of the rational and aesthetic processes that go into a built work, which must answer to the highest and most complex considerations of sculptural form and painterly light as well as to sociological and symbolic need. Architecture can then be seen as the most real and abstract, the most visionary and pragmatic, the most vulnerable and absolute, and the most totally involving art the world has ever known.

It is also a very vulnerable art; buildings are demolished and documents decay. With a few notable exceptions, architectural archives are uncatalogued and deteriorating, for lack of money and care. They are apt to languish in unlikely places if they have not been lost or destroyed. There were some surprising discoveries in the Cooper-Hewitt exhibition, such as the fine Bulfinch drawing of the Worcester County Courthouse found in the Worcester County Engineering Department. Only in recent years has there been a concerted effort to survey and record material by the Committee for the Preservation of Architectural Resources; the index has now been taken over by the Library of Congress. The new Building Museum in Washington, D.C., has opened with an exhibition of superb drawings from various federal archives but no word as to the cataloguing, collecting, or preservation of these undervalued and often threatened documents.

The Cooper-Hewitt display was followed almost immediately by a show at the Drawing Center; together, they covered a full range of American architectural history. At the Cooper-Hewitt one could see Asher Benjamin's do-it-yourself vernacu-

Eliel Saarinen

Drawing of Cranbrook Academy

Architecture that comes straight from the artist's hand, mind and eye

Cooper-Hewitt Museum/Smithsonian Institution

lar Georgian of the early Republic and compare it with the slightly later, more worldly classicism of William Strickland and Benjamin Latrobe. The High Victorian exuberance of H. H. Richardson and Frank Furness was followed by a curiously mixed bag of academic and modernist work from the twentieth century. The one characteristic that seemed to unite everything, no matter how bold a building might be in actual execution, was a consistent delicacy of perception and drawing style.

Louis Sullivan's tiny thumbnail sketches from Columbia University's Avery Library Collection, the famous ornament miniaturized and feathery, convey the full power and details of the finished product. The Greek Revival designs of James Dakin and A. J. Davis of the early nineteenth century share the same kind of serene pastel washes and precise shadows with the later Gothic Revival churches and Tuscan villas by Richard Upjohn. Marion Mahony Griffin's bird's-eye view of 1912, done in gouache on silk, transforms housing into an elegant

Japanese landscape. Bertram Goodhue's view of a craggy rise topped by a 1915 mansion suggests Wuthering Heights more than Westchester. Eliel Saarinen's pencil rendering of Cranbrook Academy in 1926 still stands as an ethereal miracle of line and tone.

This same delicate sensibility characterizes some of the most advanced of today's practice. It appears in the lyrical, Necco-wafer colored abstractions of John Hejduk, the artfully Mannerist collages of Michael Graves, and the sophisticated pastels of Richard Meier. Lauretta Vinciarelli's subtle assemblies of innocent elements have their roots in Renaissance order and 1920's formalism. Coy Howard's use of graphite on tracing paper recalls Hugh Ferriss's charcoal-shadowed studies just after World War I, but Howard's updated drama owes a lot to Cubism and Art Deco. For a younger generation, these romantic references to the recent past are perfumed by cinema and the elusive aura of a time not actually experienced.

All of these drawings are seductive. They enchant with the lightest touch, the finest ink line or pale thin washes, the most expressively shaded pencil or charcoal (casualties of Magic Markers), the most subtle tones and textures. Even the boldest skyscraper is suggested by gentle nuances. That legendary vehicle and generator of architectural genius, the drawing on the back of an envelope, continues to exert fascination. Charles Moore's "napkin" drawings are literally that, done in airport cocktail lounges while waiting for planes. Like Sullivan's miniatures, James Coote's first shorthand notations show the same thoughtful relationship of house and nature as in later detailed representations.

Under the hypnotic spell of Aldo Rossi, a whole school of drawing has appeared with overtones of Ledoux and Boullée and undertones of Marxism and nihilism; the style is Mussolini-modern suffused with the anomie of De Chirico's surreal settings. This is work that has a certain dangerous beauty. Eclecticism, Mannerism, nostalgic historicism, Pop sensibility are all being tried on for size by today's architects; too often, these pastiches of the past demonstrate a shaky passage through history. They can elicit anything from exasperation to awe. But in every one of these galleries you will find at least one drawing that enchants you, one that will haunt you, one that suggests a new world to you, and one that you will want to take away.

There is evidence that Mies was speaking for the whole profession when he said that God was in the details. But the details are often lost on the way to the finished product. The history of architecture, therefore, splits into two realities: the drawing, which contains the architectural intent; and the completed construction, which may be a markedly different thing. The drawing not only illuminates the process of design, it is also a skillful representation of what the architect wishes to convey of the spirit and appearance of his building—the information delivered by the traditional perspective rendering. The influence of drawings on the art and practice of architecture— from Andrea Palladio to Hugh Ferriss, from the seventeenth to the twentieth century—has been enormous and underrated.

The move from the architect's studio to the commercial gallery has created a new audience for the architectural drawing as an art object, rather than as an interpretive tool of a complex creative act. But today's architectural drawing attempts to do much more. It is freighted with meanings, metaphors, states of consciousness, and commentary on the conditions of our culture. This more profound and visionary aspect of the architectural sensibility has achieved a particular status in intellectual circles. A show of the work of Raimund Abraham, Emilio Ambasz, Richard Meier, Walter Pichler, Aldo Rossi, James Stirling, and Venturi and Rauch, held at the Castelli Gallery in 1977, emphasized the kind of unconventional thought and practice that stretches the definition of architecture as we know it now.

None of these architects were new to gallery exhibitions. They represented an international group of star names, and their work had already been seen in small shows at the Museum of Modern Art, the Institute for Architecture and Urban Studies, and at the Cooper-Union Gallery. Some of their completed buildings, such as those by James Stirling in England and Germany and Richard Meier in the United States and abroad, have been among the most closely watched by the profession; often they are as controversial as they are influential. Aldo Rossi's haunting scheme for a cemetery in Modena,

Italy, for which construction was begun long after his unforgettable drawings appeared, was already established as a postmodernist icon in the 1970's.

Few viewers will find this art easy, or even accessible in the currently fashionable phrase, although the gallery-going public has been well trained in the acceptance of what it doesn't understand. The architectural "codes" of conceptual sketches, axonometric renderings, and models that are closer to abstract sculpture than to a recognizable environment are understood best by those who are trained to use them, although they are often stunning objects in themselves. The subject matter can range from actual executed structures to the most subjective obscure visions.

Such proposals as Emilio Ambasz's "Housing in an Agricultural Setting" are brilliantly outrageous inventions masquerading as real solutions to pragmatic problems. Others pose totally unreal problems in the most pragmatic terms, like Walter Pichler's endless introverted concentration on the creation of his own primeval house and its timeless adumbrations of space and sculpture and being; this is minimal inner architecture that is part dwelling, part shrine, and part tomb. Much of this work is personal and metaphysical, rather than functional and utili-

Walter Pichler

"Barn"

Drawings that explore the inner environments of the human spirit

Castelli Gallery

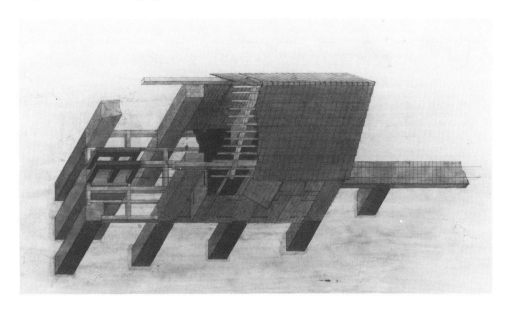

tarian. For the majority of these architects, anything as restrictive as environment, or context, does not exist. They not only create their own images, they also create their own worlds. The common denominator of these drawings is their independent existence as beautiful artifacts.

By comparison, Richard Meier's complex and subtle variations on the early vocabulary of Le Corbusier, and Venturi and Rauch's elegant interpretations and sophisticated ironies based on Pop art and taste, considered far-out by ordinary standards, are models of clarity and logic. But the impression left by most of this work is ambiguous—and deliberately so. Raimund Abraham's designs are as evocative and mysterious as the names of his projects: "House Without Rooms," "Seven Gates to Eden." Rossi's strange and suggestive world can be built, and occasionally is, but it denies familiar human needs. This is *architettura assoluta,* and the imagery touches genius. These concepts fall somewhere between architecture and the other arts, between building and poetry. They test the means and boundaries of architecture, as those boundaries are being tested in painting and sculpture today. With the line between the arts becoming less firm, divisions between painting and sculpture are disappearing and the nature of drawing is being redefined. It should be no surprise that this process involves architecture as well. In fact, some of this work deals in more than unfamiliar architecture; it approaches a new art form. There is much aesthetic crossing-over, hints of borrowed fashionable philosophies, tinges of angst and despair, and echoes of conceptual art; minimalism and earthworks are among its debts and credits. While the cultural establishment continues its tired old cry for more art with architecture, the signals, as usual, are being missed. Art and architecture have never had a closer relationship at any time in history. Occasionally, the two merge and dissolve.

At the same time, the eye and the approach of the architect are uniquely those of the constructor and problem-solver—as they have always been—even when the problems are philosophical and artistic. Within the range from the practical to the visionary, the one common factor is that everything is breaking out of the conventional or "normal" way of seeing and building, to a greater or lesser degree. With its beauty obscurity, and remoteness, what is being produced on paper can be curiously disturbing. What kind of building it may lead to, and how it will serve us, is terribly unclear. The question one cannot avoid is how much of this is obsessive self-indulgence and how much is the opening of new architectural frontiers. It is a mark of our time, of course, that the two are not mutually exclusive.

A more conventional approach to the subject of architectural drawing was taken in 1980 by Elaine Evans Dee, in an exhibition called "Spectacular Spaces: Drawings from the Cooper-Hewitt Collections." The "spectacular spaces" were equally spectacular drawings, at once delicate and bold, painstakingly detailed and enormously evocative. All were studies for buildings, interiors, monuments, festivals, theaters, and imaginary places, executed in precise pen or pencil or lyrical brush and wash. Part of the charm of these drawings is the way in which they provide a record of vision and taste; their elegant virtuosity delights the eye while their stylistic variety engages the imagination. The art of architecture has always been used to set the stage for life and history.

The Cooper-Hewitt collection is conspicuously rich in the baroque extravaganzas of the prolific Bibiena family (in both artists and drawings) and lesser known Italian work of the seventeenth and eighteenth centuries. But the examples selected for display were nothing if not eclectic. From the nineteenth century, innocently grandiose schemes of Montezuma's Palace and Hindu pagodas by Antonio Basoli had a certain Victorian coziness, while an impeccably drawn series of a Gothic-style English country house by an unidentified designer showed every trefoil and pinnacle sharply in place. In a bit of a twist, Hector Guimard, exponent of Art Nouveau in France, shared turn-of-the-century honors with practitioners of the French Beaux Arts style in the United States, Whitney Warren and Ely Jacques Kahn. The common theme of this potpourri was the art of architecture in dedicated and continuous pursuit of its most universal and controlling ideal—the creation of "place."

The impact of such places can be overwhelming. Human

Felice Gianni

Stage design

Multiple layers of Baroque spatial mystery and magic

Scott Hyde/
Cooper-Hewitt
Museum/Smithsonian
Institution

figures, when they appear at all in these drawings, are grace notes, almost invariably underscaled to a staggering array of architectural features. The eighteenth-century Bibiena stage sets convey the very essence of the baroque—a style in which the Renaissance reconstruction and reinterpretation of Roman components is used to define, not just classical orders, but the shifting and overlapping movements of multiple-focus space in what may be the most sophisticated and dramatic manipulation of enclosure ever devised. Batteries of arcades and pilasters and fanfares of stairs lead the eye up to balconies and down vaulted corridors whose columns and balustrades engage in games with solidity and transparency in a fugue of rich and elaborate forms.

Beautifully executed in black ink and subtle washes of brown, blue, and gray, these are more than the archetypal palaces that they purport to be; they are symbols and metaphors for the kind of ennobling magnificence with which man has always tried to clothe his public and ceremonial endeavors. The world of these drawings is wonderfully free of realistic restraints. One feels that beyond the picture frame there is an eighteenth century more tangible and real and complete than any of its surviving monuments, if one could only pass through to the other side.

The concepts of Giuseppe Barberi (1746–1809) are already closer to the austerities of the romantic classicism that produced the overscaled, surreal stylography of Ledoux and Boullée. But what is later pushed to the monumentally macabre by those French architects is full of light and motion in Barberi's sketches; his facile use of pen and brush infuses the massive subjects with a joyful vitality. A courtyard piled high with arches is a paradoxically weightless fantasy, with spiral columns run up by a hand that is almost quicker than the eye. There is nothing static about the regular rhythms of a Grand Palais that rush impatiently to the paper's edge.

All architecture is illusion, in the sense that it creates places and images where none existed before. Drawing is the unique instrument of illusion that serves every phase of the building art from the initial conceptual sketches to presentation drawings for the client and working drawings from which the construction is carried out. It is also the medium in which the architect records his most pure imaginative inventions. The palace doorways of Filippo Juvarra, meltingly lovely in gray and rose washes over chalk, meticulously define the details of entablatures and rusticated walls. At the other extreme, Charles-Louis Clérisseau invents a "ruin fantasy," all tumbled tombs and columns.

Between the immutable monument and the evanescent fancy, and borrowing from both, there is still another category: designs devised solely for the mood and the moment, the temporary architecture of entertainments and celebrations. These are the drawings of *tempietos* and triumphal arches run up for royal weddings and the return of heroes, the artifacts and scenery for festivals and special events. From stage sets to cenotaphs, this is the architecture of illusion at its most extravagant and free. The ultimate achievement of the genre was the royal masque—a participatory theatrical performance developed for the entertainment of the courts of England and France that combined equal parts of allegory and engineering. Inigo Jones created masques for the Queen of England for which splendid drawings survive. Princesses costumed as goddesses descended from the heavens in chariots while mountains heaved and palaces disappeared in clouds of smoke, to music and thunder and lightning. In a rendering by Girolamo Fontana (1690–1714), multiple tiers of palatial stairs rise like a *bombe glacée* from a wildly romantic grotto below; above, billowing cream-puff clouds support a draped allegorical figure. For these early sound and light shows—the first "happenings" —architects were the set designers and the special effects men. The audiovisual, smoke-filled descendants of the masque, the discos of the 1970's, couldn't hold a candle, or a laser, to the royal "cloud machines."

Architectural drawings throughout history have created special worlds in which time stands still while we contemplate their mysteries. If these are illusions, they are the dreams of which reality is made.

June 12, September 25, October 23, 1977
April 27, 1980   updated October 1985

SIDE TRIPS

IMAGE AND IDEOLOGY

H ow does one view a Fascist work of art? Is there such a thing as a Fascist work of art? And why do these questions, and the work itself, seem to hold such a fascination now, three decades after European Fascism was supposedly put to rest and its art dismissed as aberrational and aesthetically worthless? There is a discernible upswing of interest in the art of Nazi Germany and Fascist Italy among many younger historians and architectural practitioners, particularly in what passes for the avant-garde. An exhibition and symposium held at the Columbia University School of Architecture in 1980 addressed the issue of Fascist architecture with the display and discussion of a show of Mussolini-era planning and design called "Armando Brasini: Roma Imperiale." The relationship of art and Fascism was analyzed in a 1974 book by Berthold Hinz, *Art in the Third Reich,* published originally in West Germany and translated and reissued in the United States and Canada. An MIT Press publication on *Art and Architecture in the Service of Politics,* edited by Henry A. Millon and Linda Nochlin, includes excellent essays by Professor Millon and Spiro Kostof on architecture and urbanism under Mussolini.

In the highly influential but largely unbuilt designs of the internationally known Italian architect Aldo Rossi there are disquieting images of the repeated cell block and the endless arcade and a preoccupation with mortuary monumentality. These images are presented as stripped and disembodied abstractions, as "typologies" of universal meaning. The interest is clearly formalist in effect and vocabulary. But the look is chillingly close to the iconography of the public buildings of Nazi Germany and Fascist Italy—so much so that critics like Bruno Zevi deplore the work. This is a vocabulary that carries enough associative horror to dismay an older generation to whom Fascist images are no abstraction. But it intrigues the young, to whom that chapter in history is distant and blurred, with an air of sinister, seductive, and to them, poetic mystery. These evocative forms are appearing in projects of architectural students around the world.

This curious renaissance cannot be put down to simply a morbid fascination with the forces of evil; there is little evidence that it has anything to do with the terror and the tragedy that accompanied totalitarian regimes. That appeal obviously exists, fed by the escalation of violence in art and entertainment today. A good deal of this interest can be attributed to the current emphasis on revisionist history, including a preoccupation with the record of the recent rejected past, which some find too painful and others too repellent to treat with objectivity. The best of such studies are aimed at documentation and analysis; the worst, either through innocence or perverseness, can turn history on its head and black into white. But it is clear that this dark moment in human history will figure prominently in future assessments of the art of the twentieth century.

The Brasini drawings shown at Columbia were from a presentation portfolio prepared by the architect for Mussolini in 1928; they illustrate a master plan, evidently approved by Mussolini, that was to create a new Fascist Imperial Rome. A symposium that accompanied the exhibition was marked by a range of attitudes from the insistence that the scheme was patently evil and should not have been presented without a strong moral judgment (this was voiced by a very small and apparently nonarchitectural minority) to a conspicuous emotional detachment and concentration on its architectural aesthetics. That this was a long forbidden kind of aesthetics—an extravagant, theatrical, no-holds-barred neobaroque of mind-boggling vastness and scale of the sort put down by the modern movement—seemed of far greater interest to the students and some of the professors than the architecture's service to Fascist ideology, or any related values. Surely nothing could have better indicated the change in student attitudes from the involved and anguished 1960's to the disinterested and distant 80's.

Despite its documented provenance as a genuine Fascist artifact, the Brasini *oeuvre* was inconclusive. It is easy to call a scheme Fascist that involves the *aventramenti,* or disemboweling, of old working-class neighborhoods, for the "liberation" of ancient monuments and the creation of huge new monuments, avenues, and squares with the obvious names of Via Imperiale and the Forum Mussolini. But similar clearance concepts appear periodically under different regimes; Haussmann plowed through Paris in the nineteenth century, and bulldozer renewal has been characteristic of our own time. Armando Brasini (1879–1965) just happened to be the right architect in the right place at the right moment, whose vision coincided with the Duce's dream of a new Rome. He was a self-taught architect who had already devoted a good part of his life to the kind of scenographic megalomania eminently suited to the taste of an operatic Italian dictator. This does not mean to make light of totalitarianism or to beg the architect's role or responsibility. But Brasini's Roma Imperiale must be seen within the total context of his work. His product is too personal and eccentric to fit the standard totalitarian image of stillborn, overscaled, and overbearing classicism so consummately exemplified by the work of Albert Speer in Nazi Germany.

Brasini was an incredible performer in any number of styles, from neobaroque to Secession Modern; he could play to any audience. He was also a performer of considerable skill with an instinctive bravura grasp of the complex architectonic relationships of substance and scale, capable of daring high-wire acts of architectural theater. He could produce serious, subtle, and accomplished works, like the 1930 Convent of the Good Shepherd outside Rome or a thoroughly bourgeois, stodgy

Italian Pavilion for the Paris Exposition of 1925; he was prolific with the kind of picturesque stage-set buildings that suggest an Italian Addison Mizner, the architect who invented the
style of Palm Beach. In fact, Brasini began his career designing

stage sets for such epic films as *Quo Vadis?*, which gave him a leg up on fantasy and an immediate imperial style. His nimble scenographic bombast is unconvincing as serious propaganda. But it is hard to forget his phantasmagoric entry in the Palace of the Soviets competition of 1930 or the Ledoux-like fused temple and tower bridge project for the Strait of Messina.

Brasini was branded and buried by the modernists, who treated both his Fascism and his classicism with equal abhorrence. He was almost universally forgotten by 1966, when Robert Venturi cited a Brasini basilica in his now-famous manifesto, "Complexity and Contradiction in Architecture." With the eye of a disenchanted modernist, Venturi delighted in Brasini's exaggerated baroque play with inner and outer space; he found in this work the traditional richness of means and effect proscribed by modernist theory. Time has passed, and attitudes have changed with the breakdown of modernist orthodoxy. Enthusiasm is easy for those without memories of the repression and cruelty of despotic regimes.

As a Fascist architect, Brasini was a maverick and an accident of history. But the questions raised by the architecture of Fascist states still remain. Among the freedoms abrogated was that of artistic expression; modern forms were commonly outlawed as "decadent." This was not just the indulgence of the leadership's reactionary or academic tastes; in the early years of the Soviet revolution, the most radical modernism had been encouraged. The Futurist Marinetti was accepted by the Italian Fascist leadership, and the avant-garde Italian rationalists found favor right up to the aborted plans for the International Exposition of 1942. But it soon became clear to the political hierarchy that only more familiar forms could carry ideological messages to the masses. And if social and ideological homogeneity and fanatic consensus were the objectives, architecture could shape and express the desired response by the way it looked and by the way it manipulated those who used it. Monolithic societies and monolithic buildings served each other.

Albert Speer, for example, understood the uses of scale, sight lines, and drama for more than creating a setting; his plans actually established the sequence of climactic moments of

Opposite page:
Armando Brasini

Design for a bridge over the Straits of Messina

Neo-Baroque of mind-boggling vastness for a twentieth-century Imperial Rome

those public ceremonies that induced frenzied illusions of the invincibility of an all-powerful master race. At the Nuremberg parade grounds, for example, the regimented stone columns and the regimented columns of men together equated obedience and order; served by extraordinary lighting such calculated designs were given an almost divine dimension.

However, it does not follow that anything that resembled Speer's stripped classicism was necessarily fascistic architecture. The very similar romantic classicism of Scandinavia in the 1920's, as seen in the work of Gunnar Asplund, or the similar American "modern" classicism of the 1930's, does not serve or evoke totalitarianism. On the other hand, Giuseppe Terragni's masterpiece of Italian "rationalism"—one of the memorable buildings of the modern movement—was designed as the Casa del Fascio in Como, for the local headquarters of the Fascist party.

In sum, forms in themselves are innocent. But that they can be used to seduce the spirit has been understood by every age of builders. The benign expression of this truth is part of any great structure that moves us through its art. The point is that architecture has this power to an extraordinary degree, and it is an enormous and frightening power. Building is, therefore, one of the most effective and dangerous of totalitarian tools, which is why dictators have always used it so extravagantly. That is the lesson to be learned, and that is the knowledge to be carried in the conscience of the architect.

November 23, 1980

AMERICANS ABROAD

I have a profound mistrust of pictures of impressive construction in distant cities of the world. This stems from a visit to Caracas in the 1950's, and coincides with my first published opinion in the press—a letter to the editor. The letter was inspired by a favorable review of an exhibition of photographs of new architecture in Venezuela; the buildings shown were a series of dramatic towers of the most stylish modern design, dramatized even more by bold patterns of sun and shadow that highlighted the sophisticated slabs on a handsome Caracas hillside. This was new public housing, and it was meant to be the answer to the *favelas,* those shanties of cardboard and corrugated iron that housed the poor on another Caracas hillside.

The buildings, which I had just seen in the flesh—or more accurately, in the concrete and full fluorescent color (the pictures were black-and-white)—were appalling as architecture and failures as housing. The transplanted agricultural poor who occupied them did so with a combination of fear and loathing and remarkable domestic inventiveness. I think the stories of goats and crops in the bathtubs may have started there. My letter went on at some length about the shame of such architecture and the irony of its image. Its theme was a warning against the seductiveness of the architectural photographer's flattering abstractions, and their betrayal of reality, particularly in places as distant as Caracas, where the reality was not easy to check firsthand.

I am still extremely wary of impressive presentations of new architecture in far-off places; I bring along this reflex set of concerns about image, suitability and style, and the skills of propaganda. Therefore I approached an exhibition called "American's Architecture for Export: New York's Contribution" with caution. Presented by the New York Chapter of the American Institute of Architects in 1981, the show consisted of about twenty examples of work done by New York offices for those new architectural frontiers—the Middle and Far East and the Third World.

The firms prepared their own panels of illustrations and text, and two of them—Skidmore, Owings and Merrill and Warner, Burns, Toan, and Lunde—get the Huxtable broken compass award for type too small to read. The latter firm also gets the crooked **T**-square award for its absurd rationalization of the relationship of the new Rameses Hilton in Cairo (I am not making up the name)—a kind of offset tower of reincarnated brutalism—to the ancient monuments of Egypt. We are told that it has used "the 'wall' as the overriding device." True, most buildings have noticeable walls. We can do with a lot less of this kind of pretentious nonsense about "architectural recall" in the design of new buildings in old places so dear to the hearts of architects doing their own thing. Just a small ink spot goes to Liebman, Williams, Ellis for too many "hierarchicals" and similar buzz words for a generally thoughtful and sensitive housing and neighborhood development plan for Teheran.

None of these are modest projects; and except for those in Iran, which were aborted by the revolution, the majority are complete or under construction. The most ambitious are master plans for new cities and communities, such as Conklin and Rossant's National Capital Center at Dodoma in Tanzania, which is to be the country's new capital, three hundred fifty miles inland from the old one on the seacoast at Dar es Salaam. The city is projected as a series of stepped earth terraces, with staged construction of ministries, offices, shops, and a hotel.

Construction for the United States Government is a traditional category of overseas work. Consulate staff housing in Hong Kong by Davis, Brody Associates suggests a handsome group of buildings on a steep slope facing the China Sea, and the new American embassy complex in Moscow by Gruzen and Partners and Skidmore, Owings and Merrill is a ten-acre, walled American Kremlin with an eight-story, redbrick embassy office building that bears a strong family resemblance to the Gruzen firm's New York City Police Headquarters. This centerpiece is surrounded by row housing for staff, and served by an American underworld of below-grade cafeteria, shops, health facilities, and parking. Work began on this $100 million high-security community in 1979. (It was finally approaching completion in 1986, its pace slowed or accelerated by changes of temperature in the cold war.)

The range of housing is broad, from the traditional efforts to develop economical and easily constructed housing systems for developing countries to standardized workers' blocks for the international oil companies. What is new is the size and ambitiousness of housing developments that utilize the conspicuous new resources of the Moslem world.

It is the commercial construction, however, that is the most spectacular, with the palm surely going to Gordon Bunshaft of Skidmore, Owings and Merrill for his twenty-seven-story triangular building for the National Commercial Bank, which now soars over the flat landscape of Jiddah in Saudi Arabia. The exterior of the bank tower is a powerful sheer shaft faced in travertine. This extraordinary building has its facade broken only by large vertical openings for three interior courtyards hung within the building's frame, an inward-turning scheme meant to protect the offices from heat and glare. The offices themselves, in the strictly opulent Skidmore, Owings and Merrill manner, have their elegant seating arranged in the traditional Middle Eastern pattern of couches grouped around tables. The use of multiple small tables instead of one large table is the only noticeable departure from the ritual American corporate style.

This amazing design has been attacked and defended—as

unsuitable in size, shape, and scale for the flat desert-city land-scape, or as a brilliant adaptation of technology and art to a harsh climate and modern international business needs. There can be no debate about its inescapable monumentality.

Skidmore, Owings and Merrill has also developed a fascinating airport for Jiddah. The King Abdul Aziz International Airport is covered by a series of huge semiconical, Teflon-coated Fiberglas fabric roofs. These lightweight umbrellalike structures will protect an expected 950,000 airborne Arab pilgrims to nearby Mecca from the sun and heat. Nothing could speak more eloquently of change.

What strikes one most are the extremes of this exotic over-seas work. At one end is a slender, teardrop-shaped, gold glass office tower with intricate reverse curves, designed for a development in Singapore called the Golden Mile, that is the epitome of suave, luxurious, high-fashion, high-tech commercial construction. At the other pole are 750 units of concrete block housing costing $7.50 a square foot, erected in record time for the government of Cyprus to serve refugees from the 1974 Turkish invasion. The first is the work of Robert Sobel/Emery Roth and Sons, and the second is the Strovolos Community Low Cost Housing Development by David and Dikaios. Low-cost housing is meant to adapt the simplest industrial tools or native processes to urgent local needs. Stylistically sophisticated symbols of economic development are a response to the changing economics and politics of the Islamic countries and the Third World, including the inevitable desire for symbols of progress. Invariably, these building forms, styles, and technologies are borrowed from the industrialized and commercially oriented countries of the West. We are clearly in the business of exporting architectural images.

Style has always been transported from one country to another. The British brought European classicism to India with the Empire; prefabricated nineteenth-century cast-iron ginger-bread was shipped around the Horn. Some very strange buildings have been dropped into some very unusual places, with varying degrees of adaptive success.

I had a spooky feeling of familiarity with the Eggers Group's housing in Dammam, Saudi Arabia—eight rigidly clustered groups of seventeen-story towers on podiums containing parking and shopping that looked like an update of Queens, for which 12,000 tons of precast elements were shipped to Dammam weekly for sixty weeks. That's exporting an image and a technology with a vengeance. The disembodied and discredited clichés keep right on rolling along.

Planners continue to try to sort out tidy samples of the populations of developing countries according to some magical set of demographic statistics, to be served by the "right" number of schools, playgrounds, and regional shopping centers. And progress is still seen as steel and glass skyscrapers, no matter how inappropriate to culture, climate, or site. As the architect Jaquelin Robertson commented after a stint in Iran, "The export model we have been sending out is not working very well, and most of the world has a bad case of cultural indigestion." The client countries are, as usual, getting our best and our worst. There is uncertainty and ambiguity on both sides. If anything consistently marks this kind of export architecture, it is a failure of communication about means and needs. Just beware of the pictures; they always look good.

June 28, 1981

OTHER PLACES,
OTHER LIVES

MODEL ROOMS

I have spent a good deal of time in model rooms. Their evocative empty spaces have done a lot to shape my life. As a child-wanderer in museums, I discovered eighteenth-century France in the silent *boiserie* of the re-created Louis XV salons of New York's Metropolitan Museum. Those rooms worked their magic even though I knew that Fifth Avenue, not France, was outside the false windows through which a cool gray light filtered evenly, without dusk or dawn, miles and centuries away from the Paris of the *ébénistes* of the king.

And yet, in those rooms, I was transported to another time and place. Their beautiful artifacts seemed as fresh and fashionable as when they were first made and enjoyed, and they revealed to me the lilt and swing of the rococo in an intensely intimate way.

The same was true, later, in the museum's American Wing —the kitchens, parlors, and bedrooms brought from historic houses and reassembled in the galleries' contextless cocoon cast a similar spell. Dominated by portraits of their plain proud owners, these rooms exuded a sense of homely skills and virtues. A pale blue watered silk settee could express all the yearnings of the Colonies for London's distant and more sophisticated charms. The only thing left of those lives and aspirations was the furniture and its shadowy suggestions. The rooms were an epitaph, eternally still and empty. Standing behind the velvet ropes, I never felt a sense of presence just gone or about to return through carved and gilded or hand-hewn doors. In this bell jar of a place, this domestic time machine, so strangely intact and hollow, there was no sense of anyone at all; the occupants were gone forever.

"Rooms Without People," Martin Filler called them in the Walker Art Center's publication, *Design Quarterly,* in 1979. Subtitled "Notes on the Development of the Model Room," his essay is a succinct history and analysis of a subject that exerts a universal fascination.

The museum model room carries a particular cachet. It is based in part on the quality of its *objets d'art* and a scrupulous attention to "authenticity," but to an even greater degree on the museum's authority as an arbiter of excellence. Colonial Williamsburg, for example, is actually a whole collection of model rooms in model buildings—a kind of model museum. The avowed purpose of such rooms is to promote the understanding of art, history, and culture in the most direct and personal terms. A good part of the appeal of these "preserved" interiors is the chance they offer to experience other lives vicariously; to indulge in sentimental journeys of time and place; to share, voyeuristically, a richer and more elegant existence; to possess, but briefly, the artful and expensive—or merely to play house.

But to most people, model rooms are those decorators' and designers' extravaganzas that sell houses, furniture, and dreams. Their subject matter is status and expectations; their theatrical settings are invented for a life free of the impedimenta of sentiment or necessity. These are the rooms photographed in shelter and fashion magazines; the model rooms of department stores and charitable causes used to promote products and lifestyles for the upwardly mobile. In celebrated model rooms like Bloomingdale's, consummate consumerism and glamorous overreaching have been raised to a special form of art.

Bloomingdale's model rooms of the 1960's and 70's represent the culmination of a trend that gained great momentum just before and after World War II. In Lord & Taylor's model rooms and Sloane's House of Years the decorative themes were changed as a well-publicized annual event. They were also predictable and consistent. A domestic ideal of charming provincial settings or eighteenth-century reproductions was enriched by a bit of traditional Oriental exotica or enlivened by Dorothy Draper's more daring cabbage roses and William Pahlmann's painted floors. This was where young suburbia saw itself mirrored and magnified in its pursuit of the substantial proprieties. By contrast, today Bloomingdale's deals in outright fantasies, from the eclectic to the outrageous; it caters to a much trendier set of values.

My first experience of Bloomingdale's model rooms was long before they hit their psychedelic stride, and it was, surprisingly, through the museum route. In 1941 the Museum of Modern Art had a now-historic competition for something called Organic Design Furniture. The winners, with Eero Saarinen and Charles Eames conspicuous among them, had their furniture manufactured and exhibited at the museum and displayed and sold—in model rooms, of course—at Bloomingdale's.

This furniture was meant to be good for you, like all things organic. It was billed as honestly functional and honestly contemporary; that the Saarinen-Eames chairs borrowed airplane technology for their chair mounts was an indication of their enlightened design. The model rooms were simple, understated, and uplifting, with geometric prints at the viewless windows and dying rhododendron leaves in glass brick vases. (I still can't bear to have rhododendron in the house.) They demonstrated how one should live, defining the good and the beautiful in the same reformist spirit as the earlier Arts and Crafts rooms of William Morris and Gustav Stickley, or Le Corbusier's later domestic demonstrations of *L'Esprit Nouveau.*

Fresh out of school and looking for a job, I was hired by Bloomingdale's to explain and sell Organic Design Furniture, because of my art background. Many young architects and designers made the obligatory tour of the rooms; one of them noticed and married me. Like Saturday's generation, we courted in Bloomie's model rooms. Later, working at the Museum of Modern Art, I spent a good deal more time in model rooms. That was the period of the houses in the museum garden; I remember, in particular, Marcel Breuer's "binuclear" house of 1949 and the traditionally re-created Japanese House of 1952. Like most model interiors, the art wore thin as the dust grew thick.

All this is probably why I am so delighted by Filler's "Rooms Without People." Here, at last, is the definitive analysis of the model room. They are the stages we play on, superbly manipulated for a set of complex personal and cultural needs. What they are filled with is not people, but people's aspirations, associations, and desires. Model rooms are exercises in psychology as much as in design.

Filler divides model rooms into three types: the historic/nostalgic, the aesthetic/didactic, and the commercial/promotional. He traces the first to the rise of interest in the country's past after the Philadelphia Centennial Exposition of 1876, tied to the desire of a growing middle class for the proper symbols of its prosperity. As industrialization progressed, nostalgia for the past increased. The results have ranged from Williamsburg to Disneyland. Museum model rooms stand at the art/historical pinnacle of this trend. All that is missing in the painstaking, authoritative, and expensive reconstructions in museum galleries is what Filler calls "the validity of context—an essential component in shaping interior spaces of all kinds." The transported room dies an instant death; the re-created room is stillborn.

The aesthetic/didactic room began to emerge in the middle of the nineteenth century. Reformers like William Morris wanted to sweep away bourgeois clutter for a more restrained and virtuous design philosophy. "The urge to improvement" from then on, Filler tells us, was the impulse behind most noncommercial model rooms, which became vehicles for the promotion of design reform. The implications were that our taste could be raised, either by honest handcraft or intelligent mass production. These rooms tended to preach rather than to preserve.

The heyday of the aesthetic/didactic room has been the twentieth century. From the products of the Deutsche Werkbund from 1907 to the elegant exposition rooms of the 1920's and 30's by such pioneer modernists as Walter Gropius and Mies van der Rohe, design was seen as the way that the Modern Movement could combine social and industrial concerns for the good of humanity.

Running counter to this messianic aesthetic was the richly decorative "modern" style espoused by the Paris Exposition Internationale des Arts Décoratifs et Industriels Modernes of 1925, which found an echo in some remarkable "period" rooms presented by the Metropolitan Museum in New York in the 1920's and 30's. Because these rooms pleased as well as instructed, they helped to establish the bridge to the commercial exploitation of officially sanctioned styles. After that, it was a short step from the professional tastemaker to the commercial tastemaker. The commercial/promotional room was quickly understood as a brilliant response to the need to move goods. It has become, in Filler's words, "an exercise in fashion as planned obsolescence in the service of increased consumption." As such, it particularly suits a time and a society that have rejected the "eternal verities" of art for escalating sensations and a record turnover of trends.

I confess that I find most commercial model rooms a bore. But there are other model rooms that I count as almost transcendental experiences. Whistler's Peacock Room at the Freer Gallery in Washington, for example, a rich and somber masterpiece of peacock colors, gold, and ebonized wood, has remained in my mind for years with a glowing intensity. The turn-of-the-century rooms of Charles Rennie Mackintosh, re-created in the Victoria and Albert Museum exhibition of his work, may be the most ravishingly austere interiors in history—a touch of red becomes a glowing jewel; the palest lavender is a subtle explosion. I keep remembering the description of the originals of these interiors by Friedrich Ahlers-Hestermann: "Here were mystery and aestheticism, with a strong scent of heliotrope, and a delicate sensuality. Two upright chairs with backs as tall as a man stood on a white carpet, looking at each other over a slender table, silently, like ghosts."

Such rooms will always haunt me.

July 19, 1979

WAITING ROOMS

Waiting is a large part of living. Great, passive, negative chunks of our time are consumed by waiting, from birth to death. Waiting is a special kind of activity—if activity is the right word for it—because we are held in enforced suspension between people and places, removed from the normal rhythms of our days and lives.

We wait for trains, planes, doctors, dentists, business and social appointments, and services of all kinds; we stand and wait or we sit and wait; we do it in a variety of settings that range from gorgeous to grim. Real serious waiting is done in waiting rooms, and what they all have in common is their purpose, or purposelessness, if you will; they are places for doing nothing and they have no life of their own.

This makes for a remote and impersonal kind of interior design. There is no stylistic formula; the rooms where we wait can be out of Kafka or Hollywood, the work of high-priced designers or dumping grounds for castoffs. But their one constant is what might be called a decorative rigor mortis; the only vital signs are the movement of vintage magazines or the ritual comings and goings of the people who use these disaffecting spaces. In the fashionable parlance of the trade, they are *faux,* which means that they are not real places at all; the French word imbues the false thing with a false dignity and chic. Waiting, we feel equally unreal.

Some people wait constructively; they read or knit. I have watched some truly appalling pieces of needlework take form. Others—I am one of them—abandon all thought and purpose to an uneasy vegetative state. But we all fill the emptiness with an extraordinary range of emotions, anticipation, apprehension, aggravation, dread, or despair, and the cessation of feeling known as alienation or anomie.

Few wait with pleasure. This stop-time void tends to depress rather than elevate sensations. In a curious way, the waiting consciousness is raised so that attention is concentrated—fixated, in fact—on the details of our surroundings. The sofa that never, in repeated visits, lines up with the mirror above

it, the lamps with crooked shades, become exaggerated irri-
tants, and dusty bunches of dried flowers and coat hooks that
suggest peculiar perversions take up permanent unwanted resi-
dence in our minds. The more standardized facilities of travel
or commerce offer fewer distractions. But all waiting spaces
hold us captive in the disembodied settings of an altered emotional state. Call it the ambience of ennui.

Airport lounge

The universal style of anomie

Pan American World Airways

If there is no common design denominator for the waiting
environment, it is still possible to analyze it in terms of purpose
and characteristics. There is waiting for transportation—the
vigils in airline terminals, bus stations, railroad sheds, and ferry
depots. There is waiting for doctors and dentists and related
professional appointments. There is waiting for government
services—for permits, licenses, the payment of fees and violations, the ritual of benefits disbursal, and the laying on of
penalties. There is corporate waiting, with the genre peculiar
to itself—the corporation reception area.

Because waiting rooms are prisons of a sort, those who gain

from our enforced stay try to ameliorate the bleakness; they seek a calculated and spurious cheerfulness that tends to go awry. Nothing depresses me more than those upbeat medical institutions where the colors are too aggressively bright and the "art" is assembly-line abstract; it must come out of the same computers as the bills.

Where our resigned and weary presences are no more than a nuisance to those who have little interest in serving us—the government bureaucracy is the classic case—the ambience is conspicuously uncaring. In some the dismal approaches the surreal—the New York City Office of the Bureau of Motor Vehicles, for example, makes one feel like a passive participant in the theater of the absurd. The waiting is done on scarred

Bromley-Jacobsen

Doctor's office

Waiting by design

wooden benches or mismatched folding chairs in a rummage sale atmosphere with the residue of cumulative chaos and a patina of total neglect.

The one basic principle that applies to almost all categories of the waiting genre is a concern for capacity. The design unit, naturally, is the seat. The name of the waiting game is the chair count, or body count, and the seating industry has risen to the challenge. For commercial installations, chairs come in multiples; they are racked, stacked, modular, unitized and clustered, fastened together like reverse peas in a pod on single frames so that all occupants vibrate in unison, or arranged in the newest fashion, in low curving barricades. The apogee of this kind of seating-by-the-mile is the airport, and it is quite possible to trace the history of chair design in airports around the world. It is, in fact, much easier than knowing where you are, since the standardized interiors and standardized graphics only distantly evoke the names of those splendid and fabled cities that these cloned airports serve.

The seats, if they are shell-shaped, suggest Saarinen and Eames; if they squiggle across the floor like fat worms, their source is the more stylish and playful Italians. (Actually, the Italians invented the best kind of waiting, *dolce far niente.*) But wait—if I may use the word. Even in an airport there is a waiting order: special lounges for special fares. For those who pay a little more, motel decor; for those who reach the cloud clubs, all the comforts of a small-town furniture store. Here there are louvered and paneled bars, patterned and upholstered sofas, and lots of *faux* everything. While such comforts are provided on a sliding scale of ticket cost, airport waiting is still essentially egalitarian; any elitism of taste or elegance is scrupulously avoided.

Doctors' waiting rooms are, as they say, something else. Their theme, traditionally, has been the paternalistic healer; the need is for reassurance. And what is required, primarily, is a quasi-domestic look. The ideal doctor's waiting room should remind one of someone's expensive living room. The choice can range from Colonial Williamsburg to Bauhaus modern, but the level of success is often proportionate to the amount of leather and chrome and the number of original lithographs. In general, however, doctors' offices are where Danish modern went to die.

The corporate reception area, on the other hand, is meant to impress, not to make one feel at home. The objective is to convey a message of substance and solidity. The design of the corporate waiting room is as concerned with the uses of power, from the idea of dynamic but dignified leadership to the institutional put-down, as it is with aesthetic expertise. It is really not about waiting at all; it is about image. The seats are few, luxurious, and costly, part of a custom-designed interior. The style is ostentatiously unostentatious, using sleek extensive materials. This suave setting, anchored by the receptionist's "island" from which the waiting is controlled and directed, is reinforced by the proper status symbols, the approved paintings and sculpture that are also a good business investment, and the appropriately exotic tree.

For many of us, the act of waiting is among our most lasting and evocative memories. Some travelers, like my husband when he was a boy, were lucky enough to wait for ferries, where there were always the sound of ships, the smell of the sea, and the sight of wheeling gulls. He remembers plain wooden benches and the sound of voices and feet echoing from hard wooden floors and walls. The cheerful newsstand was the colorful central presence in these austere stations, before plastic and the paperback explosion. Waiting for the Dartmouth-Halifax ferry in Nova Scotia, he marveled at the size of the Buffalo *Sunday Times,* and bought the first issue of *The New Yorker,* with Eustace Tilley on the cover. Waiting, as well as travel, can broaden the mind.

March 5, 1981

DESIGN FOR LIVING

THE DEATH OF
THE FIVE-AND-TEN

It was not the marketing of opulence. It catered to anything except expensive excess. It was an idea based on frugality and the most for the least. It was, in fact, a matter of nickels and dimes; it was that great American institution, the five-and-ten.

In theory and in folklore it is still going strong. F. W. Woolworth has celebrated its hundredth anniversary. A number of Woolworth's competitors and copiers are around in one form or another. Kress's and Kresge's, Newberry's, Lamston's and Grant's, have engaged in the battle of bargains and novelties over the years as prices rose from a dime to a dollar.

But "The Great Five and Ten Cent Store," Woolworth's first successful foray into the formula in Lancaster, Pennsylvania, in 1878, is a set of faded pictures now, and the "Woolworth idea" of selling an immense variety of goods at a fixed low price is a thing of the past. The other essential part of the formula—arranging counterloads of merchandise so that customers could see and handle every item—has become a casualty of security and the packaging industry.

Corporate and marketing developments and changes in production, distribution, and lifestyles have turned the small-goods variety store into the discount supermarket that sells everything from brand-name clothing to major appliances. The price tag can run in the hundreds, and the tender is plastic credit. But this is more than a revolution in selling styles. The rise and fall of the five-and-ten involves many themes: fashions in merchandising and morality, the development of trends and tastes, and a new scale and set of standards for retail operations that have turned those who practiced a thrifty Yankee and pioneer ethic and economy into a profligate consumer society. To students of American business and culture, this is an instructive chapter of socioeconomic history. But for many of us the phasing out of the five-and-ten is a matter of pure bathetic nostalgia. The mortal illness was not just creeping inflation. The death of the dime store is an all-too-appropriate story for our times.

By 1979, the flagship stores of two of the largest competing chains—Woolworth and Kress—stood empty at opposite corners of Thirty-ninth Street on Fifth Avenue. More valuable as real estate, they have been replaced by massive new construction. Kress's was built in the popular Art Deco style as the crowning glory of "dimedom" in 1935; Woolworth's followed with an equally impressive Fifth Avenue store within a few years. The mode has been called Depression Modern by Martin Greif, and the Skyscraper Style by Cervin Robinson and Rosemarie Haag Bletter, in books of the same name that celebrate the architecture of the period. As Woolworth Modern, it continued to be the rather *retardataire* style of choice for the chain through the 1950's.

The Kress Building closed in September 1977, and Woolworth's followed in 1979. The two silent stores symbolized the end of an era. For millions of young Americans, the climax and greatest joy of every downtown outing had been the trip to the five-and-ten. For the boys it was the lure of unlimited gadgets and hardware counters that displayed every size and shape of shining hooks, nails, and screws. For girls it was the clandestinely purchased Tangee lipstick and the dazzling array of forbidden costume jewelry.

In the fall, the back-to-school counter supplied the marbleized cardboard notebooks and cedar-scented pencils, the snap-

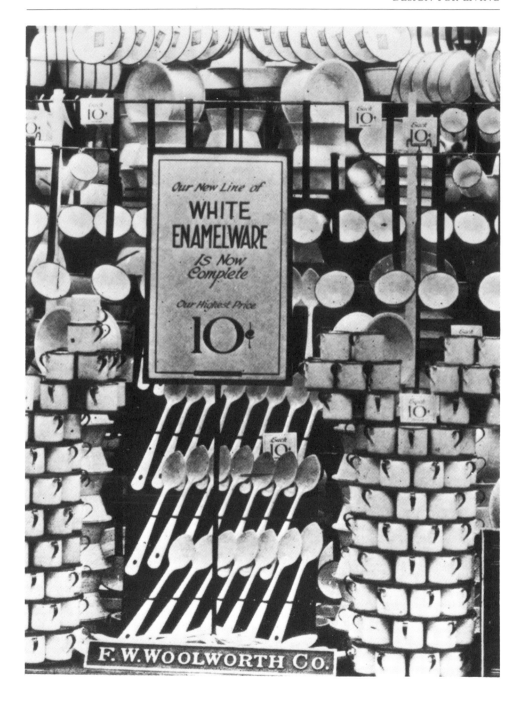

ringed loose-leaf binders, and fresh sheaves of paper that sig-
naled the season's start. There were after-school banana splits
and tricolored ice cream sandwiches enclosed in square cookie
covers with the flavor of pasteboard—a taste that became ad-
dictive. The stores smelled of sweet candies and cosmetics and
burned toast from the luncheonette counters along the wall;
they echoed to the sound of feet on hardwood floors, the
ringing of old-fashioned cash registers; and the clanging of
bells for change.

And there was the absolute saturation of the eye with every
conceivable knickknack, arranged with a geometric precision
based on the sales and aesthetic theory that more is more. Show
windows composed totally of fluted handkerchiefs, or enamel
pots, or bars of soap, were an underappreciated art form. Rows
of snap fasteners on cards and stacks of cups and saucers were
joined by novel colored plastics of infinite uses and rampant
kitsch that are now collectors' items. No one had yet invented
targeted promotions or point-of-sale displays. There was a simple cornucopia of counters. "What the bazaar was to the Middle East," the anniversary literature tells us, "Woolworth's was
to America."

"Nothing over ten cents" was the gilt-lettered message suspended from the ceiling in early Woolworth stores and embla-
zoned in gold on the carmine-red signs outside. The limit was
held even as competitors raised the ante in the search for more
varied goods, to five, ten and fifteen cents, and then to five, ten
and twenty-five cents, and finally to a dollar top. By 1919,
when Frank Woolworth died, 600,000 American babies were
wearing his ten-cent gold-filled rings. European and Japanese
imports had become common. The Kress stores, with the declared aim of making life better for everyone, introduced reproductions of art masterpieces for a quarter, and "realistic"
artificial flowers for a dime.

In 1932, Woolworth finally lifted its ten-cent limit to twenty
cents, and in 1935 all arbitrary price levels were removed.
Dollar hats and seventy-cent turkey dinners were a far cry from
the five-cent "Yankee notions" of the first stores—the safety
pins, thimbles, combs, button hooks, collar buttons, boot

*Opposite page:
Woolworth
window, 1930's*

*The five-and-ten
merchandising
creed—more was
more*

F. W. Woolworth Co.

straps, pencils, baby bibs, harmonicas, and napkins that were the Yankee peddler's stock in trade.

Small change built both fortunes and monuments. In 1913 the newly completed Woolworth Building in Lower Manhattan, the world's tallest skyscraper at the time, was flooded with light from a switch in the White House, and Cass Gilbert's Gothic extravaganza was immediately dubbed the "cathedral of commerce." The elaborate terra-cotta traceries, the facade sculpture and glittering mosaics, are said to have been paid for in cash by Frank Woolworth's nickels and dimes. The founder sat in an office that was a replica of the Empire Room of Napoleon's palace at Compiègne, except that marble was substituted for wood.

Samuel H. Kress's Fifth Avenue store of 1935, by the architect Edward F. Sibbert, featured granite, stainless steel, bronze and baked enamel, and Deco details that look like the tops of palm trees in the sunrise. Critics were less enthusiastic about its style than its functional plan, which included warehousing on the premises and fixed outlines on the floor for ladders and other movable equipment. This concern with the saving of time and energy harked back to Samuel Kress's Pennsylvania Dutch belief in "the essential rightness of conservative frugality," which also included the removal and saving of nails from crates. It was hard work and hard bargains all the way. In the early years packages were wrapped in newspaper, and "chestnuts" and "stickers," or items that did not move, were mixed with "plums" and "corkers" that produced a good profit. The dimestore men could squeeze a buffalo nickel until it bellowed. They knew, of course, what a nickel was worth in those days.

The demise of the founders and the growth of the corporate structure ushered in decades of change. Woolworth acquired other companies and expanded into fashion and foods; its Woolco Division entered the discounting field. Kress was absorbed by the fashion conglomerate, Genesco, in the 1960's, and the S. S. Kresge Company was changed to the K-mart Corporation in 1977, with K-marts accounting for 94.5 percent of the company's domestic sales.

What had occurred was a total revolution in the American way of living and buying. Stores grew to warehouse size, and aisles of goods became acres of products. With the new mass merchandising of mass-produced goods, locations shifted from Main Street to shopping centers. Buying in quantity no longer meant saving up and splurging in one glorious nickel and dime bash, or going in with two dollars and coming out with ten presents, from celluloid animals to unbelievable bric-a-brac. Even in the remaining variety stores, costly plastic packs of multiple items replaced the fun—and the economy—of being able to pick out exactly what was wanted or needed. Sales policy and its handmaidens, packaging and promotion, have a lot to answer for in the inflationary spiral.

But not only the Yankee notions went the way of the ten-cent bargain; thrift, frugality, and the time-honored concept of buying for cash are equally obsolete. Overreaching and over-paying have become the two sides of the coin that has no resemblance to small change. If I am ever radicalized, it will be done by those advertisements for $250 shoes and $90 jeans and $500 sets of cooking utensils with French names and the implicit message that without them I might as well drop dead.

Kress sold a fine drip coffeepot for fifty cents, and I have gone to wonderful parties in a pair of Woolworth "canary diamond" chandelier earrings that are as close as I will ever get to the real Cartier thing. In the dim light of a cocktail lounge, dollar hats looked glamorous with a ten-cent veil. You can't buy happiness, of course, but there was a time when you could get pretty close for a nickel or a dime.

November 8, 1979

THE DECORATIVE URGE

One of the most basic human instincts is the need to decorate. Nothing is exempt—the body, the objects one uses, from intimate to monumental, and all personal and ceremonial space. It is an instinct that responds to the eye, for pure pleasure; to the rules of society, for signals of fitness and status; and to some deep inner urge that has been variously described as the horror of a vacuum and the need to put one's imprint on at least one small segment of the world.

Embellishment is an irresistible and consuming impulse, going back to the beginnings of human history. More than just a way of changing or improving a surface or a setting, it is meant to bring about artful and magical transformations that evoke surprise, delight, even awe. All early ornament was tied to the supernatural and sublime. The decorative cycle parallels civilization; there is a line that goes right through ancient cave paintings to contemporary graffiti, with the entire history of the decorative arts in between.

Probably the strongest motivating force is the simplest: the inability of almost everyone to ever leave well enough alone. The temptation to fill a blank space is common to all; a child will scribble on a wall, and the arbiter of taste and fashion will decree those decorative parameters that establish the charmed circle of social acceptability. But one man's, or woman's, decoration can be another's atrocity, and no other art form can range from the elegant to the awful with such ease. Crimes of decoration—by the very surface or additive nature of pattern and ornament and their cumulative effect—are the easiest to commit.

Adolf Loos, one of the leaders of the modernist revolution, damned all decoration—a response understandable to any historian who has had to grapple with the excesses that spilled out of the nineteenth century and into the twentieth. Loos is famous for equating ornament with crime. Only the unschooled and savage find ornament necessary, he declared, pointing out the taste of criminals for tattooing. This, he said, is conclusive evidence that ornament is to be associated with the debased and lawless elements of society.

Still, it takes a heroic resolve to dispense with the traditional synthesis of detail and delight. One is easily seduced by the superb library-gallery of Syon House in Middlesex, England, for example, where the brothers Adam stretched a neoclassical ceiling completely across the building and filled it with a pastel rainbow of Pompeian-inspired garlands, medallions, urns, and arabesques. The message fades in the shadowed salon of a Venetian palazzo, where the reflected water-light of the green canal dances on heavy ornate gilt and blends with the greens of painted furniture, faded velvets, and frescoed ceilings filled with rosy *putti*. None of this is plain. And none of it has anything to do with savages or social misfits. Each example provides a superb decorative vocabulary that speaks the language of a particular taste and time.

There is no way to play down, or downgrade, the attractions of richness and the accouterments of style. The uses of enrichment go beyond surface decoration. The ornament on a Louis Sullivan building in Chicago defines the early art of the skyscraper by making the revolutionary structural frame visually clear while elevating it to something beyond engineering. Eighteenth-century painted rooms and nineteenth-century scenic wallpaper not only sent fashionable signals but also evoked the ambience of exotic beauties and far-off places.

Decoration definitely denies that less is more. It gilds the lily, out of choice. And while it may represent the distilled essence of the taste of the moment, in its change, say, from rococo to neoclassical, or from the Greek to Gothic Revival, it turns out to be far less transient than its ties with the world of fashion would indicate.

Surely no decorative style has been more enduring—or more adapted, bowdlerized, and revived—than the Adam; the delicacy and refinement of its ornament, furniture, and details have made it as suitable for small domestic interiors and contemporary uses as it was for the grand palatial scale of the original Adam rooms. And if Adam has been the most copied style, then the rococo has been the most vulgarized. The nineteenth century's combination of mass production, new money, ambition, and ostentation found the more elaborate styles most sympathetic; it did not matter if what was once artfully designed and elegantly hand-carved was now reduced to banality and machine-stamped as long as there was plenty of it.

The nineteenth century also explored some fascinating decorative byways. It was the century that admired, and invented, the concepts of the "picturesque" and the "sublime." Those ideas were defined in terms of the distant and the exotic, in time and place. At Olana, the painter Frederick Church's home and studio on the Hudson, sublime views of the river were framed by picturesque architectural details, in a kind of Hispano-Moresque, or casbah-harem potpourri of arches and patterned brick and interiors thick with Orientalia.

Inevitably, the twentieth century embarked on a kind of purification process. After one last serious fling with the whiplash curves of Art Nouveau, decoration was banished. It was a cold-turkey cure. But modernism did something more than deny the decorative past; it rediscovered the eloquence of space. Plain white walls and the simplest forms emphasized line and light, plane and void; the best interiors achieved a kind of minimal poetry.

The urge to decorate, although fiercely disciplined, survived, however. If there was the modern, there was also the modernistic, and the two ran parallel in the 1920's and 30's. Modernistic, now called Deco, was lush rather than austere; it was the last of the "traditional" decorative arts. But even among the most dedicated purists the need for enrichment came out in subtle and insidious ways. Sooner or later, a plain white wall had to have a painting or a piece of sculpture or, if all else failed, a tree. The suppressed desire for color and pattern remained expressed through the intrinsic ornament of visible structure. Mies van der Rohe announced that God was in the details. There was haute structural luxe with shining chrome-sheathed joints and caps for concrete beams.

Structure moved closer to sculpture. Decoration was like the thin man inside the fat man, struggling to get out. The clarity and courage of the early earnest insistence on the primacy of form over surface was lost. Even the glass box borrowed the richly patterned variety of the rest of the world for its mirrored facades.

While it is fashionable today to say that decoration is back, the truth is that it never really went away. It has simply come out of the closet, architecturally speaking. Those for whom Corinthian was a dirty word are now filling modest spaces with salvaged or mail-order classical columns. Parodies of Adam ceilings are coming from the offices of those who should know better. The vocabulary of ornament is being awkwardly re-learned. It is all a far cry from delight and caprice.

The art of decoration requires the most sophisticated and self-indulgent skills. Its aim has always been to sate the senses as gloriously as possible. That is why, when those effects become too predictable, popular, or debased, decoration moves on to something else. And it always will, because ornament is not only a source of sensuous pleasure; it supplies a necessary kind of magic to people and places that lack it. More than just a dread of empty spaces has led to the urge to decorate; it is the fear of empty selves.

May 14, 1981

CONQUERING CLUTTER

There are two kinds of people in the world—those who have a horror of a vacuum and those with a horror of the things that fill it. Translated into domestic interiors, this means people who live with, and without, clutter. (Dictionary definition: jumble, confusion, disorder.) The reasons for clutter, the need to be surrounded by things, go deep, from security to status. The reasons for banning objects, or living in as selective and austere an environment as possible, range from the aesthetic to the neurotic. This is a phenomenon of choice that relates as much to the psychiatrist as to the tastemaker.

Some people clutter compulsively, and others just as compulsively throw things away. Clutter in its highest and most organized form is called collecting. Collecting can be done as the Collyer brothers did it, or it can be done with art and flair. The range is from old newspapers to Fabergé.

This provides a third category, or what might be called calculated clutter, in which the *objets d'art,* the memorabilia that mark one's milestones and travels, the irresistible and ornamental things that speak to pride, pleasure and temptation, are constrained by decorating devices and hierarchal principles of value. This gives the illusion that one is in control.

Most of us are not in control. My own life is an unending
battle against clutter. By that I do not mean to suggest that I
am dedicated to any clean-sweep asceticism or arrangements of
high art; I am only struggling to keep from drowning in the
detritus of everyday existence, or at least to keep it separate
from the possessions that are meant to be part of what I choose
to believe is a functional-aesthetic scheme.

Really living without clutter takes an iron will, plus a certain
stoicism about the little comforts of life. I have neither. But my
eye requires a modest amount of beauty and serenity that
clutter destroys. This involves eternal watchfulness and that
oldest and most relentless of the housewife's occupations, picking up. I have a feeling that picking up will go on long after
ways have been found to circumvent death and taxes.

I once saw a home in which nothing had ever been picked
up. Daily vigilance had been abandoned a long time ago.
Although disorder descends on the unwary with the speed of
light, this chaos must have taken years to achieve; it was almost
a new decorating art form. The result was not, as one might
suppose, the idiosyncratic disorder of a George Price drawing,
where things are hung from pipes and hooks in a permanent
chaos of awesome convenience. This was an expensive,
thoughtful, architect-designed house where everything had
simply been left where it landed. Pots and pans, linens and
clothing, toys and utensils were tangled and piled everywhere,
as well as all of those miscellaneous items that go in, and
usually out, of most homes. No bare spot remained on furniture or floor. And no one who lived there found it at all
strange, or seemed to require any other kind of domestic landscape. They had no hang-ups, in any sense of the word.

I know another house that is just as full of things, but the
difference is instructive. This is a rambling old house lived in
for many years by a distinguished scholar and his wife, whose
love of the life of the mind and its better products has been
equaled only by their love of life. In this very personal and
knowledgeable eclecticism, every shared intellectual and cultural experience led to the accumulation of discoveries,
mementos, and *objets de vertu,* kept casually at hand or in un-
studied places. Tabletops and floors are thickets of books and

overflow treasures. There is enormous, overwhelming, profligate clutter. And everything has meaning, memory, and style.

At the opposite extreme is the stripped, instant, homogeneous style, created whole and new. These houses and apartments, always well published, either start with nothing, which is rare, or clear everything out that the owners have acquired, which must take courage, desperation, or both. This means jettisoning the personal baggage, and clutter, of a lifetime.

I confess to very mixed reactions when I see these sleek and shining couples in their sleek and shining rooms, with every perfect thing in its perfect place. Not the least of my feelings is envy. Do these fashionable people, elegantly garbed and posed in front of the lacquered built-ins with just the right primitive pot and piece of sculpture and the approved plant or tree, feel a tremendous sense of freedom and release? Have they been liberated by their seamless new look?

More to the point, what have they done with their household lares and penates, the sentimental possessions of their past? Did they give them away? Send them to auction galleries and thrift shops? Go on a trip while the decorator cleared them all out? Take a deduction for their memories? Were they tempted to keep nothing? Do they ever have any regrets?

This, of course, is radical surgery. The rest of us resort to more conventional forms of clutter combat. Houses have, or had, attics and cellars. Old apartments provide generous closets, which one fills with things that are permanently inaccessible and unneeded. In the city there is stolen space in elevator and service halls. And there is the ultimate catchall—the house in the country.

Historically, clutter is a modern phenomenon, born of the Industrial Revolution. There was a time when goods were limited; and the rich and fashionable were few in number and objects were precious and hard to come by. Clutter is a nineteenth-century aesthetic; it came with the abundance of manufactured products combined with the rise of purchasing power, and the shifts in society that required manifestations of status and style. Victorian parlors were a jungle of elaborate furnishings and ornamental overkill. The reforms of the Arts and Crafts movement in the later nineteenth century only substituted a more "refined" kind of clutter—art pottery, embroidered hangings and mottoes, hand-painted tiles and porcelains, vases of bulrushes and peacock feathers. There were bewildering "artful" effects borrowed from the studio or atelier.

Clutter became a bad word only in the twentieth century. The modern movement decreed a new simplicity—white walls, bare floors, and the most ascetic of furnishings in the most purified of settings. If ornament was crime, clutter was taboo. Architects built houses and decorators filled them. Antiques were discovered and every kind of collecting boomed. There were even architects of impeccable modernist credentials—Charles Eames and Alexander Girard—who acquired and arranged vast numbers of toys and treasures. They did so with a discerning eye for the colorful and the primitive that added interest—and clutter—to modern rooms.

Today clutter is oozing in at a record rate. Architect-collectors like Charles Moore are freewheeling and quixotic in their tastes; high seriousness has been replaced by eclectic whimsy. Nostalgia and flea markets coexist on a par with scholarship and accredited antiques. Turning the century on its head, the artifacts of early modernism are being collected by the postmodernist avant-garde. At the commercial level, sophisticated merchandising sells the endless new fashions and products embraced by an affluent consumer society. The vacuum must be filled. And the truth must be told. Our possessions possess us.

February 5, 1981

AS YOU LIKE IT

The well-publicized Design Collection of the Museum of Modern Art, established in the 1930's, has managed to make a lot of us feel uneasy or insecure. Those suave and startling furnishings and objects that the museum espoused as the ultimate marriage of art and technology have rarely fitted into the ad hoc accumulation of our lives without showing up the expedient crumminess of our domestic styles. They shattered any tenuous claims we might have to leading lives of aesthetic coherence. Those who were young or bold enough could start with a clean slate; those who were trendy enough could dispose of everything and start fresh. The rest of us were left with the conviction that our own tastes were messy, irrelevant, or *déclassé.*

I am not knocking the museum or beautiful and useful objects of any definition or persuasion. The Design Collection is a significant contribution to the archives of modern art. But I am pleased to report that the new revisionist way in which we are looking at everything from art to history is finally affecting our understanding of the field of design.

Since design is the spin-off of the creative process that touches all our lives and almost every aspect of our existence, this change has its aesthetic and cultural significance. The exhibition called "Take Your Choice: Contemporary Product Design," held in 1979 at the Cooper-Hewitt Museum, the Smithsonian Institution's Museum of Design, was no more than a tiny sampling of appealing and interesting design objects, but those objects were selected and presented in a way that would have been virtually unheard of a decade ago. Organized by Richard Oliver, the museum's curator of contemporary architecture and design, it was a limited but delightful display. Visitors seemed to share the affectionate rediscovery of the comfortable old Wearever aluminum coffeepot and the clunky Juice King orange squeezer; there was rejoicing among those who had kept the jazzy streamlined Toastmaster. The transformation of these objects from *dernier cri* to kitsch to historical artifact is now complete.

It was clear that the Cooper-Hewitt's interest in design extended beyond the traditional and very fine decorative arts of its earlier collections to the processes and products of the twentieth century. And it was also evident that this interest was both historical and analytical, in contrast to the Olympian proselytizing that has marked the pronouncements of the design apostles of the modern movement. There was perspective, wit, information, and innuendo here, as well as objects you could love or hate.

The title, "Take Your Choice," immediately suggested that no single approved model of anything was being enshrined, an impression borne out by the fact that the half dozen or so objects in each of ten categories—toasters, telephones, cameras, calculators, typewriters, coffee makers, juicers, radios, clocks, and chairs—offered a variety of solutions, deliberately and intriguingly juxtaposed. Nothing was enshrined as "best." But the selection was not as simple or random as it seemed. These objects illustrated a basic point, which was that design is a process that responds to so many variables that the number of acceptable ways to shape, house, define, or style (a taboo word for the modernists because of its cosmetic implications) any item, at any particular time, is almost limitless. Consumer preferences, in fact, grow out of a large cultural context and have a good deal more to do with the options offered than with designers' or museums' standards. Consumer judgments are made on the basis of subjective feelings, individual needs, and emotional responses skillfully manipulated by marketing, rather than on any objective evaluation of how close the design may come to some hypothetical ideal. The fact that the hypothetical ideal could lose out to next year's model was the great miscalculation of the modern movement.

A typewriter may be chosen because it corrects mistakes, not because its handsome housing won a prize; a coffee maker will be bought because it has radically altered the brewing process no matter how it looks; a clock is selected for novelty as often as for readability. Objects may be chosen to blend inconspicuously with their surroundings, or to stand apart as symbols of newness or status. An expensive hi-fi will be designed to look as slickly "engineered" as possible and a giant TV projection system makes its presence felt like a Cadillac in the living room.

According to Oliver, these choices are far from arbitrary. He isolates four factors that consistently influence the consumer: innovation, process, materials, and imagery. Some products are genuinely innovative because of the development of new techniques or materials. Others offer different features to different people so that the selection is made on the basis of use or process according to individual needs, as in cameras for amateurs or professionals. Where use does not vary, materials will. But the way the product looks, its style, or "image" may ultimately carry a stronger appeal than anything else about it, even overriding function.

This made for some entertaining setups in the museum's display cases. Take clocks, for example. There was a handsome nineteenth-century timepiece with all of its intricate brass wheels exposed to view next to the latest version of a clock with exposed works—a rectangle of clear plastic that revealed the circuitry of modern digital design. With these were two artful Deco digital models perceived as radical in the 1930's and accepted as period pieces today. For sheer utility, there was the Big Ben alarm by Henry Dreyfus that woke up America in the 1930's and 40's, and for sheer stylishness, a tiny, numberless, bright-red plastic Italian clock of up-to-the-moment daunting chic. Take your choice, they all tell time.

We are beginning to have a much more inclusive and interesting view of the art of design. The twentieth century has revolutionized the objects that surround us through the use of the machine, the explosion of technology, the mobility of society, the invention of consumerism and marketing, and the rise of income and expectations. The choices are limitless and revealing. This is a rich field for the study of cultural history and society's self-image—the latest word for taste.

April 29, 1979

THE JOY OF ARCHITECTURE

THE JOY OF
ARCHITECTURE

very age cuts and pastes history to suit its own purposes;
art always has an ax to grind. Classical Rome became
the Renaissance in the eyes of the fifteenth century.
Every great artist is re-created in the chosen image of a particular time. No "historic reconstruction" is ever really true to the
original; there is neither the desire nor the courage to embrace
another era's taste. We keep what we like and discard what we
don't. In the recent past the nineteenth century has been disdained except for a limited interpretation tailored to modernist
taste and beliefs, for a fascinating, if somewhat hobbled, history.

Fortunately, great art contains enough to satisfy each generation's needs, and there is always pleasure in the process of
rediscovery. The news is that the Academy wasn't all bad, and
the action wasn't only in the world-class cities; Peoria and
Dubuque may have been in the mainstream after all. The
realization is growing that a great deal has happened outside
the conventional centers of power and culture and there is a
whole world of architecture between New York and San Fran-
cisco and beyond Charleston and Savannah, lost in the shadow
of the Chicago skyscrapers. It has been there all along, but the
tendency has been to write it off and out of the history books.

The immediate gain is for architectural scholarship. We are undoubtedly suiting our own biased vision again, but we are achieving a richer and broader mix, enlarging experience and aesthetic response. The emphasis is on the material that is the most troubling to modernists—the kind of sentiment and ornament in Frank Lloyd Wright's work, for example, that the nineteenth century admired and the twentieth century banished. Bypassed achievements and unfamiliar or unsettling aspects of familiar work are being explored enthusiastically.

In a curious way, the door has been opened for serious study, not just by revisionist scholarship, which has been operating quietly for some time, but by the relaxation of conventional "received" standards. This includes the fashionable vogue for nostalgia and camp; the trivia of the recent past has become an enormously popular stylistic dig. No earnest and involved intellectual justifications are offered for the vigorous pursuit of the novel and the new; the objective is pure perverse delight in artifacts bound to shock those whose values are being challenged. There is nothing so far out, the new tastemakers seem to be telling us, that it cannot be embraced. There is nothing so antimodern that it cannot be accepted. There is nothing so totally rejected that we cannot admire it now, and if that means rewriting history, we will do so.

But the game is not a scholarly one alone. As with so much else in our determinedly hedonistic society with its emphasis on short-term satisfactions, the consistent theme is pleasure. There is so much more to see, to experience, to understand, to enjoy. There are worse ways of pursuing today's liberated sensibility. *The Joy of Architecture* must be on some publisher's list by now.

February 5, 1978

334

INDEX

ABOUT THE AUTHOR

Ada Louise Huxtable, the first full-time architecture critic on an American newspaper, was *The New York Times* critic from 1963 to 1982 and a member of its editorial board from 1973 to 1982. In 1982 a MacArthur Fellowship enabled her to retire and devote herself full time to writing. She is well known throughout this country and Europe and has received more than thirty professional awards and over twenty-five honorary degrees.